The Presentation Design Book

2ND EDITION

Tips, Techniques & Advice for Creating Effective, Attractive Slides, Overheads, Multimedia Presentations, Screen Shows & More

Margaret Y. Rabb

VENTANA PRESS

The Ventana Design Companion(TM) Series

Rabb, Margaret Y.
        The presentation design book : tips, techniques & advice for creating effective, attractive slides, overheads, multimedia presentations, screen shows & more / Margaret Y. Rabb. -- 2nd ed.
            p.   cm.
        Includes bibliographical references and index.
        ISBN 1-56604-014-0
        1. Computer graphics. 2. Business presentations--Data processing.
        I. Title.
        T385.R33 1993
        001.4'226'0285--dc20   93-9554
                                                                        CIP
Book design: Karen Wysocki
Cover design: John Nedwidek, Sitzer: Spuria
Cover illustration: Katherine Mahoney
Illustrations: Laura Farrow, Brenda Currin, Anne Valentine and Margaret Rabb: Southern
    Media Design & Production, Chapel Hill, NC.
Index services: Dianne Bertsch, Answers Plus
Editorial staff: Patricia Frederick, Marion Laird, Linda Pickett, Pam Richardson, Cabell Smith
Production staff: Rhonda Angel, Brian Little, Midgard Computing, Karen Wysocki

Second Edition 9 8 7 6 5 4 3
Printed in the United States of America

Ventana Communications Group, Inc.
P.O. Box 13964
Research Triangle Park, NC 27709-3964
919/544-9404   FAX 919/544-9472

Limits of Liability and Disclaimer of Warranty
The author and publisher of this book have used their best efforts in preparing the book and the programs contained in it. These efforts include the development, research and testing of the theories and programs to determine their effectiveness. The author and publisher make no warranty of any kind, expressed or implied, with regard to these programs or the documentation contained in this book.
    The author and publisher shall not be liable in the event of incidental or consequential damages in connection with, or arising out of, the furnishing, performance or use of the programs, associated instructions and/or claims of productivity gains.

TRADEMARKS

ABOUT THE AUTHOR

Margaret Rabb practices what she preaches—usually—in Chapel Hill, North Carolina, working 16 years as design director for Southern Media Design & Production. Thanks to her real-life clients (fortunately, most like to drink coffee), she has learned to listen closely, to overlook the stage of despair when casting about for an answer, then to imagine and envision solutions using both new and old media. It's the obstacles in the path that teach us the most.

In addition to designing, Margaret also writes books and articles. With Chris Potter, she is co-author of *The Harvard Graphics Design Companion* (DOS and Windows editions) for Ventana Press, and *Dynamite Design: Practical Power for Desktop Publishers and Presenters* (with Richard Scoville) for *PC World*. Life will ever be the same.

ACKNOWLEDGMENTS

My gratitude and love for Carolyn Kizer haven't dimmed a bit in 20 years. Thank you, my teacher.

Thanks also to Chris Potter, Anne Valentine and Meghan Lubker for their daily support, good humor and wonderful eyes and ears. To editors Linda Pickett, Patricia Frederick and Marion Laird for entering into the spirit of the book, as well as the words. To Pam Richardson for keeping us all in line, even halfway around the world. To Karen Wysocki for a generous world view and clean book design. To Elizabeth and Joe Woodman for carrying it all. To Blake and Arwen Potter for an unending supply of third-grade jokes and stories. To Regina McDuff, Lee Anne Nance and Rich Beckman for waiting an extra day or two on their projects when time got tight. Good gracious, bless you all.

Dedication

For you—

Merry meet again.

CONTENTS

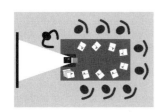

Dynamic Dressing
The tie that shines...
The right tie could make the difference between a new promotion...
...and waiting forever on your current rung of the corporate ladder.

4 DESIGN & LAYOUT   55

He cannot choose
BUT HEAR;

5 UNDERSTANDING TYPE 81

6 EXPLORING COLOR 111

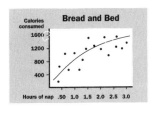

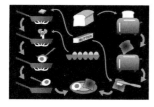

USING DIAGRAMS 193

MOVING INTO MULTIMEDIA 215

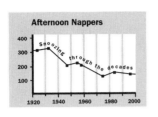

A FINAL GLANCE   263

INTRODUCTION

SWIMMING INTO VIEW

You're not alone. Every day thousands of us stand and deliver. We present ideas, information, arguments and reviews. We project our enthusiasm and interest outward—toward five co-workers or a hundred professional peers. We know we have something important to say, but we want to be sure that our audiences hear it, receive it, understand it and remember it.

We're all surrounded by information, confronted by instant electronic communication wherever we turn. Yet as a presenter you may feel daunted; it may seem that this constant tide of details is an impossible backdrop from which to pull your own brief moment. But you have one enormous advantage: your presence. Your individual perception of the world and the topic at hand has brought your audience into the room.

WHAT ARE PRESENTATION GRAPHICS?

Presentation graphics are nothing more than the visualization of information and ideas—representations that allow others to see your points quite literally. They support your message and clarify its meaning. They add depth and even beauty to your work. They help to engage the audience. When your presentation graphics stand behind you, you're not up there alone.

WHO MAKES PRESENTATION GRAPHICS?

Not so long ago, presentation graphics were considered luxuries. After the initiator of the project provided the content and concepts, the visuals were actually produced by professional photographers and graphic artists. Not only did these professionals command handsome compensation for their skills, but often they were at a disadvantage in being unable to grasp the full meaning of the concepts presented in the materials. Consequently, they made mistakes and false starts; time was wasted; tempers flared.

With simplified, automated production techniques, more and more people are writing, designing and producing their own presentation graphics. If you're one of those working solo to tell your story, congratulations! You'll get a lot of satisfaction from designing your own graphics, start to finish. And, of course, for the times when you really want to "knock their socks off," you can still call in the professionals to help with decisions and special effects.

On the other hand, if you're a graphics professional, you've probably worked primarily with print-related materials. You already know how page layout software can liberate you from technical pens and paste-up adhesive. Now you can apply your experience to the design and development of dynamic slides, overheads, screen shows and multimedia programs—exciting and invigorating extensions of the designer's vision.

In either case, you'll need information about the new media and processes. Color choices, type specifications and image density on film or computer monitors will differ from those used on the printed page. And you'll probably need new suppliers, since most printers and print-related service bureaus don't offer film processing or transparency mounts. You'll find information and illustrations to help you in all these areas in *The Presentation Design Book*.

WHO NEEDS THIS BOOK?

If you have a detailed message to deliver—even if it's just one detail—*The Presentation Design Book* is for you. The venue might be a sales seminar, an executive board meeting or a scientific symposium. Whatever the topic, wherever it's presented, you can learn how to put clear, effective visuals in front of your audience.

Like any interpretive process, presentation graphics require the interpreter, the presenter, to have a basic understanding of the subject to be explored, the media used to present it, and the audience's expectations. As a presenter, your own imagination and intelligence are also essential ingredients. And then there are the designer's tools that help you express your understanding in words and pictures. This book offers you the tools to get your message across, so that you will show as you speak, delivering a truly powerful presentation.

The graphics tools described in the following chapters aren't used exclusively in presentations. They'll come to your rescue in a number of other situations, from lengthy reports to snappy bulletins. However, when you bring text together with graphs, diagrams or motion video and display—or even combinations of these in multimedia—you create that magic called *presentation graphics*.

HOW TO USE THIS BOOK

The Presentation Design Book is written with the assumption that you have some experience making presentations and working with tools for creating computer-generated graphics. While a computer certainly isn't a prerequisite for designing effective presentation graphics, the material set forth here is intended for computer users.

If you've made and used presentation graphics before and already know how to analyze a project, you may want to skim the first two chapters and get right into media choices. If your media decisions are already cast in concrete because of other considerations, you can skim the first three chapters for presentation tips, then delve into the basics of layout and design.

LET'S GET STARTED

The Presentation Design Book is organized to help you review areas you've already mastered, and concentrate on learning new or unfamiliar techniques and skills. I've included a wide range of examples that will trigger application ideas without tying them to specific products. The design principles are universal. If your software doesn't automatically comply with my recommendations, explore ways to customize the program. Software companies recognize that flexibility is important in solving complex design challenges, and they're moving toward accommodating a wide range of visual choices.

The examples in this book aren't elaborate. I've left the razzle-dazzle for later, and concentrated on the basics. My intention is to cover the ground rules of presentation design and give you the confidence to experiment and explore. With each presentation you make, you'll learn more about the interaction between ideas, audiences and visual design. As you extend your design skills, your presentations will communicate more effectively. It's a long and fascinating road: *bon voyage!*

Margaret Rabb
Chapel Hill, NC

FOR STARTERS

S ince the day your first-grade teacher wrote the alphabet on the blackboard, you've been exposed to hundreds, maybe thousands, of different presentations—from chalk drawings to sophisticated multimedia shows. Some held your interest, while others bored you silly. One was so low-key it hardly happened at all, while the next was outrageously overblown. Which presentations kept you captivated? Did they rely on the speaker, the subject matter, the presentation materials—or a charismatic combination of the right choices in all three areas?

Figure 1-1: We learned early that visuals make a presentation more interesting.

The benefits of watching as well as hearing a presentation are, well, easy to see. Slides, overhead transparencies, computer graphics and flip charts clarify the spoken word, help the audience identify the most important points and rivet attention on the topic at hand. Subject matter is often more interesting and easier to understand when illustrated. Abstract information—statistics, plans, concepts and processes—can be particularly hard to communicate, especially to a large group of listeners, until you picture the ideas for them. Colors, motion and visual organization bring facts and figures to life.

Figure 1-2: **From the blackboard to the keyboard, graphics make abstract information easy to understand.**

Personal computers can now handle most of the production tasks involved with presentation graphics, from generating an outline to creating a file that can be imaged on paper, film or screen. Yet the design of an attractive, persuasive presentation is a craft in itself, with time-honored, tried-and-true rules that often differ from those of other branches of graphic design.

Good presentation design is neither a luxury nor a mystery. Nor are graphic decisions difficult to make when taken one by one. They aren't based on arcane secrets of the art world, beyond the grasp of the layperson. They're sensible, and with a few guideposts you'll be able to relate them to your own experience.

The most effective designs solve the daily communications challenges you deal with in the office, on the road or in the classroom, boardroom or auditorium. They convince real people, throw light on their efforts, move them to action. That's why this book takes a practical approach to helping you produce attractive images your audience will really read, understand and remember. Media, type and charting decisions are explained simply and clearly so you can learn quickly to make powerful presentations.

WHAT'S INVOLVED?

Most books on basic design urge you to "get organized"; so this maternal advice is nothing new. And, in fact, forethought pays off handsomely in presentation design and production.

While you're creating your presentation, you spend quite a bit of valuable time, tie up resources and often ask for help from others. It makes sense to plan first in order to avoid false starts, missed deadlines and the added expense—in both stress and dollars—-of last-minute remakes.

For starters, list the objectives of your presentation: clarify your intentions, both for yourself and for others involved with the project. They give you a goal to focus on as your presentation takes shape and you concentrate on narrower issues. And they give you a benchmark by which to judge your final accomplishments.

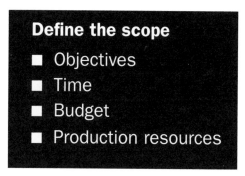

Figure 1-3: **Get organized by first listing the objectives of your presentation.**

Work from your objectives to create a content outline you'll use as the preliminary structure of your presentation. What's the most interesting point you have to relate, the crux of the argument, the heart of the matter? When you know where you're going and why, you can arrange all the supporting material in elegant, logical ranks behind their banners.

Next, you'll have to find a balance between what you want to do and what you can do within the constraints of time, budget and production capabilities. Be realistic! If you're asked on Tuesday to present an update on your department's projects at a staff meeting on Friday, you just won't have time—nor (we hope) will you be expected—to create elaborate artwork or complicated animated effects. Fortunately, clean and simple graphics have a great appeal of their own.

Achieving good design and creating the visual support to carry it out requires plenty of time and effort—much more than the hour or two at the computer you can work into a busy schedule with a minimum of bother. A complete, satisfying presentation consists of at least several elements. Production is more demanding than merely creating artwork; it involves many steps, from reviewing thumbnail sketches to proofreading the frames and assembling speaker's notes. Even before you sit down at the computer, you'll have invested several hours sketching frame designs and arranging the contents in an effective progression.

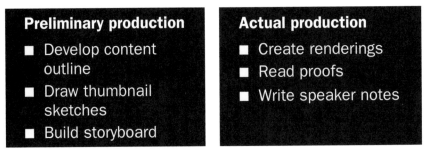

Figure 1-4: **Create a content outline as your preliminary structure.**

Graphic consistency helps tremendously in the struggle to unite disparate material into a seamless presentation. Settle on a typeface, color palette and layout grid structure for the whole presentation. Your audience will learn quickly how to "read" the frame for important information, as long as the individual parts of your show bear a family resemblance. A hodgepodge of design styles, on the other hand, only irritates the hapless viewers; they'll lose track of your message while trying to decipher new visual clues.

When you've designed and rendered the images to your satisfaction, they're ready for transfer from computer screen to the final medium (slide film, overhead transparency or paper) or for assembly into an electronic on-screen presentation. Remember to factor this final step into your time frame; it's no big deal to produce a few black-and-white overheads from your laser printer, but if you send PostScript files to a service bureau, you'll have to consider turnaround time, too.

Before moving into design and related issues, find out relevant facts about your audience. It's also important for you to know who will be responsible for each step of the production process.

DEFINING YOUR AUDIENCE

Imagine that the people who will attend your presentation are filing into the room right now. Observe them closely. Focus on two or three of them. What do they expect to achieve by attending your presentation? How does your presentation meet their expectations? Evaluate your overall style and individual frames in light of your audience's background, attention level and sense of engagement. Appeal directly to their interests. Tell your story in a way they'll remember.

Say you're making a few overheads to clarify your weekly status report to your staff of six. What will help them visualize the current workload in a constructive and engaging manner? What vocabulary and images do you share? What will draw the group together and encourage cooperative working relationships?

On the other hand, maybe you're planning to address 500 of your peers at a major conference. The tone of your support slides, as well as your tone of voice, will change to accommodate a more polished and formal setting. Even intangibles like the projected size of the images will affect the audience's reaction.

Whatever the setting, try to recall the presentation graphics that have worked best for you. Develop a mental "clip file" of presentation techniques and sketch out particularly effective visual techniques to use in an appropriate situation.

Assess the audience's familiarity with your topic. Are they already acquainted with your subject, or do they need an introduction to it? Think about their background, education, experience and work environment (factory line, cubicle, executive suite) so you can anticipate their questions and hold their attention. Remember how annoying it is when someone talks down to a group that's thoroughly familiar with a topic, and how frustrating it is to keep up with technical material beyond your realm of expertise.

Base your presentation decisions on the level of your audience's understanding. When your listeners need an introduction to your subject, be generous with explanatory diagrams and other visual background information. But don't get bogged down—make a smooth transition into the main topics of the presentation.

Concentrate on basic information and don't overwhelm the audience with a lot of data for which they have no reference. Don't rush; avoid abbreviations and acronyms; and don't use jargon specific to a narrow field. Leaving people behind at this point only puts them off the entire presentation and prevents them from grasping and remembering the most important points.

HOW MUCH TIME DO YOU HAVE?

A speaker frequently must convey information or ideas to the audience in a limited amount of time. Somehow, it's never enough!

Whether you have ten minutes or half an hour, it behooves you to organize your presentation to cover the key concepts efficiently and economically. You can always return, time permitting, to any points you particularly wish to emphasize. This way, your audience will feel they've been led through the full story, amplified with interesting depth in some areas.

Avoid even the possibility of feeling, or appearing, rushed and ragged: your audience will identify this feeling with the issues at hand. Practice the core presentation until you can deliver it consistently with at least five minutes left over. Neither technical hitches at the meeting site nor other speakers' excesses will fluster you, and you'll reap the most benefits from those exciting presentation graphics!

WHO DOES WHAT?

Some speakers prefer to create their own presentations from start to finish, while others work with writers, designers and producers to craft their visual materials. Working independently gives you the freedom to inject your personal taste and even sense of humor into the presentation; it allows greater latitude in managing content and design, and provides for total control as well as complete responsibility over the presentation. But unless you have wide experience, it's helpful to consult with others, at least informally. In fact, the more experience you gain, the more likely you are to check out your graphics with a trial audience.

Figure 1-5: **When you design graphics for other people to present, aim for a neutral style to accommodate a range of personalities.**

As soon as you've created one successful presentation and your fame spreads, you might well be called on to create a show that someone else will present. In this situation, sensitivity to your speaker's needs is a must. Try to put yourself in the speaker's place before you start the project. Catch his or her tone of voice, gestures, natural pacing. This person represents your first and most critical audience.

Presentations you plan for other people to deliver are typically a bit more detailed and formal—you don't want to project your own personality. To ensure a smooth fit between speaker and graphics, allow the materials to take on a more neutral style.

Suppose you're the national sales manager for a coffee and tea company. You're designing a presentation for your seven regional offices to introduce a new line of organic coffee to prospective retail customers. Since at least seven different people will present the material, you aim for a neutral tone that will accommodate a wide range of personalities. You concentrate on depicting the health benefits of organic beans, demonstrating the market's current demand. This way, you'll be answering the retailers' questions and giving them valuable information about their customers.

You can still offer the speakers suggestions for engaging the audience, relating interesting anecdotes and making the presentation come alive. Encourage each presenter to personalize the presentation, and show where such embellishment would fit into the overall plan. Try grouping your ideas in a "Notes for the Presenter" section of your speaker's notes.

If others must approve the content and format of the show, determine early in the process who will have the final say on content decisions; confer with this person at intermediate stages to keep the program on the right track. The farther into a project you move, the more complicated and costly it will be to make changes.

Likewise, find out who has the last word on design decisions. Take corporate design guidelines into consideration *before* preparing your templates. It's great if your project team includes the talents of a professional graphic designer, but don't assume that this person will be the final arbiter of all design choices. Many times, the project manager wants to be involved and expects to pass judgment on all aspects of a presentation, content and design alike. Be aware of the politics and personalities related to your project; it's dreadful to find out at the eleventh hour that the boss abhors the color green. Color proofs of sample designs have saved many presenters from this fate.

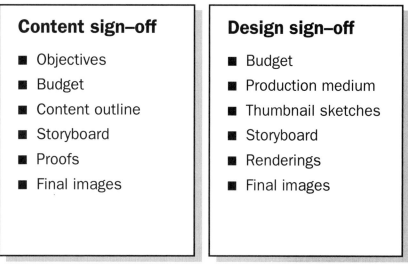

Content sign–off

- Objectives
- Budget
- Content outline
- Storyboard
- Proofs
- Final images

Design sign–off

- Budget
- Production medium
- Thumbnail sketches
- Storyboard
- Renderings
- Final images

Figure 1-6: **Confer with the final decision-makers at an early stage to avoid complications later.**

MOVING ON

Plan ahead! Outline your presentation's objectives. Get a clear idea of who will be in your audience, what you want to say to them and with whom you'll be working. Ask yourself how much time you have to accomplish all this.

Decide on a graphic theme to tie your presentation together. Planning lays the foundation for your project and minimizes problems that might crop up along the way.

Now it's time to start thinking about how to compose and visualize your message. Let's get started...

THE MESSAGE 2

The message you deliver to your audience is the reason for any presentation, no matter how elaborate or basic the supporting graphics. That's why you're doing this—to convey new information, or explain existing facts more completely, or look at familiar ideas in a new light. The logical first step, then, is to determine the most important points you want your audience to retain.

With this in mind, set specific objectives. Keep the list short and the wording brief. You may have only one *goal*: to communicate the benefits of organic coffee, for instance. But your *objectives* are the specifics you want your audience to grasp: coffee tastes vastly better without chemical overtones, it's much healthier to drink coffee without herbicides and pesticides, and local agriculture benefits from renewable organic growing practices.

Learn as much as you can about the information you're going to present. You'll become the resident expert on growing organic coffee and on coffee-tasting procedures. The better you understand coffee cultivation in Sumatra, or the physiology of discerning flavor, the easier it will be to organize and visualize concepts, ideas, facts, figures and relationships. Even though you're probably impatient to start creating your show, restrain yourself until you've planned the conceptual outline.

Figure 2-1: **The more focused you are at the start, the more effective your presentation will be.**

Such an outline will aid and abet you—it needn't be dry and dull if you go about it in a creative, imaginative way. Start by jotting down ideas as they occur to you, without order or priority. Allow one point to suggest others. Look over your notes and highlight three or four main topics. Cluster the others around them. Ask yourself which subpoints make significant contributions to your message and which don't. Where are the gaps? Then establish a flow between the groups and a hierarchy within each cluster, using the traditional outline format.

EXPRESSING INFORMATION

...With Words

Most presentation graphics you see are text frames, with words as the only visual elements. These frames can present a real challenge to the designer who must create a flexible, dynamic and engaging format to accommodate a range of bullet lists, key words and narrative concepts. The building blocks of successful text frames are type style, color palette, simple elements like lines and bullet shapes used wisely and consistently, and a well-developed sense of proportion.

Choose your words carefully. Limit yourself to the points that are most important to the viewer, and eliminate extraneous content. When you have more than four or five lines, divide the broad concept into a couple of logical components.

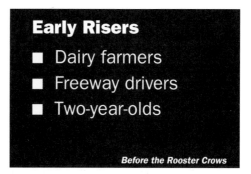

Figure 2-2: Keep the content of your text frames crisp and to the point.

...With Numbers

Because people like to count things and use the results to back up conclusions and proposals, statistics are the second most commonly presented type of information. Entire state and federal agencies have been established just for the purpose of counting—the Census Bureau, Internal Revenue Service and Bureau of Economic Analysis, to name just a few.

Our organic coffee growers in Sumatra, for instance, might expect a yield of 10,000 kilos this year. But when they review the crop figures from the last 20 years, they see that production tends to be cyclical. It shouldn't be a surprise, they conclude, if their yield drops off significantly this year.

Figures help us predict, plan and forecast, but they're very abstract. Written numbers help make the concepts more concrete; they're easier than spoken numbers for the audience to grasp and compare. But don't be a slave to exact quantities—learn to approximate, round off and contrast. Cite precise figures only when they truly serve an important purpose.

Coffee Drinkers		
	1990	**1991**
Instant	541	580
Perk	453	476
Drip	622	690
		Coffee Consumer Reports

Figure 2-3: **Using numbers graphically can clarify your message—but don't overdo it.**

...With Other Relational Information

While numerical values frequently form the basis of relationships and comparisons, they're only one part of a much broader category of information. Some ideas can be expressed best simply— through links, hierarchies and relative size or position. Flow charts and organizational diagrams are examples of standard treatments for such concepts.

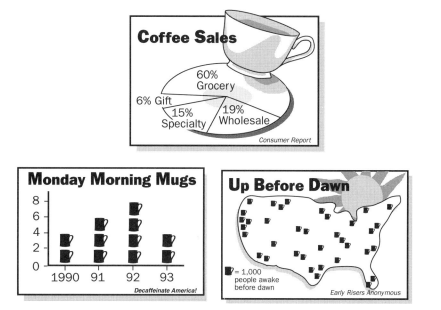

Figure 2-4: Depict relational information by using pie charts, graphs and maps to show how subjects are linked.

Imagine, for instance, the flow of work on a coffee plantation as a simple diagram. While it might be confusing to talk about the way individual tasks relate to the total operation, a visual overview can clarify the whole process at a glance.

Other relational data deals with temporal and spatial relationships, events that occur over time or in different places. Maps, graphs and diagrams illustrate these correspondences and show how time or events are linked and interrelated. The yearly cycle of the coffee tree—from flowering through bean maturation—would make an excellent timeline diagram.

...With Motion

Nothing shows change so well as motion. Animating a line graph, growing a piece of a pie chart or drawing a connecting link is almost as much fun as zipping to the top of the big ladder in your old Chutes and Ladders game. Be sure that change is the concept you want to emphasize in a set of data, though; the motion effect carries attention away from more subtle considerations and details. For instance, the dramatic increase in the demand for organic coffee lends itself readily to motion graphics because the point is to emphasize growth rather than precise starting or ending values. We follow a steep upward curve with ease as it traces across the screen.

...With Artwork

Many helpful drawings and diagrams reflect actual objects in the world around us: an anatomy diagram, a cutaway view of a jet engine and a visual comparison of cloud types are all examples of representational art. While most of us find this type of illustration relevant and easy to understand, it takes a good deal of skill to render a lifelike, detailed representation. Since we expect the drawing to look exactly like what it represents, the results, especially with computer drawing tools, can be disappointing.

Figure 2-5: **Computer-generated representational art can be disappointing.**

As an alternative to a strictly realistic representation, try a stylized graphic stripped of details. Flat, bold images emphasize one aspect of the subject matter and convey selected information without extraneous elements. They help you "telegraph" the message to your viewers. The concept of drinking coffee, for instance, can be conveyed effectively by a cup and a face. This simplified graphic style is easy to apply to any illustrated frames of your presentation, building a consistent program; it's much more difficult to maintain consistency with detailed representations, however, especially if you must create all the artwork from scratch.

Your presentation certainly doesn't have to include pictures for everything. Resist the temptation to flip through the clip art files for inspiration. Generic pictures can draw attention away from the information you're trying to communicate. Instead of pulling up a telephone graphic when discussing telemarketing projections, for instance, try for a visual translation of the important concepts—the costs, benefits, strategies or projected profits.

Figure 2-6: **Ensure immediate recognition by using flat, bold images to convey information.**

A word about electronic clip art files: Caution. You can perform miracles with clip art, but only if you take the time to work these images into your overall frame design. Successful clip art images support the scale, color palette and typography of the presentation. They need a consistent context and placement in the frame—as background elements, repeated images or special icons. Give them the same careful consideration you'd give original drawings.

...With Photographs

Photographs are the extreme of realistic artwork, so they're very helpful in showing specific people, places and things. Incorporate them into your presentation when you want to represent a particular location or an exact moment. Effective presentation photographs focus clearly on one main element in the foreground. The stages of coffee beans ripening, for instance, would make an excellent sequence of photographs.

Because the audience will have little trouble grasping the import of a good, clear photograph, you can show a series of photographs and tell a story quite rapidly. Experiment with combining graphics and photographs; scan or ask your photo lab to insert a photo detail into a text frame, for instance, or use a photographic background for your title frames. Both techniques are excellent additions to your stylistic repertoire.

Keep your format in mind when planning photography: will you end up with horizontal 35mm slides, an electronic screen show or a vertical black-and-white flip chart? How will the photographs be integrated with the other frames? Choose locations, backgrounds and key colors carefully.

Figure 2-7: **The best presentation photos focus clearly on an element in the foreground.**

...With Graphic Style

Allow the content of your presentation to set the tone for the visual style. Describe for yourself and others in the project team the character of the presentation; use words like *friendly* or *polished*, *warm* or *cool*, *high-tech* or *low-key*. Translate these concepts into background treatments, color palettes, type styles and layout grids. Make sure each visual element, down to the lines and dots, works with you to communicate your message.

The tone and graphic style of a consumer-oriented presentation about organic coffee, for instance, might best reflect the human values of health and good taste with vibrant colors and informal type. The visual approach to a presentation for investors, on the other hand, might emphasize fiscal reliability with a more subdued palette and restrained typeface selection. Graphic style congruent with content goes a long way toward convincing your audience that the points you make are sound.

...With Variety

Break out of the same old format, even if it has worked well in the past. It's easy to get stuck on a favorite graphic treatment and use it for show after show, regardless of the kind of information in your message. Some people get hooked on bullet lists, others like graphs. Pie charts have become so popular in recent years, someone must be running a special on them! Although most information can be shown adequately in a variety of ways, you can choose the graphic form that represents it best only when you understand the content thoroughly.

Suppose you want to show production data for the 10 largest coffee plantations in Sumatra. You could make a map to show the spatial pattern, a graph to show temporal patterns, a pie chart to show how each plantation relates to the whole, a table to show exact population numbers or a keyword list to highlight the points you want to stress. Think about where you're leading the audience with this information before you choose an interpretive device. Your goal is to focus on the message and create a visual presentation that supports the whole flow of information as well as each point along the way.

INFORMATION SOURCES

As you work to refine your message, don't lose track of the information sources from which you've drawn your material. Occasionally, one person is responsible for the content of a presentation from start to finish. But more often you'll be assembling data gathered by a number of people, groups and agencies. Keep source references firmly attached to each bit of information, so you know who is accountable for its accuracy. The audience looks to you, the presenter, for reliable facts and figures—be sure you're passing along verified data.

Early Risers
- Dairy farmers
- Freeway drivers
- Two-year-olds

Before the Rooster Crows

Coffee Drinkers

	1990	1991
Instant	541	580
Perk	453	476
Drip	622	690

Coffee Consumer Reports

Coffee Sales

- 60% Grocery
- 6% Gift
- 15% Specialty
- 19% Wholesale

Consumer Report

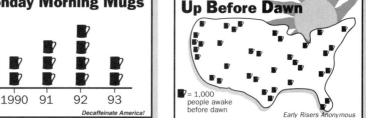

Monday Morning Mugs

Decaffeinate America!

Up Before Dawn

= 1,000 people awake before dawn

Early Risers Anonymous

Figure 2-8: You're responsible for giving accurate information to your audience, so be sure you know the source of every fact and figure.

As you gather information from the people within your organization, prepare a package about the presentation to give each source person. Include a description of exactly what information you need, and state your deadline. When it's appropriate, support your request with background materials on the presentation, such as the audience analysis, objectives and content outline.

Determine if your audience will benefit from knowing about your sources. Make it clear to them if you're presenting opinions and speculations or documented information derived from respected studies. Think about the enormous difference we perceive between data generated in research funded by a tobacco company and figures supported by the U.S. Surgeon General's office.

The nature of your sources can affect your graphic treatment as well as your presentation of content. Findings from a preliminary study, for example, might not be annotated in precise units but instead sketched in quickly with a broad brush to indicate trends and tendencies.

Certain situations call for your judgment in providing some background about the information you're presenting. Let your audience know how current the data is, so they can evaluate its worth at the moment. Indicate whether your figures are forecasts or known values. And, of course, it's never a good idea to deliberately conceal information. Respect your own credibility.

Because verbally crediting sources can be cumbersome, some presentations benefit tremendously from a standard format for citing sources on the presentation graphics. When you implement this format throughout the program, the audience will know exactly where to look for attribution and date information.

TRUTH IN PRESENTATION

Have you heard people say that it's easy to fool an audience with fancy materials and a slick presentation? Don't you believe it. People aren't that easily snowed; in fact, some audiences won't tolerate fancy graphics at all. They've become sensitized to hypesters who've tried to pull the wool over their eyes with expensive productions and misleading information.

Audiences are savvy. Refresh them with the materials you'd like to see if you were on the other side of the podium. Be truthful, straightforward and scrupulously honest.

CONCENTRATING THE MESSAGE

A presentation graphic is the visual accompaniment to the spoken word or, more precisely, to many spoken words. You can't begin to cover as much territory in the graphic as you naturally can in speaking. Concentrate the language in the visuals to the essential words or phrases; plan to use different, more expansive language for the verbal presentation. Your audience will appreciate the fact that, rather than reading to them, you're amplifying the basics on the screen.

When writing the text for your graphics, think "tight and concise." Extract the critical points and distill them into a few key words. Aim for titles and headings that can be read easily without losing the thread of the speaker's words. Complete sentences or (worse!) entire paragraphs interrupt the listener's concentration, demanding a different kind of visual attention.

Once you've extracted the key elements, assign them a particular function. These visual- and content-oriented distinctions are most important to maintain throughout the presentation. In a bullet list, for instance, the title is clearly differentiated from the bullet items by position, size, typeface, color or other design choices. Attribution lines, explanatory notes, labels, reference values and other identifiers all work best when managed as separate graphic entities with particular style attributes.

Consistency in the application of your design to each frame will maximize the overall punch and pizzazz of the presentation.

Titles

Remember the strength of well-stated, well-placed titles when you write the text for your presentation. You can think of the title as the linchpin of the graphic: it's the key to understanding the material. Your viewers won't be as familiar with your subject as you are, so help them out by stating the point of each frame as clearly as you can. Try to capture it in two to five words, leaving out such unnecessary phrases as "Graph of" (people see that it's a graph) and "Percentage of" (that information will appear on the graph scale). Since a presentation is a temporal event, moving through time under your control, it's unnecessary and distracting to include a figure number or other reference in the title.

Subtitles

When you find you need more than a few words to describe the subject of a frame, employ a subtitle. This handy division of labor allows your viewers to absorb the ideas in two stages, organizing the message for them. Try to include something in the subtitle that will intrigue your viewers and make them listen more closely.

Reread your titles and subtitles from the audience's point of view. Say them aloud. Think of the poor presenter with a chart— showing statistics on male and female demographics by different age categories—titled "Population Broken Down by Age and Sex."

Punctuation

On a printed page, punctuation marks signal the reader to prepare for a break in the flow of ideas. Because the ideas in presentation graphics are already grouped and arranged visually, the punctuation requirements are quite different. We rarely need a period or colon at the end of a title or bullet line, since these are discrete ideas on the screen. Your formatting—size, type style and weight, position and color—reveals the organization of the material.

Parentheses can be particularly annoying in presentation graphics. Keep them to a minimum, especially in titles, where you don't need to give your audience the impression that you're whispering over your shoulder. If an idea is so subordinate to the main title that you're tempted to enclose it in parentheses, drop it to the subtitle or eliminate it altogether. Keep your titles strong and clear.

Figure 2-9: **Avoid using punctuation if possible. An alternative visual treatment can be far more effective.**

If you find yourself peppering your text with quotation marks, break the habit! Presentations aren't the place for indicating "so-called" phrases. If you're citing someone directly, be sure you know whom you're quoting and whether it's a verbatim citation or a paraphrase before you reach for the quote key. Consider using alternative graphic treatments for these passages—italics or contrasting color, for instance. Make punctuation work in your favor by using it very sparingly and only for clarity.

Abbreviations

For some audiences, a presentation that relies heavily on abbreviations and acronyms will look like gibberish; for others, a presentation must include such phrases in order to appear professional. In introductory-level programs you can't go wrong spelling things out, even if that makes your material slightly more bulky. Audiences already acquainted with the subject are used to reducing familiar terms to acronyms and abbreviations, so key in to this common lingo. When you're not sure, spell it out. Practice reading the graphic out loud, using both the abbreviation and the full phrase. Do both make sense and sound right to you?

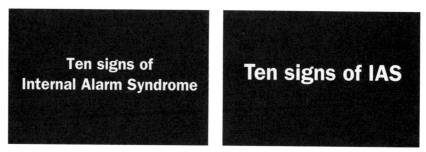

Figure 2-10: Spell things out sparingly, but use acronyms only if your audience is familiar with the subject.

Viewers will have a hard time remembering new abbreviations explained in the first slide and used thereafter. The terms must be meaningful enough to them to stand alone throughout the presentation. Consider that you'll have at least one latecomer or daydreamer and ask yourself whether that person will understand the abbreviations you're using. As an alternative to abbreviations, replace wordy phrases with simple graphics and diagrams.

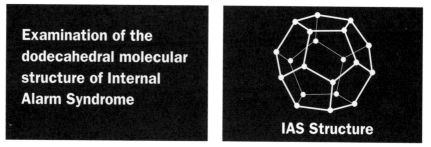

Figure 2-11: Sometimes, a simple graphic treatment can pack more punch than a wordy phrase.

Your goal is to keep the character count in each image to a minimum, but you shouldn't accomplish this merely by abbreviation. There's a big difference between distilling a message to its essence in a few words and cramming a lot of words into a few characters. Go for simplicity!

MOVING ON

Put yourself in your viewers' place. Can you follow the message clearly? Is it concise or rambling? Does it flow smoothly and logically? Is it interesting to you?

Once you've developed some concrete ideas about your message, you'll want to decide which medium will suit your presentation situation and audience best. In Chapter 3, "Presentation Media," we'll examine these options and their relevant characteristics.

PRESENTATION MEDIA 3

W hen the presentation medium fits the environment, harmonizes with the content and speaks effectively to the audience, your chances for successful communication increase a hundredfold. Finding the right match doesn't require a master's degree in media, but familiarity with the options helps you choose wisely.

ENVIRONMENTAL CONSIDERATIONS

If you're preparing a presentation for one particular event, you may have the luxury of examining the environment in detail. The size of the room and the flexibility of the lighting control are major factors. Is there a whole wall of windows with only filmy curtains? How many people will be in the audience? How will they be seated—in rows or around tables? What is the distance from the projection area to the screen?

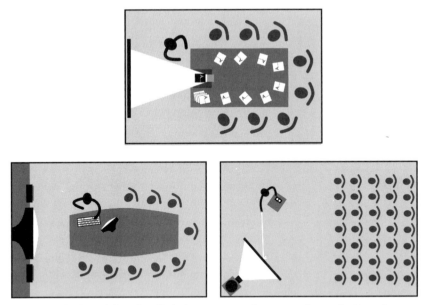

Figure 3-1: **Consider the lighting, room size, number of attendees, seating configuration, and size and clarity of your visuals.**

The presentation environment influences even something as simple as the size of your type. The illustrations and type in your visuals must be big enough for the people in the back row to read. On the other hand, they can't be so big that people sitting in the first rows are engulfed in graphics. As a rule of thumb, the distance between the monitor or projection screen and the last row of the audience should be no more than eight times the height of the screen; the distance from the projection screen to the first row should be no less than two times the height of the screen. Clearly, then, computer display monitors are in their element with small groups; for larger meetings, match lenses and throw distance with slide, video or overhead projectors. The quality of the image plays an important role in legibility as well. Low-resolution images, even when they are large, can be blurry and grainy. Video projection of computer screens is hot these days, but the quality of details and small type is not. That's because video images are made up of pixels—blocks of colors—that are coarser than the tiny points that make up high-resolution graphics like those in the PostScript language. When projected, these chunky areas of color are enlarged further. Post-Script film recorders overcome this difficulty by imaging extremely fine points of color on slide or overhead transparency film—but they produce only static images, not the catchy animated effects and transition devices, like wipes and fades, so easily produced in electronic presentations. Multiprojector slide shows provide the best of both worlds—high resolution images and motion effects—but they require dedicated computer programming hardware and software, as well as healthy budgets.

EQUIPMENT

It definitely pays to think ahead about presentation equipment. Practice your presentation with all the hardware and software in place, so you'll have firsthand experience with the equipment. Unless you're providing it yourself, make absolutely sure all the equipment you need will be available on-site. Whenever you can, check it out the day before. If you're traveling to present at a conference or other large gathering, you can often meet the technicians as they're setting up the evening before the event. Unless they're tearing their hair over an obstinate projector or balky sound system, they'll be pleased to run through your visuals. Take the opportunity to walk yourself through each stage of the process: where you'll put your notes and essential items like remote control, pointer and extra transparencies, where you'll stand and gesture, how you'll maintain eye contact with your audience. Think how much better you'll sleep, familiar with the remote control buttons, projection situation and organization of space.

In this chapter, we'll consider the elements that influence your most basic decisions: which medium is best for your content, audience and venue? How will you shape your presentation to take full advantage of that medium's communication potential?

35-MILLIMETER SLIDES

Characteristics & Qualities

For sharp images, intense colors and easy transportation, 35mm slides are hard to beat. With your carousel tray of tried-and-true slides in hand, you can rest assured that unpleasant surprises won't interrupt your presentation. Well-designed slides always convey a sense of preparation and professionalism. They may not be as dynamic or trendy as electronic presentations, but neither are they subject to crashing systems or complicated interfaces.

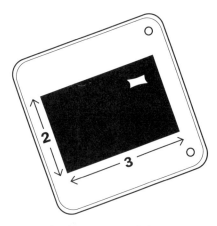

Figure 3-2: **The aspect ratio for 35mm slides is 3:2.**

Presentation slides typically make use of a horizontal format with an aspect ratio of approximately 3:2. Prepare your artwork in that proportion to make use of the full image area. If it suits your content, and your projection situation allows the audience to see the entire slide, there's no reason why you shouldn't opt for a vertical 2:3 format. Just stay consistent! Mixing horizontal and vertical slides in the same presentation conveys a thrown-together quality, shifting the audience's expectations about the part of the screen that's the live area. You're also more likely to lose part of your image off the screen if the projector has been set up for horizontal slides.

Because you can easily incorporate photographic slides into your 35mm presentation, this medium offers a distinct advantage for communicating certain kinds of information best shown with pictures. Again, be sure to maintain the same horizontal or vertical format with all slides—graphic and photographic. In your photos, work for the rich tones that look best with the intense colors of computer graphics. Simplify backgrounds and create a strong point of focus.

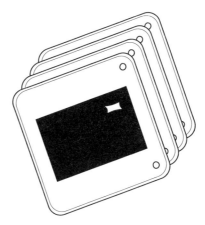

Figure 3-3: **Don't mix horizontal and vertical slides in the same presentation.**

Production

Slide production involves three stages. First, the frames are designed, produced and saved as computer files. Next, the files are imaged on 35mm film, using a digital film recorder. Finally, the film is processed in the same kind of chemical development as your 35mm snapshots.

Presentation software programs are set up to help image your files, and most offer a specific software link with one of the national service bureau groups. It's important to contact your service bureau early in the process; you may need to choose particular items and enter values from the Setup or Print menus before you begin to produce your frames on-screen. You're not limited to "chain" service bureaus, however; consult local vendors for competitive pricing with your particular software. Be sure to ask how their resolution and color fidelity compare with the norms of the national service bureaus. Send some of your more complex files to both for a detailed comparison. Be aware, too, that the color shift between your monitor and the final film image can be dramatic, even from the highest-tech equipment. It's sound advice to run a test slide to see what your color palette really looks like on film.

Quite often, organizations find it profitable to invest in their own in-house film recorder. Follow the instructions for file preparation to the letter, and consult others who have wrestled with the beast. Ask the sales rep to give an on-site demonstration of the process if you have any questions. Its always better to make a trial file and ask for help than to struggle alone at the brink of a deadline.

You aren't limited to presentation programs when creating high-quality slides. PostScript film recorders image any PostScript file—from page layout or drawing programs, for instance. Remember to set your page size to match the 35mm aspect ratio of 3:2 (try 9 x 6 inches, for example) and call your PostScript service bureau for details. The beauty of this approach is the freedom to use any typeface you wish, to fine-tune your type and design elements more completely than your presentation software may allow, and to work in a program with which you're familiar. Artwork and layouts you've already created for a print application can be imaged easily on film.

Don't stint on film processing! Your service bureau will automatically process the film they image, and they're usually excellent. Send the film you record in-house to a reputable photo lab with high-quality equipment for processing 35mm transparency film. Inspect the film for water stains, scratches and dust—they can ruin all your hard work. Just as important, make sure your slides were cut and mounted correctly. Open the mounts of your test frames to check that the film chips are straight and that the black strip on either side of the image is the same size. If film returns to you with dirt in the emulsion or misaligned frames, find a new processing lab. These errors can recur at the most inconvenient times.

To hold your film chip exactly in the focal plane of the slide projector, you'll want to request glass mounts. When individual frames stay in the projection gate, exposed to the hot lamp, they warp and quickly go out of focus. The very thin panels in glass mounts hold the film flat and keep the image sharp from corner to corner. If your slides are more than ephemeral—you'll be working with the same set of slides over the course of several presentations, say—you'll also appreciate the way these mounts protect the film from dust, fingerprints and scratches.

Workarounds

Over the years, folks have tried just about everything to get images from the computer onto film. If the standard film recorder route won't work in a particular situation—if your program lacks a film recorder driver, for instance—one of the following techniques might come in very handy. Be sure to test your workaround before relying on it for an important presentation.

Shoot the screen.

That's what you're tempted to do anyhow—so aim an ordinary 35mm camera at the computer screen and take a picture. However, the image will only be as crisp as your screen itself, which is probably quite a bit coarser than standard digital film recorder resolution. While you don't notice this when working at the computer (since you expect a computer display to show pixels), it's much more apparent on film. Further, your success will depend on your ability to control focus and lighting. The curve of the screen requires a good depth of field to hold focus. Make sure your camera lens is parallel to the computer screen and centered in the middle of the image area. Since the glass is very reflective, turn off all the lights in the room before you set your exposure and shoot. The light from the screen can be a bit tricky for a camera's light meter to read, so bracket your exposure by several stops over and under. Don't close in too tightly on the image area; allow yourself some leeway in case the camera shaves a little from what you see in the viewfinder.

Shoot flat artwork.

With a relatively simple copy stand setup, you can work with laser print output from a black-and-white or color printer, or sheets from a high-resolution color plotter. Your copy stand should include tungsten-balanced photographic lights on each side of the image and a tripod or stand to hold the camera parallel with the artwork on paper. Use tungsten-balanced film to match your lights. Kodalith film will reverse black type on white paper to a dense black background with clear type. Again, allow for any size discrepancies between what you see in the viewfinder and the image on film.

Work color magic with black-and-white.

A full-service photo lab can make color slides from your black-and-white laser printer output. They'll guide you in preparing separate, prealigned layers for each color on a slide; then they'll photograph the layers with gels and composite them. The advent of digital film recorders has greatly reduced the call for lab services like this, but they still can be useful in some circumstances.

Presentation Environment

Slides project best in the dark—the darker the room, the snappier the colors. The closer the projector can be placed to the screen, the brighter the image will appear. Long throws benefit from special, extra-bright projector bulbs.

Light figures on a dark background are easy for audiences to look at, and they show up well with the lights off and windows covered. Be aware, though, that darkening a room separates the speaker from the audience so that interaction within the group is limited and note-taking restricted.

Rear-screen projection brings the projector close to the screen and keeps the image bright. The viewing room should be dimly lit to bring out the most from your slides. Be sure no light is falling on the screen from either direction.

Using the Medium

Most projectors accept the standard carousel-type tray. Always use 80-slide trays because they're much more mechanically sound than the jam-prone 140s. A slight additional investment in covered trays will protect your slides from dust and accidents. Find out if your slides will be projected from the front or rear and arrange them accordingly. Rear-screen projection requires loading the slides "backward," unless a mirror system is used.

Confirm the availability of a 35mm projector before you plan your show. Some presenters make it a habit to verify that a back-up machine is readily available. Be sure you have a spare bulb and know how to change it. Some projectors have spare bulb modules that allow you to slide in the new bulb without disarranging the projection setup. Always switch to the high lamp setting for brighter illumination.

Slide frames advance smoothly, so feel free to use a series of images when telling a complex story. Compared with overheads, the typical slide show will have more frames, each one relatively simple in amount of information and focus of content.

Use the slide changes to pace your presentation. As slides drop, they establish a rhythm. Use a break in this rhythm to emphasize a point or make a transition from one topic to another. Dissolve units can be added to your projection arsenal to fade between images on alternating projectors, making slide changes virtually seamless. These systems add polish to your presentation, but most make it impossible to move backward in your slide trays from a remote control.

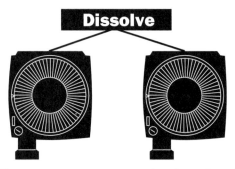

Figure 3-4: Lend finesse to your presentation by using dissolve units with two or more projectors.

Because they're very small, slides are easy to carry and store. You don't have to store them in carousel trays—many space-saving products like sleeves, drawer units and boxes are available to help organize and view your slide library. Fading isn't a problem; under the proper storage conditions of temperature, humidity and protection from dust, the colors in slides stay strong and crisp for years.

Slides are easy and inexpensive to duplicate. That's an important consideration when you'll need multiple copies of a program. Most professional photo labs offer fast, inexpensive copying services. Wise presenters carry a duplicate set of "insurance" slides sleeved in viewing pages, just in case. While a duplicate is never as good as another original from the film recorder, slide copies can come very close. Examine your duplicates next to the originals on a color-corrected light box, looking for loss of detail, gain in contrast or shift of colors.

OVERHEAD TRANSPARENCIES

Characteristics & Qualities

Overhead transparencies are a terrific presentation medium, often overlooked in favor of slides or electronic shows. The great advantage of overheads is that you can project them in normal room light, facing the audience. That means you can establish eye contact and rapport with your audience, and check their reactions during the presentation. In fact, in certain corporate cultures, the level of preparation for a meeting is gauged by the stack of overheads in hand. While this is a rather limited view, take a cue from these high-preppers—don't overlook the humble overhead.

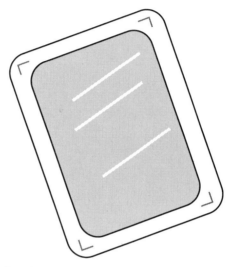

Figure 3-5: **Consider the virtues of using overheads instead of slides.**

Some informal situations are tailor-made for black-and-clear overheads straight from the laser printer. But don't stop there! Move up when the circumstances allow it. Try quick-and-dirty overheads printed on a color laser printer at a resolution of 300 lines per inch. Or go all the way to full-color, high-resolution overheads imaged through a film recorder at 2,000 or 4,000 lines per inch. Your budget, production time and audience expectations will guide you in choosing the appropriate type of overheads.

Production

When you're working with monochrome overheads, take time to experiment with a range of midvalue grays by mapping screens and patterns on your laser printer or final output device. This exploration will help you avoid two problems. When screen values are too fine, the dots will clump together, causing blobs that make your graphics look dingy and low-budget rather than crisp and clear. On the other hand, screens and patterns that are too coarse can make your graphics resemble an eye doctor's test chart. To spiff up a black-and-clear overhead, add color by hand with markers that stick to acetate (Vis-à-Vis, Sharpee), or transparent adhesive film made specially for overheads. These embellishments look best as highlights when a sketchy, hand-drawn style adds impact to the transparency as a whole.

The same production stages outlined for slide graphics apply to overheads imaged from desktop presentation software packages. First, design, produce and save the frames as computer files. Be sure to set the aspect ratio correctly for overhead transparencies (4:5). Next, image the frames on a film recorder and process the film. Some systems require a slide or slightly larger transparency as intermediary to the final overhead; your service bureau can advise you on production specifics and relative costs. Always have your overhead transparencies mounted in cardboard or plastic mounts to hold them flat and keep them from curling under the heat of the projector.

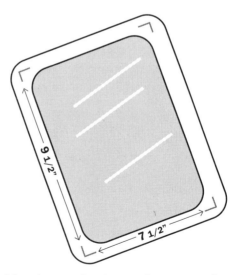

Figure 3-6: **Consider the production and presentation advantages of using overheads instead of slides.**

To make your presentation even more interesting, it's possible to include overheads made from photographs. A film lab will work with a 35mm slide or larger, medium-format photographic transparency. If you decide to mix graphic with photographic overheads, plan to maintain your overall presentation size and orientation.

The "live" area of an overhead transparency measures roughly 7.5 x 9.5 inches. The dimensions of cardboard and plastic overhead frame mounts vary slightly from one manufacturer to another, but you can safely plan on an aspect ratio of approximately 4:5.

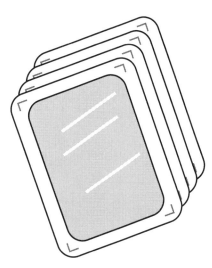

Figure 3-7: **Keep a consistent orientation throughout your presentation.**

Presentation Environment

If you'll be projecting on a horizontal screen or presenting in a meeting where horizontal slides will be used as well, you'll want to produce horizontal overheads. On the other hand, if your screen is square or vertical and you don't have to worry about other presenters, you're free to consider vertical overheads. Frequently that orientation will be more practical for the information you're communicating. Make sure no room light falls directly on the screen, and keep the projector fairly close to the screen for the brightest image.

Overheads are often the best choice for small and medium-sized working groups. Regardless of the dimensions of the viewing room, overheads give a speaker full control over the medium. Since the projector stands very close to the screen at the front of the room, the speaker can change or rearrange graphics quickly and easily.

Because overheads are used in a partially lit room and don't require complete darkness, there are minimal interruptions as the speaker shows the visuals. Listeners can take notes and communicate with the speaker easily. Group discussions that would be awkward in a darkened room can be carried out comfortably. The speaker can interact with the graphics by using a light pointer, walking toward the screen and even marking on the transparency. These techniques help engage the audience; changing the overheads themselves helps pace the presentation, signaling a transition or change in information level.

Using the Medium

Most businesses have overhead equipment, so it's a safe choice for a corporate setting. Make sure the projector, cart and spare bulb will be available when and where you need them. While you are at it, check to be sure a screen will be provided, although a smooth white wall will do in a pinch. The surface of a genuine projection screen is highly reflective and brightens your images for greater clarity and snap. Since attention wanes quickly when audiences are exposed to dim visuals, line up the best available equipment. Before your presentation, learn how to change bulbs and work the basic controls. If you're making a very important pitch that relies heavily on the graphics, consider reserving a backup projector.

Overhead frames are changed by hand—although it needn't be *your* hand. Think about enlisting a helper to handle the frames so you can concentrate on content. While the frame-changing operation should be smooth and easy, even the most experienced speaker can't guarantee a perfect alignment every time, so expect to make occasional adjustments. Clear space around the projector for at least two piles of overhead frames: the "to show" batch and the "already shown" batch. Locate each pile in a comfortable spot for moving onto or off the projector.

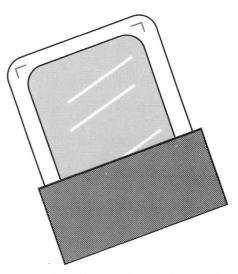

Figure 3-8: **Build an overhead image by hand: reveal each point by simply moving a piece of cardboard down the frame.**

The longer break between images and the slightly cumbersome changing procedure may limit the number of frames you use. With a series of slides, you can build a bullet list one point at a time. Instead of shuffling lots of overhead frames on and off the projector, try moving a piece of lightweight cardboard down the list, revealing each new point as you discuss it.

Another helpful technique is to amplify single frames with multiple layers. While they require a bit more time and resources, these additional flaps and overlays prove extremely effective as you can fold them down in sequence to build a complex idea. Try your hand at constructing an overhead with a surprise ending!

Figure 3-9: **Flaps, or overlays, can enhance a presentation, but using them skillfully requires experience.**

Overheads aren't the easiest presentation material to haul around. Thirty mounted overheads can fill a briefcase. Furthermore, the transparencies themselves are somewhat fragile; they scratch easily and should be interleaved with soft paper when stored. It's a good idea to remove these papers before beginning a presentation, since it's hard to deal with all those extra sheets. After the show, reinsert the protective papers if you'll use the presentation again.

ELECTRONIC PRESENTATIONS

A great momentum is building, supported by rapidly changing software programs and hardware interface cards, to use desktop computers for the display as well as the production of presentations. The advantages are quite convincing: the program is ready immediately, without sending files to a service bureau or output equipment; all the motion effects, animation, multimedia clips and transition devices are easily accessible; and changes can be made to your files for immediate updating. The down side has always been related to the limits of the computer screen itself—the relatively low resolution and the difficulties of setting up in the presentation environment.

Figure 3-10: **Use computer images and video for special effects in informal presentations.**

Advances in technology are overcoming many of the reservations we've had about electronic presentations. There are now fairly reliable display options for most every size and style of presentation, from large-screen monitors for small groups to active-matrix LCD panels that work with overhead projectors to capture motion for large audiences. Large-screen video projectors, rapidly becoming standard equipment in corporate boardrooms and auditoriums, accept computer output signals and generate a crisp, high-resolution image.

Characteristics & Qualities

Computer video works with "component" red-green-blue signals, called RGB. Video and television, by contrast, generate and accept "composite" NTSC signals. To move from one world to the other, your computer must be outfitted with a special board to translate incoming NTSC video to RGB, and to provide the NTSC output to video from the computer's internal RGB. These boards are becoming more sophisticated and less expensive by the minute. If you plan to work frequently with multimedia or wish to interface your computer-generated materials with videotape, keep a weather eye on these devices.

The computer screen and video aspect ratio is 4:3—horizontal, of course—slightly taller and narrower in proportion than the 3:2 slide format, but not as close to square as overheads.

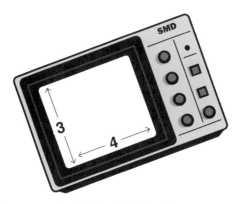

Figure 3-11: **Video aspect ratio is 4:3. Monitors vary, so allow room to avoid cutting off text or graphics.**

The resolution of even the best computer monitor is not as good as a digitally imaged 35mm slide, but it is better than a traditional television screen. Thin horizontal lines that look fine on a computer display will dance or flicker on a television screen. Expect some loss of definition when you output images to tape or to a video monitor. By the same token, video images you grab and bring into a multimedia program may look rather gritty compared with the resolution of your graphics. If you plan to broadcast your images, allow a 10 percent safe area around the outside edges.

To offset the problems of low resolution, flicker and glare, design bold, simple graphics. Weight your line elements so they're thick enough to resolve on a video monitor—at least two pixels wide if your system allows measurement in pixels.

Set your type in simple sans-serif faces, fairly large and with generous letter spacing. Thin, dark drop shadows can help clarify the letters. Colors that read well on your computer screen don't necessarily come across well on television monitors: reds and magentas tend to smear and pure white can cause contrast problems. If you plan to use an LCD display panel, project a sample palette early in your design process to check out any color shifts.

Production

Make images for electronic presentations somewhat coarser and more simplified than images for slides—don't rely on intricate graphic detail to make your point. Keep in mind that even a very small audience gathered around your computer screen will be farther away than you are when you're designing the frames. Compensate by dividing your content into lots of frames and by playing directly to the medium's strong suit, emphasizing motion with animated effects and transition devices.

Figure 3-12: **High resolution allows some fairly intricate detail in slide frames, but the lower resolution of video and computer screens requires simpler, bolder images.**

Devote some thought to the sequence and pacing of your images. How many times can you comfortably prompt a new image from the keyboard? When do you want to run a brief sequence of images automatically? Be aware that while you can back up in an electronic presentation, most programs don't handle going backward the same as moving forward. Don't try to view the presentation by backing up; just return to the point of origin and replay the sequence going forward.

Motion effects can use lots of memory; they also make heavy demands on your computer's processing speed. We once designed an animated sequence that looked great on a 486 machine— registers spun and plugged into electronic meters like clockwork. Unfortunately, it ran like molasses on our client's slower laptop models. The moral of this sad story: keep your display equipment firmly in mind when designing your program.

Presentation Environment

The display platform for your electronic presentation will depend on the size of your audience and the equipment available to you. Gather very small groups of two or three people around your computer screen. Darken the room to minimize glare and contrast problems. If you're lucky enough to work on one of the larger 16- or 17-inch screens, you'll be able to include a few more people. For slightly larger groups, consider one of the large-screen 33-inch or 37-inch monitors. These CRT displays handle video input as well, so check out your company's corporate communications department as a possible source.

Once your audience grows beyond ten or twelve people, your options require more hardware. LCD projection panels throw your computer display onto the screen, hooking to your computer and fitting on overhead projectors just like transparencies. They offer lots of flexibility in a lightweight design about the size of a notebook. With your laptop and a projection panel, you're ready to hit the road—only the overhead projector, a fairly standard piece of corporate gear, remains to complete the setup. Passive matrix panels have a fairly slow refresh rate, which makes them suspect for motion graphics. Active-matrix LCD models, by contrast, work well with animation and effects. Both types of technology are available in a range of models that vary in the way they handle contrast and display color. Naturally, better contrast and larger color palettes mean bigger price tags.

While LCD panels offer the advantages of audience rapport associated with overhead presentation, video projectors can produce an even higher quality image. Especially when the projector is already installed in your presentation space, or when your meeting features live or taped video as well as computer-generated presentations, video projection is the way to go. If a projector is at your disposal, be bold! Conceptualize your program to take full advantage of the display medium: take a tip from rock concerts and feed live video signal to the projector to capture people from the audience asking questions or interacting.

Using the Medium

If you've been experimenting with multimedia applications, you already know the difficulties of working with large files. Those same disk crashes and glitches can happen in front of a live audience, too. That means the presenter must be more than familiar with the file structure, names and access route for the presentation program. Run through disaster scenarios to develop a relief plan, and always prepare a backup file.

When you invite a few people at a time into your office to see a presentation on your computer display, your needs are simple—comfortable chairs and coffee. Electronic presentations on a larger scale are equipment-intensive. Setup can take time and specialized assistance.

Adjust video monitors for the color balance and contrast that present your graphics best. Video projectors are quite delicate and must be carefully aligned after they're moved by someone trained to register their three-gun configuration. In all cases, check the electronic projection equipment with your program as far in advance of your presentation date as possible. The wrinkles probably will be easy to iron out, given enough time to recognize and work around them.

POSTERS & FLIP CHARTS

Don't neglect paper as an effective presentation medium. Some situations don't lend themselves to projected images yet still require big, high-impact graphics. In these cases, remember posters and flip charts. Posters are individual sheets, usually mounted on stiff backing board; the sheets in flip charts are unmounted but bound together at the top. Tabletop flip books are a smaller version of the easel display variety, useful when viewers can come closer to the pages.

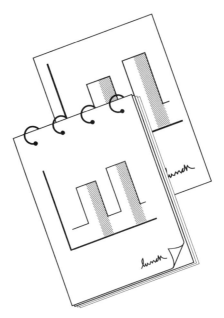

Figure 3-13: **Sometimes posters or flip charts can be better than projected images.**

Characteristics & Qualities

The graphic quality of posters depends largely on the resolution of the printer or plotter you use to image your type and artwork. Remember that when you enlarge these images photographically, you enlarge the resolution-related jagged edges as well.

Audiences tolerate viewing posters or flip chart sheets for a longer period of time than slides or even overheads. Therefore, each can represent quite a large chunk of the content and include a fair amount of detail. Legibility is still important, however; you would never want to make a poster as dense as a printed page. Normally you'll require fewer poster frames than projected media frames to cover the same amount of material.

Production

Poster art can be printed to the size your printer allows, then photographically enlarged. The imperfections of the original become much more apparent at larger sizes, so start with the highest-resolution output you can. A Linotronic 300, capable of over 2,400 lines per inch, would be a good choice. Film negatives allow enlargements printed to very large sizes. Check your local graphic arts camera services or blueprinters; both make excellent resources for large-scale reproduction.

A less expensive and more immediate solution is available if your software offers "tile" under the print menu. Tiling creates a mosaic of your image at the correct final size when it's pasted or taped together. Unfortunately, the paste-up lines are usually fairly obvious. Trim each sheet carefully with a matte knife and make sure any crossover lines match exactly.

Add color to these monochrome posters or flip chart pages using markers, colored pencils, paint, adhesive papers or vinyl. Mount posters on foam-core board or gatorboard: they're lightweight and won't sag or buckle when placed on an easel. Gatorboard has a tough surface, which helps prevent bowing and denting. Dry-mount or use spray adhesive with care, and always store the panels flat and away from heat or high humidity, to prevent warping and buckling.

You can attach flip chart sheets to a large clipboard, or hold the sheets to one sturdy backing board with clips or rings across the top. Triple-ply chipboard or masonite make good supports; lightweight illustration board adds heft to the individual sheets if they seem flimsy or difficult to handle. Drill or punch holes for the rings, which are available in a variety of sizes to match the thickness of the final stack of sheets. Practice flipping the sheets to be sure they turn easily.

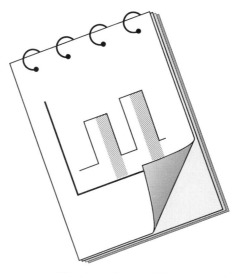

Figure 3-14: **Be sure your flip chart is sturdily constructed, and practice flipping the sheets to make sure they turn easily.**

The size and shape of posters and flip charts aren't limited by any predetermined standard, so your artwork dimensions can reflect the needs of the content. Work with the most demanding frame first; then set a consistent size for your frames, based on the requirements of that one. Take into consideration your display method, distance from viewers, construction process and media to determine the overall dimensions for your work. Ask for price guidelines from your graphic arts camera operator or blueprinters, who charge by sheet size.

When you spend a lot of time or money producing a beautiful set of posters, especially if you add color by hand, consider shooting 35mm slides of the posters as a permanent record of your presentation graphics. These slides are likely to see a lot of use, since they allow a wider distribution of your final presentation if you receive more requests than you can handle personally. Sheets in the 2 x 3-inch format exactly fill the slide image area.

Presentation Environment

Use posters and flip charts when projection and electronic media just aren't feasible. For example, a set of posters would be the right medium for a courtroom exhibit, where a witness might testify about the details represented in one image for a considerable length of time. You may be asked to make a presentation where no projectors are available, or electrical outlets aren't where you need them. Some conferences call specifically for poster sessions. When only a few frames are needed, it's overkill to set up projection equipment merely to display one or two visuals.

Posters and flip charts make ideal solutions for presentations during which you may want to add to—or strike out—your original information. These dramatic elaborations can really grab an audience's attention. If you wish to save the basic poster, tape a sheet of nonglare clear film or acetate over the poster and use film markers.

Moreover, working in this medium allows you to display a series of posters in the room before, during or after your presentation, giving your audience direct access to the information they contain. In the days following your live presentation, you can display the posters in a high-traffic area (like the cafeteria) where they can be seen and read again.

Once mounted on foam core, posters are rather cumbersome to carry and store. They're easily damaged and don't age gracefully. Their size makes them hard to wrap effectively; corners need protection and even the best mounting job will develop bubbles or come unglued. Colors added by hand can fade in time, and photographic prints can yellow.

Using the Medium

In contrast with equipment-intensive electronic presentations, the equipment requirements of poster and flip chart presentations are minimal. That advantage alone can make a tremendous difference when you're tight for time, money or display options.

Pin your poster displays to a wall or rest them in the trough of an easel or other prop. Check the walls and ask for permission in advance if you plan to attach your graphics to them; some conference room walls are designed for Velcro or other special systems. Be sure to bring pushpins or other secure fasteners with you. You may want to travel with markers or a pointer for emphasis.

Since you'll move through print graphics more slowly than projection or electronic graphics, consider consciously developing additional pacing devices like gestures and movement, redirecting your eye contact and changing vocal emphasis. Anecdotes and stories also can be very effective during a poster or flip chart presentation: the graphic anchors the content but doesn't demand a strictly linear approach.

HANDOUTS

Although paper handouts may be distributed before or after a presentation and often contain versions of graphics that a speaker shows the audience, they are not strictly presentation media. Rather than leading a group through the speaker's points, they're designed as pages to be perused at the reader's leisure.

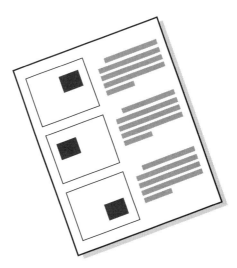

Figure 3-15: **Handouts supplement a presentation by bringing the comments and graphics together in a complete statement.**

Visual displays used during a presentation include intentionally incomplete statements that supplement what the speaker says. By contrast, handouts must stand alone as complete concepts, incorporating information from both the speaker's comments and the graphics.

MOVING ON

Now that you've considered the message and media in relationship to your audience and presentation environment, it's time to concentrate on the design and layout of your frames. In the next chapter, we'll examine some of the core concepts that will help you produce an effective, well-integrated program.

DESIGN & LAYOUT 4

In essence, design is simply a visual plan to achieve a desired goal or effect. That means everybody is a designer in one way or another. When you're putting together your presentation graphics, you're the designer for every frame you create. As you arrange the basic elements on the screen, you'll have to make an incredible number of design decisions on position, size, color, shape and texture. Fortunately, understanding just a few fundamental design concepts will help you make the right choices for the project at hand. Don't be daunted by the visual world—you participate in it every day. Effective presentation layout relies on design principles that help you to compose attractive, informative frames and to sequence the individual units into an integrated and compelling program.

Examine the design of anything you find especially outstanding, from a building or car to a poster or brochure. Chances are good that it combines the old and the new. The tension created by blending the traditional and the innovative keeps us involved and tells us something interesting about the way we perceive the world. It gives us a ground for understanding but wakes up our aesthetic sense. By avoiding the cliché and the bizarre, good design strikes just the right note for the audience and subject matter.

Although you can organize graphic elements into infinite combinations, the actual marks you can put on paper or the computer screen are limited to points, lines, shapes and letter forms. Each of these elements is associated with the attributes or properties of color, size, texture and position. Elements and their properties, specified during the design process, are the building blocks of presentation graphics.

The finished frame is nothing more than a record of many small choices. Your design's success reflects the attention you gave each decision along the way.

FOCUS & CONTRAST

We've all experienced indifferent presentation graphics, ho-hum frames that leave us cold. What was missing? Usually, dull graphics lack focus or the selection of one particular element as the most important point. When nothing is more important than anything else, or when our attention is drawn to several equally weighted elements, we're confused. We don't know where to look first.

Frames with a clear focus draw the viewer into the visual world of information. We need direction to feel that a frame is organized. Use the graphic elements at your disposal—type style, size, alignment and weight; design devices like rules, boxes and open space; color choices and illustrations—to direct viewers to the single most important point. Engage the eye, moving into the rest of the frame in a smooth transition from the focal point.

Contrast is your ally in creating a focused frame. Contrast in size, color or weight attracts the viewer's attention—but resist the urge to use all three at once! In this context, less is definitely more. Extra open space around a particular element will sharpen the contrast and heighten its importance, even without other changes. Try it yourself and see.

THE IDEA STAGE

When we see and appreciate a speaker's presentation graphics, it's natural to assume that the visual concept somehow dropped out of the sky and the designer knew exactly what to do at the outset of the project. Too bad, but that's rarely the case. Well-made images look so finished, it's hard to imagine that other solutions were considered and rejected before a satisfactory constellation of elements and attributes was found. Relax. Almost no one—not even the experts—-can arrive at the perfect design solution without some trial and error. That's what keeps this work interesting.

As you generate ideas for your presentation, remember your objectives and evaluate each idea with them in mind. Work from your content outline, visualizing different ways to present each point. There's no single "right" way to approach your subject. Experiment; develop several alternative approaches. Evaluation and selection will come later. Don't try to get from start to finish in one giant step. Just let the ideas flow and see where they take you.

Thumbnail Sketches

While rendering your graphics on the computer is much easier than with traditional methods, sketching the initial designs is not. Computer images look too finished to have that experimental feeling, and you might find yourself accepting even a design you don't like simply because it looks "done" and you put considerable effort into creating it. Instead, start experimenting by making thumbnail sketches. These are simple, small-scale pencil drawings set down quickly on tissue paper.

It's not necessary to write all the words on your sketches. With a few simple strokes, indicate where type will be placed and the approximate size you expect to use. Similarly, block out graph areas and artwork in basic shapes and lines. The overall relationships between text and graphic elements are most important at this stage.

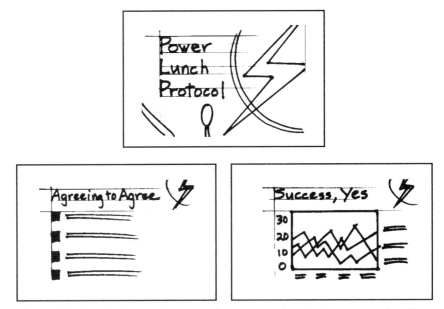

Figure 4-1: **Begin by making thumbnail sketches to help you visualize the concepts.**

Think with your pencil. The main purpose of this step is to get a sense of how the graphics will look, translating the vision in your mind's eye. Sketch out several types of frames in the presentation to see if the overall layout will work with all your material.

It may surprise you that even the best hardware and software in the world can't replace pencil and paper at this beginning stage. You don't need training in studio art to sketch a few simple elements. Don't worry if your concept sketches aren't masterpieces. Finished art comes later in the game. At that point you'll appreciate the computer's precision; right now, you're just jotting down visual notes.

Storyboards

The storyboard is a visual and verbal outline of your presentation. A helpful tool both for your own use and for others who might need to evaluate your plans, the storyboard shows the underlying structure of the presentation in frame-by-frame sequence. Titles and illustrations are consistently sized and placed; relative type size and line-length patterns can be indicated.

Figure 4-2: **A storyboard will help you evaluate the structure and impact of your presentation-in-the-making.**

The storyboard answers many structural questions. What points will you need to amplify, and where should one frame be split into two or more? How will you indicate major shifts in emphasis and keep your audience oriented? Is the presentation nicely balanced with the right number of frames for each point, based on its importance and complexity?

You may find it helpful to sketch out a storyboard using thumbnail drawings. You can prepare a rough storyboard on paper to check the program for continuity, adjust sequences and insert or delete frames.

If you have a storyboard option on your software system, ignore it at this point. It will prove much more helpful during the actual production phase of your show. Save this feature to check your sequences as you develop them, to review consistency and flow, and to revise by shifting sections or individual frames to different positions in the presentation.

Design for the Medium

Each of the presentation media discussed in Chapter 3 brings its own inherent qualities and properties to the project—that's why it's so important to choose your medium early in the conceptualization process. Design with your medium's particular characteristics firmly in mind and you'll realize the greatest return on your efforts. Although the basic graphic elements are the same for all media, their applications are quite different. And be sure to keep in mind the fundamental difference that separates presentation media of all varieties from print media: presentations accompany and reinforce the speaker's live delivery. They're team players rather than stand-alone components.

The physical characteristics of each presentation medium are different. Check your orientation—horizontal or vertical—and the aspect ratio, or relationship between the width and height of the image. Maintain the same orientation throughout a presentation, or you'll destroy design continuity and risk severe projection problems. Proportion your art to match the aspect ratio required by the medium.

When you use the same artwork for more than one presentation medium, or to carry it over into the print world, differences in aspect ratio can give you some headaches. On one hand, it's delightful to create a complicated drawing once and then use it in a multitude of applications, importing and incorporating it into various files. On the other hand, you must design carefully to preserve the integrity of the image. When you make artwork serve two media, plan the design primarily for the more important use. Let's say you're planning to tour the country with both a slide presentation and a take-home report on organic coffee. Design the time-consuming diagram of an organic coffee plantation as a 3:2 horizontal for the presentation, since it's more vital to your program's success. Then adjust the design to best use the 8 1/2 x 11-inch vertical space in the report. But design for page layout if you just need to make a few overheads of illustrations from a brochure to review information with a group that will refer frequently to the printed piece.

Printed pages frequently work best with black type and colorful images on a white background; projected media are more effective with light type on a dark ground. When you use artwork from a slide presentation for a printed page, try reversing the background and type colors as well as adjusting for aspect ratio before importing the image.

LAYOUT DECISIONS

Your audience will never see your most important design tool, and probably they won't even be aware that you're using it. But they'll be very much aware of the results: clear and organized presentation frames. This mystery tool is the grid, the layout structure on which depend all your decisions about sizing and placement of various elements.

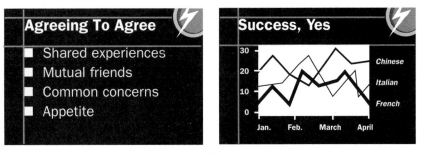

Figure 4-3: **Use grid blocks to establish a consistent structure for your layout—the simpler the elements of the show, the simpler the grids.**

Early in the design process, establish the grid that will underlie each frame in your presentation. This pattern, like coarse graph paper superimposed on the image area, does more than any other tool to make your show a coherent whole.

Simple shows need only a few divisions to show where to place the basic elements; larger and more complicated shows call for more complex grids. The grid lines and intersections give you spatial anchors for positioning headings, bullet lists, graphs and illustrations. The more elements you plan to use, the more detailed your grid must be.

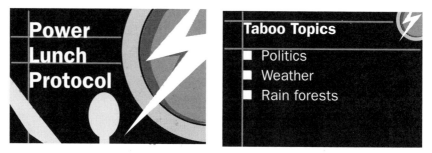

Figure 4-4: **When you stay with the same basic grid for each frame in your presentation, you create an underlying visual pattern that ties everything together.**

The grid establishes the frame's working area, inside the safety zone of margins. These outside border areas ensure that no important content will be lost to poorly projected edges. Within the live area, divide the space into columns and rows to organize the elements of your frames.

Suppose you're designing a simple, brief and informal show, and you plan to follow a title slide with six bullet lists. Your grid will help you plan the size and placement of three kinds of elements: the main title, the heading for each bullet list and the bullet items themselves. The layout will include spacing between lines of type and between bulleted items, and the distance between bullet symbols and the first word of each line. Although the title slide is the only one of its kind, it is laid out on the same grid pattern as the text frames, incorporating it into the design of the show. That way, it won't look radically different, like an orphan from another program.

Another important consideration in establishing your grid format is symmetry. If your content lends itself to formal balance, you may want to try an even number of grid columns to organize the frames. If, however, you'd like to open up the frames and introduce a more dynamic type of balance, an asymmetrical design based on an odd number of grid columns adds contrast and interest to the graphics.

Alignment

The alignment scheme you choose for each presentation dictates whether the elements will line up along a left-hand margin or grid line, along a right-hand margin or grid line, or smack in the center. Consistent vertical alignment contributes to unity and continuity. It sets up a clear pattern to help the viewer find information in each frame and so creates a sense of clarity in the graphics.

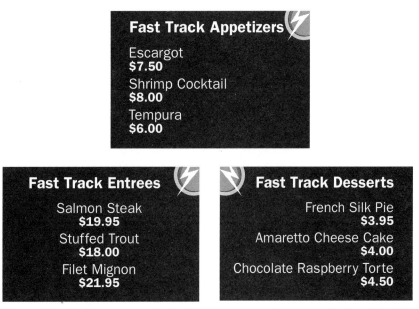

Figure 4-5: **Keep your vertical alignment consistent—whether it's left, centered or right—to give your presentation continuity.**

Flush-Left

Because it's the style of vertical organization with which we're most familiar, a flush-left, ragged-right alignment scheme seems natural and easy to follow. Type and other elements line up along the left-hand margin or against another grid line, resulting in a crisp, clean left edge to the type block. The "ragged" right edge results from naturally varying line lengths. Our eyes are accustomed to following text with a consistent left-hand margin in everything from business letters to phone books. When moving away from a left-aligned organization, be sure you have a clear reason to depart from convention.

When you're designing frames with a flush-left format, you need not always align each text block to the same vertical axis. Instead, use your grid to define a series of vertical axes you can use for left alignment of headings, subheads, text or bullet lists, charts, tables, artwork, attribution lines and other elements.

Flush-left alignment establishes a solid visual anchor for the viewer. The ragged-right edge keeps the frame from becoming too evenly balanced, static and boring. It's easy to lay out and to read, making it an excellent choice for most presentation graphics.

Centered

It can be tempting to center lines over one another or over other elements like illustrations and charts. This layout style makes both left and right margins ragged, with the axis in the middle. Thus, there is no strong vertical stroke defined by the elements themselves. Think of a traditional wedding invitation: it's hard to create effective contrast and emphasis, since each line tends to have equal visual weight unless it's surrounded by quite a bit more open space than other elements.

The most formal and conservative alignment format, centering is a safe choice but not often interesting. Without a distinct visual anchor within the graphic, it can be hard to read more than two or three lines of type. The left and right edges aren't well defined, and odd-shaped areas of negative space are created. Try out a flush-left alignment alternative on one or two frames of any presentation you're considering centering, just to see the difference.

Flush-Right

The opposite of flush-left alignment, a flush-right layout forces lines of type and other elements against a right-hand margin or grid line. Legibility is affected by the ragged-left edge, since eye-tracking from one line to the next becomes more difficult. Align type flush-right only when you want to create a strong visual effect with relatively few lines of type. Align graphics and illustrations flush-right only when you have a strong right vertical from which to work.

Justification

When type is justified, the lines are flush along both edges. Newspaper columns are a prime example of justification. This technique doesn't work well with presentation graphics, because presentations require larger sizes of type, shorter line lengths and fewer words than newspapers. Justification works by dividing the space after the last word into equal increments between the words on the line. When there are only a few words, the extra space makes unsightly gaps and breaks up the even flow of text.

Figure 4-6: **Justified type can mean trouble in presentation graphics.**

If you've followed our advice and condensed your message into key words, your graphics won't have enough type to warrant justified alignment. Flush-left, flush-right or centered alignment will produce more attractive and readable frames.

Even on page layouts, justified columns look best when the line length and type size are carefully matched. Many designers are moving away from justification, since it looks more mechanical and less compelling than a flush-left layout. The inconsistent word spacing may also make justified columns more difficult to read.

Organic Layout

Occasionally it's refreshing and rewarding to break out of the established grid and position type and other graphic elements according to some internal logic or pattern indicated by the elements themselves. This organic approach can be applied much more effectively to one or two graphics rather than to an entire series of frames. Following the irregular edge of a particularly dramatic drawing, for instance, can tie type and illustration together. Diagonals represent another strong source of organic alignments. If you think an organic layout would work with one of your frames, sketch and experiment until you find an arrangement that pleases you with its informal balance; there are few rules to follow beyond working with the natural movement of the eye from top to bottom and left to right.

Figure 4-7: **Occasionally an organic layout can be striking, but it's tricky to find the right informal balance in each frame.**

As you watch other presentations, you may notice layouts that mix alignment styles. Sometimes heading lines are centered in the frame while labels for graphs or tables are placed flush-left. This works as long as the graph or table area defines a space for the centering; centered headings over flush-left bullet lists can look very odd indeed, because the bullet lines usually don't fill up the entire line length available for them. Some presenters even incorporate three axes—flush-left, flush-right and centered—to good effect; the results depend a great deal on the content and the particular elements in the frame. The only way you'll know how this type of layout will look is to go ahead and try it.

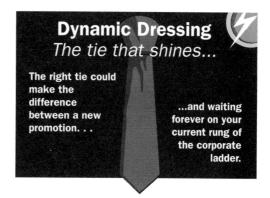

Figure 4-8: **Experiment with layout variations by mixing vertical axes.**

Units of Measure

Most software programs offer a variety of measurement systems. People who work extensively with type use points and picas (see Chapter 5, "Understanding Type") for everything, including the page width and depth, grid size and margin widths. If you're not accustomed to working in picas, choose a unit of measure for which you already have an intuitive sense.

Inches are familiar and comfortable to most of us. While you've probably been using rulers with eighths and quarters of inches since grade school, you might give decimal inches a try if you like to size and scale with a calculator. Some programs use only their own measurement systems based on rasters or pixels, which are proportionate, not fixed, units. It will take a while to adjust to these increments, but soon you'll find you've learned to speak their language.

Integration

In order to construct a layout structure that will work for your whole presentation, list all the various components that appear in any frame so you can give each kind of element a uniform graphic treatment. For example, almost every slide will have a heading, so that's a start. Will some frames need subtitles? How about a corporate, product or project logo? If the images include illustrations, can they all have the same size and location on the frame? Could you group several smaller illustrations to fit the same space as a large one?

How will the main title frame of the presentation relate to section titles throughout the show? Should they receive similar visual treatment? How can these "guidepost" graphics work as a unit to help viewers understand their role?

Figure 4-9: **As you integrate the graphic components of each frame, strive for a visually coherent presentation.**

Will it be possible to design all the charts and graphs in your presentation so they can be sized similarly and placed into the same area of the frame? By keeping the layout treatments consistent, you'll be able to integrate all the different ideas and information into a visually coherent presentation.

In spite of all your efforts, you may find one or two oddball frames that just don't work with your overall layout plan. If you must redesign an image, carry over the most obvious visual properties of the common structure—color palette, type size and type style, heading placement and alignment. Then this frame will slip much more easily into the rest of the pack.

Suppose your show will be composed of bullet lists and bar graphs, except for one pie graph. How can you integrate that round shape with its scattering of labels? See if it works to use the left-edge location of your bar graphs for a callout list of pie labels. That will probably be enough to rope in the maverick frame.

Figure 4-10: **Use your creative ability to integrate a "maverick" into your frame series.**

Don't panic when you run across an element that doesn't appear to fit your plan. Evaluate the importance of that nonconforming element, then work with color, size and position to integrate it. A program with a strong foundation can absorb a few tremors.

If all your images start to seem like renegades, however, it's time to reevaluate your structure and devise a more graceful graphic plan that will allow for continuity between frames. You may need to go even further back and re-think the content and the points you want to convey at each step.

GRAPHIC DESIGN DEVICES

As you establish the overall design of your presentation, you may find that you'd like to incorporate graphic devices such as rules, borders, boxes and open space into your frames to separate elements or to direct attention. These devices become part of the layout of each frame and should be used sparingly and consistently.

Refrain from adding merely decorative applications that will clutter the frame and interfere with understanding. Decree laws for their use and follow them! If headings will always be underscored by a 4-point rule 18 picas long, placed flush-left and 12 points below the heading base-line, don't drop the rule because it interferes with a chart in a particular frame. Adjust the chart; shift the position of the rule on each frame—fine-tune to make the frames work smoothly together.

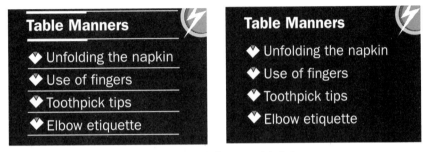

Figure 4-11: **Too much** *(left).* **Much better** *(right).*

Rules

We don't mean rules that you follow here—we're talking about rules that you draw—horizontal and vertical lines. This kind of rule can add clarity and consistency to frames throughout a presentation, especially when space is tight. Rules are extremely adaptable: draw them across the whole frame or just between certain points of your grid; choose from a whole constellation of widths, textures and colors.

While rules help distinguish one category of information from another, they're not as effective as you might think in creating visual emphasis. We tend to think underlining will bring a point to the viewer's attention, but sometimes the extra clutter has just the opposite effect. Try changing the type color or weight rather than adding a rule where it's not necessary.

Traditionally, rules are measured in printers' points (72 points to the inch). Your program may allow you to select weights from the thinnest hairline to a hefty 18-point rule that measures about a quarter-inch. Begin with rules on the lighter end of this spectrum, between 1/2 point and 2 1/2 points or so. When rules are set in a bright accent color against a dark background, even a very fine line will "pop." Thicker rules need less contrast with the background to be effective.

Borders

Like rules, borders act as separators, but their impact is even greater. They convey the unmistakable message that whatever is inside the borders doesn't belong with what's outside.

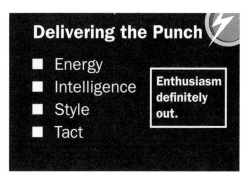

Figure 4-12: **Borders separate more than they emphasize.**

Depending on the specific graphic treatment you give them, borders can create a range of effects, from delicate picket fences to thick stone walls with barbed wire coiled along the top.

Presentation graphics rarely benefit from a border around the whole frame. Projected images define their own space very well without extra help, and screens are already framed and bordered by the monitor's hardware.

Borders don't make a statement look as important as we expect they might. In fact, framing an element can actually decrease its impact by cluttering the visual field.

Draw borders with thin, thick, double or dashed lines; turn corners as 90 degree angles or rounded fillets or even special twists and curlicues. But the clean, sharp line and corner are usually most effective since they're less obtrusive. Unless you have a specific reason for using them, avoid effects (like radius corners) that are joining the long list of desktop publishing clichés.

Boxes

A solid-color box set against the background offers a good alternative to a border. No outline box rule is necessary in most cases. If the box and background colors are close in value, the low-contrast definition of the enclosed space can be pleasantly soft and subtle, yet still do a good job setting off the content. Low contrast is especially good for slides and electronic shows, where color is rich and saturated and definition is crisp.

Figure 4-13: **Low-contrast boxes enclose and set off an element of the frame without cluttering the foreground.**

Be careful when setting gray boxes behind type or other delicate graphic elements when the final frame will be laser printed. Laser printers use screen patterns of black dots to simulate gray. When you overprint on this pattern, be careful to preserve contrast. Dark grays work best with type reversed to white, while light grays can usually support black type. In either case, the type won't be as sharp as it would be with solid black-and-white contrast, since the screen dots tend to clump on the letters and make them look ragged.

Open Space

From the time you could hold a pencil, you discovered that making pictures is a matter of marking surfaces. You probably described your pictures in terms of the marks you'd applied to the surface of the paper—the positive elements. You might not have thought much about the areas of the paper that have no marks at all—the negative elements. These open or blank areas are actually integral parts of the whole picture.

When we see three lines of type together, evenly spaced and consistently sized, it's fair to assume that they form a single statement. If the third line is pulled down, away from the other two, the relationship changes. The only difference between the following two frames is the use of space—but the effect is profound. This illustration exaggerates the use of space to make a point; you can easily use less space to emphasize and draw attention.

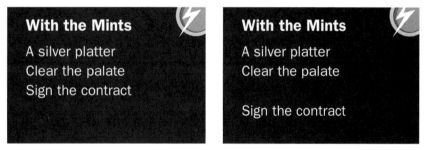

Figure 4-14: **Negative space can produce a profound impact.**

It may seem contrary that open space will direct your viewers' attention. We're more accustomed to *adding* marks to clarify a message. Presentation graphics work differently. Instead of loading the frame with arrows, rules, borders and boxes, remove all extraneous elements and simply make small adjustments to the size and placement of the remaining essential elements.

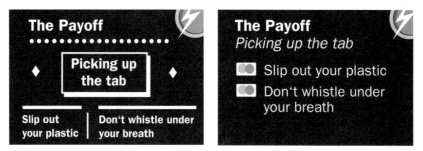

Figure 4-15: **Extraneous elements** *(left).* **Clean image** *(right).*

You might take it as a warning sign if your frames are generally so tight that you must rely on rules and borders. They're probably just too loaded with information. Try spreading the content over more frames. Be generous with the materials you need to get the job done.

MOTION & ANIMATION

Electronic presentations offer designers the wonderful ability to control the viewers' attention with motion effects. Allow your audience a chance to become oriented to the frame before the motion begins—they'll miss the point if they don't catch the heading and main ideas before the bars start to grow or the flame transforms into a phoenix.

Motion with animation or other changes is a powerful tool; because of this power, concentrate doubly hard on focus and reserve movement for the central ideas or concepts of the frame. Don't allow this device to turn counterproductive just because it's fun. Plan and justify each effect, then orchestrate the presentation with movement for emphasis within frames and for maintaining con-

GROUND RELATIONSHIPS

Whether they're slides or electronic shows, presentation graphics are by nature flat and two-dimensional. Yet a sense of depth, order and back-to-front definition can be extremely important. To achieve this *trompe l'oeil*, use tools like color, value, hidden lines, shadows, transparency and perspective drawing.

Figure 4-16: **Use three levels—foreground, midground and background—to establish relationships within your composition.**

Think of your frame composition in three levels of depth: foreground, midground and background. The differences between the figures and ground or figures and field form the basis for the relationship between these three levels.

Unlike most other graphic techniques we've discussed, the tools for establishing figure and ground relationships may be mixed at will. There's no need to limit your choices; in fact, a combination of attributes is often the best solution.

Color

Use color to suggest distance by putting blues behind the subject and yellows, oranges and reds in the foreground. Cool colors appear to recede; warm colors seem to approach. A world elevation map is a good case in point: lowlands are represented in green, the highest mountain peaks are red, and the graduated spectrum of colors between green and red indicates intermediate elevations. This color scheme creates the illusion of bringing the highest areas much closer to the viewer than the low-lying valleys. The only reason the progression doesn't start with blue, the coolest color, for the lowlands is that cartographers usually reserve blue for bodies of water.

A progression from dark to light suggests movement from far to near, since an object viewed at a distance appears darker than the same object seen at close range. If you want to emphasize the third dimension, assign lighter colors to foreground elements and darker colors to the midground. When working with full color, be sure your foreground colors are full-strength and saturated, while colors for the midground and background grow less saturated. That's how we actually see color.

Opacity & Transparency

A clever way to define or imply relative distance is to hide some of the midground behind opaque foreground elements, revealing only a portion of the midground object's outline. You can also use transparency to create veil-like effects. But remember, these effects require advanced drawing skills.

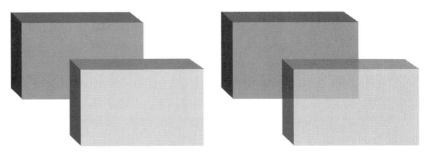

Figure 4-17: **Opacity** *(left).* **Transparency** *(right).*

Shadows

Shadowing is an extremely useful technique for generating dimension—and it's a desktop presentation standard. Shadows must be cast in a consistent manner to be effective, and they must really look like shadows. Imagine a light shining from a front corner of the frame. Foreground objects catch the light and cast darker shadows on objects lying behind them.

Shadows can be drawn either flat or in perspective. Flat shadows, called drop shadows, are easy to draw with most software. They imply that foreground objects are floating above a flat background plane. Like rounded box corners, use them with care to avoid plugging into a visual cliché.

Three-dimensional shadows are imaged in perspective in order to suggest shapes with volumes and flat planes at angles to one another. Think about the shadow cast by an upright column or billboard sign. Create the form of these shadows using any perspective drawing technique.

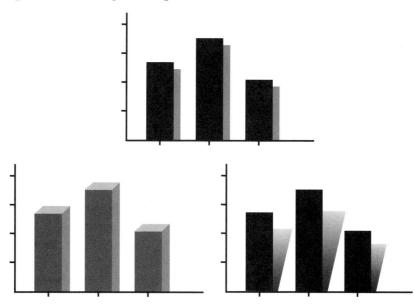

Figure 4-18: **Flat drop shadow** *(top)*. **3-D shadow** *(left)*. **Graduated shadow** *(right)*. **Each style creates a different effect.**

Graduated shadows are the most like the light patterns cast by real objects. But be careful: the angle of graduation is critical to the success of the illusion.

Perspective

Perspective drawing techniques can be applied to presentation graphics to make elements appear to occupy different planes in space. Simple parallel projection is probably the easiest method, with the greatest relevance for presentations.

Occasionally, one-point perspective comes in handy, for situations like a checkerboard pattern that disappears into the background. But even this easy vanishing-point technique is pretty elaborate for information graphics (see Appendix C).

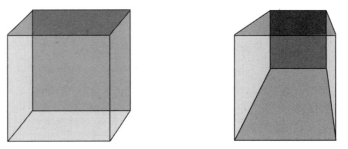

Figure 4-19: **Parallel projection** *(left).* **One-point perspective** *(right).*

Heavily worked perspective illustrations aren't necessary for most presentations. Concentrate on your original objectives and the techniques that support them most directly.

USE RESTRAINT

Most audiences sincerely appreciate graphic simplicity. People decide to attend a presentation because they want to reach a new understanding of the topic, not to be wowed by fancy pictures.

Figure 4-20: **Graphic overload** *(left).* **Effective communication** *(right).*

Software programs are loaded with features that can seduce you into graphic overload. The vast array of color choices and graphing formats, for instance, makes it tempting to go wild and use more features than necessary to get your point across. Just because you have the capabilities for unlimited typefaces, shadows, patterns, decorated corners, borders and tapered lines does not mean they'll contribute to your communications goal.

To test for graphic overload, stand back and start paring down the design devices. If you can remove anything without sacrificing content or clarity, keep going!

MOVING ON

Good graphic design is invisible. Well-made images are never contrived or forced. They call attention to the focal point of the content rather than to themselves. They serve simply to convey the message without distractions. In fact, the better you do your job as a designer, the less your audience will be conscious of your craft and skill. Practice a light touch.

Next, we'll look at typography. Typefaces and type styles are important graphic ingredients; your choices can make or break the effectiveness of your design. Now that you have lines of type roughed in and positioned on a grid, go ahead and give your thumbnail sketches final form.

UNDERSTANDING TYPE 5

The printed word is a staple of information graphics; almost every frame of any presentation makes its point with text or numbers. An overwhelming percentage of presentation graphics relies exclusively on type: bullet lists, tables, key phrases and titles account for more than three-quarters of all frames produced each year. And even graphics that rely primarily on charts, diagrams or illustrations would be meaningless without type. Words and numbers carry the message—they're absolutely fundamental to your presentation. The more you understand about typographic design, the more effectively you'll be able to harness the tremendous power of this vital element. When you choose your typefaces and styles wisely, you set the right tone for the entire presentation, supporting both the content and the design concept.

Typefaces differ radically in detail, yet we're able to recognize and read each letter immediately. As we decode the type, abstracting the basic form, we receive subtle design messages. Our reactions to the presentation before us are influenced by details like the relative sizes of the letters, how tightly the lines of type are packed together, what weight and force the letterforms carry, and whether the strokes get thinner as they round curves. We notice if the lowercase letters are nearly as tall as the capitals, and whether the individual letters look round and fat or thin and spindly. Our eyes take in the delicate cross-strokes that finish some letters. Most important, we respond to legibility—how easily can we read this type?

In this chapter we'll explore typographic terminology and basics, the main categories of typefaces, rules of thumb for their effective use, and the fundamental reasons behind those rules.

SETTING TYPE IS NOT TYPING

Because most presentation programs use proportional typefaces, you should follow the rules professional typesetters observe. These will give your presentation typography a distinctive polish and forestall the "desktop" label. The most important typographic differences are the use of special characters for curly apostrophes and opening or closing quotation marks, the long "em" and shorter "en" dashes, and ellipsis marks (dot dot dot). These special characters are produced with a combination of Option/keystrokes on the Macintosh and through Alt/keystrokes or ASCII characters on the IBM platform.

Always single-space after a period or colon. Rather than indenting the second and third lines of a single entry, work with extra between-line spacing to separate two or more ideas. Instead of relying on preset tabs, manually set the space between a bullet and the left edge of the text that follows to give just the right amount of breathing space. True fractions can be difficult to set correctly in presentation programs, but usually you can specify a bit smaller type for them. Examine a brochure or annual report that seems especially attractive typographically: have the typographer's choices in these subtle areas made a difference?

TYPE TERMINOLOGY

Typefaces

A typeface interprets the letters of the alphabet with a particular style and an individual set of design rules. The term originally referred to the printing surface—or face—of metal type. Hundreds of electronic versions of traditional and newly developed typefaces are available. Each one has design strengths and weaknesses; no single face can work for every presentation situation. While one face might make efficient use of space, another was created for legibility and to prevent eye strain. Some are crafted especially for unusual papers and inks; others work best in long, dense documents.

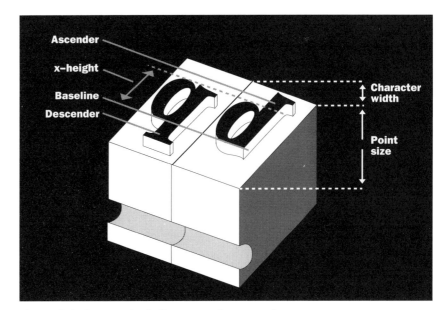

Figure 5-1: Anatomical diagram of a type character.

   Most typefaces were designed in their first incarnation for the printed page, so we must reevaluate them for presentation media. As a first step toward understanding the vast array of faces from which we must choose, we'll group them into general categories and families. Once you recognize the guideposts, the journey down the typographic road isn't really difficult at all—in fact, it's a trip through a varied and fascinating landscape.

Serif Faces

Serifs are the small finishing strokes at the ends of the main character stems. Originally, they were developed to tidy up the rough appearance of letters chiseled into stone. They also emphasize the baseline of the line of type by flaring most consistently toward it; this helps keep the reader's eye on the right line. In handset metal or wooden type, serifs played an important functional role, bracing the thin letter strokes to keep them from breaking under the tremendous force exerted by early printing presses.

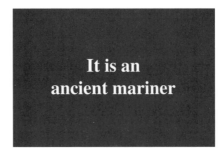

Figure 5-2: Use serif type for easy reading over long lines.

These days we choose serif type because it's easy to read in quantity—most newspapers and books are set in one serif face or another—and because it's useful for creating certain effects. If you have a presentation that requires your audience to concentrate quite hard on rather dense type, for instance, you may consider a serif face to help establish the baseline and draw the reader's eye along it.

Serif typefaces can be classified further according to their place in the history of type design (Old Style, Transitional, Modern or Contemporary, for example) or by the specific shape of the serif:

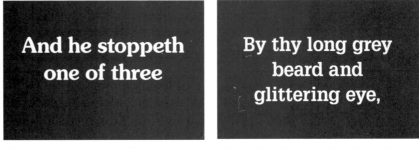

Figure 5-3: Round serifs.

Figure 5-4: Square (slab) serifs.

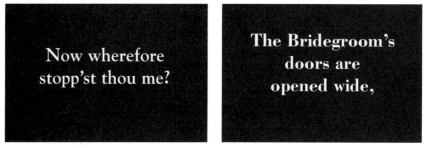

Figure 5-5: Cupped serifs.   *Figure 5-6:* Thin (hairline) serifs.

Most serif typefaces combine thick vertical strokes with thin horizontals; this contrast ehances their readability and appearance on the printed page. The tension between the straight and curved portions of the letters adds to our often unconscious appreciation of the pattern of typography. Projected by a strong light source or displayed on a luminous monitor, however, thin or delicate serifs and horizontal strokes tend to drop out, giving the letter an odd, disjointed look. Robust serif faces work best for presentation graphics, unless the type is extraordinarily large.

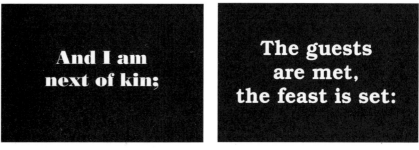

Figure 5-7: Bodoni Poster: exaggerated thick and thin strokes.

Figure 5-8: Bookman Demi: more evenly weighted strokes

Sans-Serif Faces

Letterforms without terminal cross-strokes belong in the sans-serif group of typefaces. Because they tend to offer less contrast in thick and thin strokes, sans-serif faces are rarely used for books or other text-intensive materials. But the various sans-serif families give presentation designers a wonderful variety of shapes and tones with which to work. As a group, sans-serif faces appear rather heavier or bolder than serif faces of the same size. They stand up well to projection and electronic media, remaining legible down to point sizes that would obliterate serif type.

Figure 5-9: **Avant Garde**

Many sans-serif faces are available in a wide range of weights, from light through extra bold or heavy. While you'll want to exercise caution at both extremes, it's a real luxury to increase or decrease weights until you find exactly the right combination of heading and text type for your material, size limitations and line length. Italic or oblique sans-serif faces will prove to be useful when you want to convey a sense of dynamic forward motion, or when you want to loosen up the tone of the presentation.

Figure 5-10: **Helvetica**   *Figure 5-11:* **Optima**

The simplicity and neutral style of many sans-serif faces make them perfect partners in presenting information in a business or scientific setting. Some, like Optima, retain the grace and inflection of serif faces with a suggestion of flare at the end of letter strokes and a modulation in width around curves. Others, like Avant Garde, maintain a strictly uniform line and geometric shape. Look closely at the faces available to you, so you can match their personalities with your message.

Script Faces

Script typefaces are modeled on handwriting, with letters that appear to connect. While they're slanted like italics, script faces serve an entirely different purpose—one that's generally well outside the milieu of presentation graphics.

Figure 5-12: **Ordinarily, script faces are too ornamental for use in presentation graphics.**

It's usually good advice to save scripts, with their flowing lines and flourishes, for wedding invitations and other occasions when an ornamental face looks just right. Like all rules, however, this one should be broken when the content and design demand it. We've designed some very effective presentations that use simple, legible brushstroke script fonts for short headings, choosing them as design elements that reinforce the content.

Display Faces

We usually sacrifice a degree of legibility in favor of style when we incorporate a display typeface into a presentation. These faces are designed to be printed in large point sizes for elements like headlines and initial caps. In presentation graphics they're suitable for titles or other special applications, provided they work harmoniously with the overall design and the text type. They're definitely not the workhorses you'll need for graphs, diagrams and bullet lists, but they can add a real flair when used sparingly.

Figure 5-13: **Use display faces for special elements like titles, head- lines and initial caps.**

What's in a Font?

In Gutenberg's day, a font meant a drawer full of characters made of lead or carved wood in a given size and style. The printer's devil sorted the letters into the proper compartments of the font drawer after each page was printed, so they'd be ready for the next job. The specifications for printing a document might include one typeface—Garamond, for instance—and two fonts—perhaps 9-point and 18-point Garamond.

Nowadays, digital type has taken over from lead, and while the world of typography is still full of characters, we hear the terms typeface and font used interchangeably. In computer-generated type, a font is the binary file of geometric coordinates defining the form of each character. When your software program uses Post-Script fonts, the PostScript language describes the geometry of the characters' outlines, so they can be imaged at extremely high resolutions. A single outline file prints any size of a particular face. PostScript type is the desktop industry standard, producing extremely smooth curves and fine details. Type management utilities like Adobe Type Manager allow you to see clear letter-forms on the screen, no matter what their size. The program refers to the PostScript printer files for information on how to draw the sharpest letters possible at the screen resolution.

On the other hand, if your system requires bitmapped digital type, you may need a separate file for each size of type. The sharp-ness of the letters will depend on the bitmapped resolution rather than on the capabilities of the film recorder or printer.

Along with character outlines, or bitmaps, font files include intercharacter information, which proportions the space between letters to produce a smooth and readable visual effect. As font files and desktop typesetting programs increase in sophistication, so does the built-in character spacing.

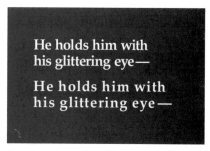

Figure 5-14: **Kerned (*above*) and unkerned (*below*) Palatino.**

Kerning is the process of adjusting the space between certain character pairs to minimize gaps for the best appearance and readability. Systems with automatic pair kerning work by including several different intercharacter space values for each letter, then adjusting the spacing to match the surrounding letters. When this kerning feature is not available, the type is metal-spaced like handset lead type. This can occasionally lead to problems in words like "Yes," where the Y and the e can seem miles apart.

Families

A type family includes several fonts that are variations on the same typeface design theme. Smaller families include roman (regular-weight type, not slanted), italic, bold and bold italic. When you select from these four family members, you can give special treatment to headings, subheads or particular words and phrases without using a second, "outsider" typeface. Some far-flung type families, like Helvetica or Frutiger, have many members; others are more tightly knit and rely on only a few weights.

Figure 5-15: Goudy

Figure 5-16: Goudy Bold

Figure 5-17: Goudy Italic

Figure 5-18: Goudy Bold Italic

Restrain yourself when you assign roles to members of a type family. Too many weights, sizes and italic variations can clutter your work and confuse your message. Don't combine hairline, outline, inline, condensed, extended and extended bold italic simply because they all carry the same family name. Maintain consistency throughout a presentation by using the same face for the same function from frame to frame.

Your Best Face Forward

Be practical. Out of all the hundreds of typefaces available, you really need only one or two at a time. So, how do you choose?

Type is meant to be read: legibility is priority number one. Second, you don't want to call attention to the type itself during your presentation—type's job is to communicate ideas, facts, concepts or statistics in an energetic and nearly transparent manner. When people notice the type rather than the content, you're drawing their attention from the central concepts to a peripheral element. And finally, the letters must fit, both vertically and horizontally, into the space you've assigned them in your sketches.

We'll run through some examples and descriptions of particular typefaces to help you get going with the selection process.

Helvetica

Helvetica makes a logical starting point, since it's the most widely used typeface in the Western world and it's probably already available on your computer system. Designed in Switzerland in 1957, soon after the introduction of phototypesetting, it has a bold, clean look and is easy to read in lowercase with initial caps. All-uppercase Helvetica is so uniform that it reads rather poorly.

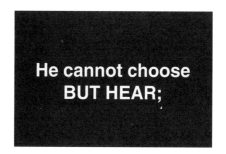

Figure 5-19: **Helvetica: one of the largest type families available on the desktop.**

Neutral in shape and restrained in tone, Helvetica includes no distracting elements. Of course, that makes it less interesting for some applications—and its very omnipresence means it has begun to wear a bit thin for some audiences. But for many purposes Helvetica remains an excellent choice. Even in small point sizes, the lowercase characters are relatively large when compared with most other typefaces. The Helvetica family offers another advantage: scope. It's one of the largest type families around, including extended, condensed, italic and many other cousins. As you expand your typeface library, remember to add depth to your Helvetica holdings. You'll be amazed at the versatility extra weights create in your type arsenal.

If you refrain, as you should in presentation work, from setting successive lines in all-capitals or justifyied type, Helvetica makes a safe, unimpeachable type solution. Just remember that hundreds of other presenters are choosing it for the same reasons. You'll have to rely on another design element to individualize your presentation when you work with Helvetica.

Optima

Nearly contemporary with Helvetica, Optima brings grace, clarity and stylistic subtlety to the sans-serif arena. Herman Zapf modeled this type on the lettering of Renaissance sculptor Luca della Robbia, and it retains a clear, classical flavor, particularly in the capitals. Close observation of the letter stems shows that they flare just a bit where you might expect a serif. The strokes modulate between thick and thin without going to extremes.

Figure 5-20: Optima: a readable sans-serif, with beautiful uppercase letters.

For short headings, Optima works well in all-uppercase. Try setting them with plenty of letterspacing for an open, airy look. The combination of upper- and lowercase generates energy and interest. The characters are generous and full, but they combine to set compactly. Large or small, the letterforms hold up quite well; the purity of their shapes tempts you to use individual letters as design elements. As an extra bonus for presentation designers, the useful bold weight successfully translates Optima's subtleties.

Futura

Although designed some thirty years before Helvetica and Optima, Futura still looks modern and functional. The precision of its rigidly geometrical letterforms based on straight lines and circles can redound to your benefit; on the other hand, you can find it detracts from your overall design by insisting on its unmistakable shape. Where Helvetica tempers strict geometry toward more traditional letterforms, Futura will have no compromise. That's both a strength and a danger.

Figure 5-21: Futura: uncompromising—for better or worse.

Select Futura for presentations where you aim for cool, crisp lettering surrounded by plenty of space. These letterforms demand balancing open areas, or else they'll appear to compete with other design elements. Apply Futura carefully, and it will reward you with its unique style.

Times Roman

Widely available with software programs and resident on many laser printers, Times Roman was designed to set legible, compact lines of type in newspaper columns. The very attributes that make it effective for the press—legibility at small sizes through shapely serifs and carefully modulated thick and thin strokes, as well as a tight set with a relatively tall x-height—limit Times's usefulness as a presentation face.

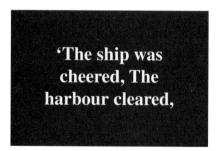

Figure 5-22: Times Roman: good for page graphics, posters, flip charts.

In presentation graphics, each word counts; we're not concerned primarily with how many characters we can fit into a line of type. Times Roman can look awkward when asked to do the kind of work demanded by presentations; the headings don't seem strong enough, and the short, telegraphic bursts of type essential to bullet points can appear cramped and stiff. When you're designing page graphics, posters or flip charts, however, look to Times for help in dealing with text blocks.

Century

If we characterized type as we do wines, we'd call Century vigorous, pleasant and lively. Due to low contrast between thick and thin strokes and generously sized characters, Century makes a legible, open presentation face. It sets a bit bulkier than some other serif faces, but that can help establish its presence in the frame.

Figure 5-23: **Century: a legible, lively typeface.**

Century's lowercase italic font is somewhat ornamented, so you may avoid it for engineering or scientific presentations. Take a look at Century for clear, traditional and unremarkable serif text. If you want to branch out, consider one of the faces we recommend next.

Some of My Favorites

There are so many exciting typefaces available as PostScript or Speedo fonts, I encourage you to branch out and try some of my favorites. Start with Palatino, which may be familiar since it is resident on many laser printers. Palatino's lively letterforms are based on calligraphic shapes, gracefully translated; it's easy to see the influence of the pen in the serifs and contrasting line weights. And yet Palatino hardly ever looks too informal or lacks seriousness. The italic and bold italic fonts are treasures in their own right and add depth to the roman fonts.

Choose another serif face, Stempel Schneidler, particularly in the bolder weights, to add elegance and to borrow the authority of the printed word. The original letterforms have been reinterpreted for digital imaging, and they translate graciously and beautifully.

The Stone family was designed specifically for desktop applications; the Stone Sans sans-serif fonts make engaging presentation faces. They're generously proportioned and require plenty of space around each line. The italics preserve the open, clear shapes while adding a sense of motion. When you'd like your type to speak colloquially, try the Stone Informal fonts. The semibold weight makes an interesting choice for very casual or "work in progress" presentations.

Gill Sans breathes life into sans-serif letterforms, making it an excellent alternative when Helvetica and Futura start to look repetitious and mechanical. Because it was developed to work well as signage for a railway, Gill is at home in presentation environments.

While Zapf Dingbats aren't exactly a typeface, they are delightfully useful shapes that can be set just like letters. Dingbats make bullets more fun and interesting; they give you control over spacing and sizing. You can create lots of great effects for backgrounds, too, with dingbats. Print out all the dingbats and keep your type chart close at hand to remind yourself of the endless design possibilities made available by shapes that act like letters.

Palatino... Aa Bb Cc Dd Ee Ff Gg Hh Ii Jj Kk Ll Mm Nn Oo Pp Qq Rr Ss Tt Uu Vv Ww Xx Yy Zz

Schneidler... Aa Bb Cc Dd Ee Ff Gg Hh Ii Jj Kk Ll Mm Nn Oo Pp Qq Rr Ss Tt Uu Vv Ww Xx Yy Zz

Stone... Aa Bb Cc Dd Ee Ff Gg Hh Ii Jj Kk Ll Mm Nn Oo Pp Qq Rr Ss Tt Uu Vv Ww Xx Yy Zz

Gill Sans... Aa Bb Cc Dd Ee Ff Gg Hh Ii Jj Kk Ll Mm Nn Oo Pp Qq Rr Ss Tt Uu Vv Ww Xx Yy Zz

Figure 5-24: Palatino, Schneidler, Stone, Gill Sans and Zapf Dingbats

Avant Garde... Aa Bb Cc Dd Ee Ff Gg Hh Ii Jj Kk Ll Mm Nn Oo Pp Qq Rr Ss Tt Uu Vv Ww Xx Yy Zz

Helvetica... Aa Bb Cc Dd Ee Ff Gg Hh Ii Jj Kk Ll Mm Nn Oo Pp Qq Rr Ss Tt Uu Vv Ww Xx Yy Zz

Optima... Aa Bb Cc Dd Ee Ff Gg Hh Ii Jj Kk Ll Mm Nn Oo Pp Qq Rr Ss Tt Uu Vv Ww Xx Yy Zz

Futura... Aa Bb Cc Dd Ee Ff Gg Hh Ii Jj Kk Ll Mm Nn Oo Pp Qq Rr Ss Tt Uu Vv Ww Xx Yy Zz

Figure 5-25: Avant Garde, Helvetica, Optima and Futura.

Galliard… Aa Bb Cc Dd Ee Ff Gg Hh Ii Jj Kk Ll Mm Nn Oo Pp Qq Rr Ss Tt Uu Vv Ww Xx Yy Zz

Times Roman… Aa Bb Cc Dd Ee Ff Gg Hh Ii Jj Kk Ll Mm Nn Oo Pp Qq Rr Ss Tt Uu Vv Ww Xx Yy Zz

Century… Aa Bb Cc Dd Ee Ff Gg Hh Ii Jj Kk Ll Mm Nn Oo Pp Qq Rr Ss Tt Uu Vv Ww Xx Yy Zz

Goudy… Aa Bb Cc Dd Ee Ff Gg Hh Ii Jj Kk Ll Mm Nn Oo Pp Qq Rr Ss Tt Uu Vv Ww Xx Yy Zz

Figure 5-26: Galliard, Times Roman, Century and Goudy.

TYPE DISTORTION

Many drawing and presentation software programs include features for skewing, shearing, stretching or reshaping graphic objects—including type. Please save these features for occasional special effects. Don't rely on them for condensing type to fit the space available. Excessive electronic distortion can easily detract from the quality of your work. Your audience may not know exactly what seems odd about the frames, but they'll be disturbed by stretched or skewed type, even when it's less than obvious.

Type designers work at an exacting level of detail. They consider the geometry of each angle and the curve of every letter, number and punctuation mark. Tiny refinements of stroke width or arc can make the difference between letters that look lumpy or static and those that flow gracefully from one to the other. Distorting carefully designed characters may easily degrade the aesthetics and readability of any typeface.

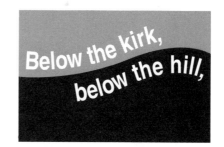

Figure 5-27: While distortion often works against good type design, it can enhance the overall design when used for specific purposes.

You may think that condensed or extended fonts are merely compressed or stretched versions of a basic typeface design. In fact, type designers actually create completely new drawings for condensed and extended type, adjusting each character stroke to the proper weight. Likewise, italics are much more than oblique or slanted versions of roman faces. It will pay off handsomely in your overall design to respect the original type designs. When you find you must adjust them electronically, do so with care and close attention.

Electronic manipulation entices us with features like outlining and shadowing; evaluate these effects by asking whether they contribute to the overall legibility and power of the frame design. Make sure you're not turning to them to disguise a more funda-mental design problem. Use them sparingly, to further a clearly conceived visual purpose. For example, letterform distortion can work effectively when type matches with a background object that's skewed or slanted, or when the letterforms themselves are used as three-dimensional objects with shadows or other depth-enhancing graphic treatments.

Figure 5-28: **Try resizing type rather than distorting letterforms.**

If you find yourself about to distort type simply to fit the words into the space allocated in your design, go back to the drawing board to redesign the frame layout or—ingenious thought!—edit the text.

When you distort type, you create a separate typeface that no longer matches the type in the rest of your frames. For the sake of consistency, you must distort the equivalent elements of each frame in the presentation—quite an undertaking. The distorted face counts toward the limit we recommend of two typefaces per frame, with no more than two or three weights or versions of a single face in each graphic.

TYPE SIZING

In spite of the dramatic changes the digital revolution brought to typesetting technology, we still use most of the original terminology, including the units of measure. Specifications for printed materials are given in points and picas: approximately 6 picas or 72 points to the inch, with 12 points to the pica. The maximum length for lines in the text column you're reading is 22 picas. Points and picas measure the depth as well as the width of text blocks. The minimum vertical space required for a 36-point line of type is roughly half an inch, since 36 is half of 72. As a frame of reference, the text you're reading now is set in 11-point type.

Figure 5-29: **36-point Helvetica requires about half an inch.**

Most drawing and presentation programs allow extremely fine tuning in type size. Some refer to standard point sizes, while others use their own proportional sizing method. In any case, you'll want to standardize on a type size spec for each sort of typographic element in your presentation.

Line Spacing/Leading

Years ago, when type was set with individual lead characters, printers added spacing between lines with thin strips of lead. While line spacing is digital today, the term "leading" (pronounced "led-ing") is still standard. The increments of space between lines of type are usually expressed in points. Extra leading in the text of this book makes it much more legible and accounts for the fact that six lines fit into an inch and one-eighth rather than a single inch. Every line has three extra points of leading.

Most drawing and presentation programs allow you to choose the amount of space you want between lines of type. If you don't specify the amount of leading, the software will usually set a default leading, approximately 120 percent of the type size. Usually you'll want to change this to allow slightly less leading between multiple lines of a single bullet entry and more space between different bullet points.

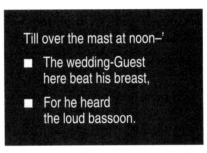

Figure 5-30: **Allow for extra leading between bullet items.**

Minimum leading requirements are influenced by characteristics of the typeface itself. In order to appear open and uncrowded, faces with tall lowercase letters, or x-heights, require more leading than those with small x-heights. For example, 18-point Helvetica or Stone Sans require at least four extra points between lines of presentation graphics. The relationship between type size and leading is expressed as a ratio: 18-point Helvetica with 22 points of leading is shown as 18/22, read as "18 over 22."

Figure 5-31: **Helvetica set solid** *(left),* **18/18, and with four points of leading** *(right),* **18/22.**

A second guideline holds that as type size increases, leading requirements do not increase proportionally. Optima set in 24 points might work well with six points of extra lead (24/30), but type twice that size wouldn't require twelve points of leading. In fact, it may work very well with only eight points (48/56).

Line spacing is a matter of proportion, and finding the pleasing relationship between type size, line length and leading. It's safe to start by adding 20 percent to your type size, but be sure to experiment with increasing (or occasionally decreasing) the leading. After a certain point, more isn't necessarily better. It's rarely easy to follow the type from line to line when the leading is more than half again the character size. When you do want to separate ideas, however, more space is a relief.

Type Measurement Terms

The following terms, and many others used in the typographer's lexicon, originated in the printing trade. However, they have "stuck" over the centuries and are still used today.

> **Baseline:** the imaginary line upon which type rests. Descenders fall below it, giving variety and character to lowercase type.

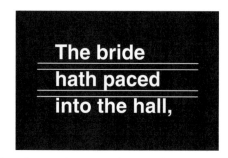

Figure 5-32: We've drawn inner and outer lines to demonstrate type size and point size.

x-height: literally, the height of a lowercase x in a particular typeface. The ratio of the x-height to the body size determines the visual importance of lowercase letters for a given typeface. Different faces set in the same size appear to be larger or smaller, depending on their relative x-heights. Futura, for instance, has a small x-height when compared with Helvetica.

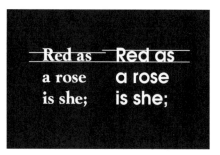

Figure 5-33: The x-height of different faces will vary, even when they're both set in 14-point type, as Goudy *(left)* and Avant Garde *(right)* show clearly.

Point size: the distance from the lowest point of the longest descender (such as p or g) to the highest part of the tallest ascender (such as d or b) is known as the *type* size. Because metal type couldn't be cast to the very edge of the block it was mounted on, the *point* size includes a small space for the "shoulder" of the block that carried each letter.

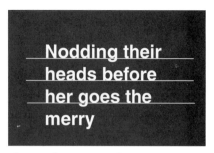

Figure 5-34: We've drawn lines to indicate "imaginary" baselines.

Em space: a square space equal to the point size. An em space in 12-point type measures exactly 12 points by 12 points. An en is half the width of an em. Ems and ens are convenient measuring units for paragraph indents (one em is standard), dash lengths (em—or en–dashes) and bullet size (12-point or 8-point).

SIZING TYPE FOR PROJECTION & DISPLAY MEDIA

Specifying type sizes for printed materials is an art in itself, but it seems straightforward when compared with sizing type for projection or electronic media. We review presentation frames as screen displays, as laser-printed proofs, as slides or overheads and as projected images. Through it all, we must evaluate the effectiveness of our typographic choices in communicating with the audience.

Proportional Sizing

One way to start designing typographic elements is by working out percentages of the overall image height. This will give you a guide to their relative sizes, rather than the exact point size of each element. Keep in your mind's eye a vision of the way the displayed image will look to an audience.

Some designers and presenters prepare and image sample type-size charts to use as references when specifying type. These samples give a good idea of how various sizes, weights and fonts look when imaged on different media and projected to various sizes.

Figuring height by percentages isn't as complicated as it might sound. Work with the fullest frame in your presentation so you can use the same type specs throughout. For example, you might be making an overhead with nine lines of type. One of those lines is the heading, which should be larger than the others and should be followed by more leading than separates the following eight bullet entries. Each of the eight is weighted evenly. Count the basic type size as 10 percent. If the heading will be half again the size of the bullet entries, it counts as 15 percent. Follow the heading with a 5 percent space.

Figure 5-35: **Title, extra leading and type sized by proportion of total image area.**

Measure the overall height of your "live" image area in printer's points or whatever measurement system your software uses. Multiply this height by the percent value for the maximum type size. Work down from this size to allow for leading, extra room at the bottom of the frame, and other spatial considerations.

Finding the Right Size

Audiences shouldn't have to strain to read your message, so be sure your type specifications result in words that are large enough to read easily. As a rule of thumb for determining minimum type size: keep your point size larger than 2.5 percent of the height of the image area. On an overhead transparency eight inches (576 points) high, the smallest letters should be about 14-point type.

For a quick legibility test with slides, hold the slide out at arm's length. If you can read all the type without magnification, it will probably be clear to your viewers.

COPY FITTING

A further wrinkle in type specification is the fact that typefaces don't all set the same, so they're not interchangeable. The same line set in five different faces will measure five different lengths.

The designs of some faces make more efficient use of space, while others require plenty of room for their knees and elbows. For example, a heading composed in 16-point Helvetica bold italic upper- and lowercase might produce a line 20 picas long; the same words composed exactly the same way in Century bold italic would set 22 picas long. When space is tight and text long, choose a compact face like Helvetica.

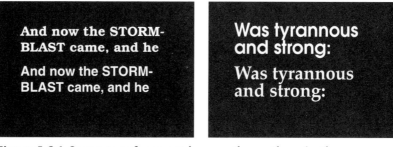

Figure 5-36: **Some typefaces set longer than others in the same point size.**

You'll find quite a wide variation in height between different fonts, because of their internal proportions; this is true even comparing the same characters at the same point size. Look closely at the height of the capitals and the length of the ascenders and descenders. These individual qualities influence your typeface selection; and once you've chosen your typeface for the presentation, they help you plan how much leading you'll need to set off the lines most effectively.

SPACING

Judicious spacing between individual letters and words, as well as between lines, contributes significantly to the legibility and the overall success of your presentation graphics.

Letter Spacing

Many software programs offer an adjustment for tighter or looser spacing between letters, through tracking choices. While you may routinely set your type for print fairly tight, presentations frequently benefit from some generosity of space between characters. Unless your type is extremely large, it's easier to read when set a bit more open.

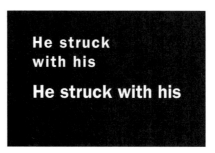

Figure 5-37: **Use more generous letter spacing for projection media** *(top line)* **and tighter tracking for the printed page.**

These increases should be tiny, hardly discernible. If the type comes out looking as if it had lost a few teeth, go back and tighten the tracking. If your system doesn't offer tracking adjustments, don't worry. The manufacturer's spacing values will probably be open enough for easy legibility.

Occasionally, you'll notice a disproportionate gap between two letters, especially in heading type. When your software allows, go in and make kerning adjustments to this pair of characters. Kerning takes a tuck in the letter spacing and helps to bring the letter pair into harmony with the rest of the frame. When you're working on precise kerning, check your results frequently on a laser proof—it's hard to see exactly what's happening onscreen.

Word Spacing

Any font you choose will automatically insert a space between words when you press the keyboard space bar. This spacing is tied to the tracking adjustment, when that feature is available, so the word spacing increases as the letter spacing expands. You can also add or remove minute bits of space manually through kerning controls. Here again, check your results on a laser proof. Your goal is to provide just enough space to indicate the end of one word and the beginning of the next.

Line Length

Long lines can be awkward to read, and can defeat your goal of working with key words that the audience will absorb at a glance. Newspapers and magazines use short, parallel columns to help the reader stay oriented. Presentation graphics should be written for the screen, in short bursts of information. Consider line length as a tool to assist your viewers as they take in your material.

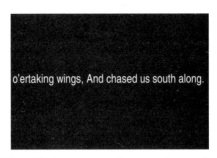

Figure 5-38: **Consider 40 characters the maximum line length for slides.**

Occasionally, a heading, attribution line, quote or other statement must be broken into more than one line. Carefully position the line break to follow the sense of the text, avoiding a very long line followed by only one or two words on the second line. Experiment with your typographic choices to find the best line length for the face and size you've selected. Use your grid layout system to position the type blocks.

As a quick rule of thumb, consider 40 characters per line as the maximum for slide graphics and 60 characters maximum for overhead transparencies. That's considerably longer than the ideal tight, condensed phrase, however, so please exercise restraint.

MOVING ON

Typeface selection and specification exerts a tremendous influence on frame design. The right type treatment will enhance your message, while an inappropriate choice can cancel out lots of hard work. Tread carefully!

The next chapter concentrates your attention on another important design element—color. We'll consider why, when and how to use color in presentation graphics, based on the inherent properties, emotional effects and effective combinations of colors. As you apply these principles to your presentation media and overall design scheme, you'll amplify the effectiveness of your message.

EXPLORING COLOR 6

Color can be the juiciest part of presentation design. Carefully developed color palettes enhance your message, provide richness and depth and put a personal design stamp on your work. We live in a colorful world, and it's natural to portray concepts and ideas with color.

WHY GO FOR COLOR?

The most obvious reason for using color in presentations is to show things the way we see them in the world: green trees, blue water and orange sunsets, for example. Abstractions like statistics, ideas and proposals may have no intrinsic colors, but they are enriched through color associations: red for warning, danger or financial loss; blue for calm; green for growth. Pink with powder blue puts us in the nursery, while orange and black suggests Halloween.

It would be prohibitively expensive to print a glossy, full-color brochure for an audience of one hundred. But now, with access to a full range of vibrant colors, your presentation frames can take full advantage of color. The impression created by a carefully arranged palette will remain with your viewers. Desktop presentations allow you to keep the content and the style of the graphics current and compelling.

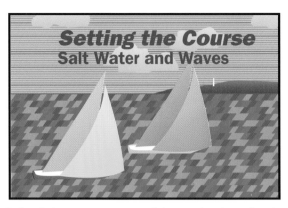

Figure 6-1: Color brings zest to graphics—whether they're natural objects or abstractions.

CODING WITH COLOR

Color Associations: Advertisers try to establish an association between certain colors and consumer products or sports teams. Businesses choose corporate identity colors. You can benefit from color association by developing signature color schemes in your presentation graphics.

Color Differentiation: Colors vividly distinguish like and unlike elements. To clarify a flow chart, show files in red and programs in blue. Similar classes of information can be subtly differentiated using light and dark tones of the same color. Consistent graphic elements should be linked from frame to frame with consistent application of color.

Color Hierarchies: Indicate levels of importance or a progression of data by increasing the color value and saturation level. Dark-to-light or gray-to-bright sequences are excellent ways to represent increasing significance. Chromatic or rainbow color series show development in a series.

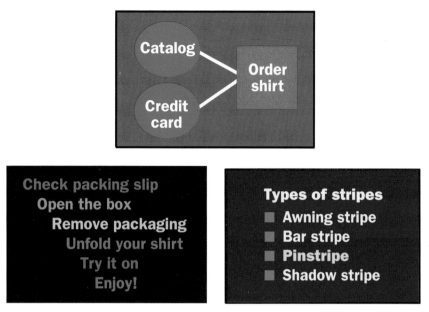

Figure 6-2: **Differentiate with color** *(top).* **Establish priorities** *(bottom left).* **Emphasize** *(bottom right).*

Color Emphasis: Focus attention on one particular element in your frame by assigning it a color that is brighter or lighter than the rest of your palette. The principle of contrast will work to draw your viewers' eyes to this element. Suppose you want to emphasize one entry in a bullet list. On a dark gray, blue or black background, set most of your text in light yellow or cream. Highlight your important line with full, bright yellow. Alternatively, pure white will create a subtler contrast by lightening the text color. One word of warning: use this effect sparingly. Don't try to emphasize more than one or two elements, and don't set up competing bright colors that will cancel each other out.

Audience Appeal

Color sets a mood; it can even evoke an era; it can be "in" or "out" of fashion. In the '60s we were devoted to avocado green and harvest gold. In the 1980s, grays, mauves and muted turquoise were popular.

Figure 6-3: Color palettes tend to shift with the fashion every decade.

Be sensitive to cultural biases as well as association with trends and periods. Some people just can't accept pink as a serious color. That doesn't mean that the various shades of pink, from magenta through rose, aren't valid presentation colors. In fact, these are strong, serviceable colors; however, if they push the wrong buttons they'll undermine your efforts. Before including them in your palette, research your audience. Combine them with other colors that emphasize their vibrant, warm qualities and play down the negative, frilly associations.

Will your audience assume that your presentation will be in color? For a weekly sales meeting, color may be seen as expensive overkill (even though the cost of color imaging is quite low). Laser-printed transparencies may serve you better. The setting, subject matter and your audience's experience with presentations generate expectation levels. Unless you're bringing a laptop unit, your viewers will usually find color quite appropriate for on-screen electronic presentations. Weigh all these factors before you decide on a color or monochrome palette.

Legibility

Never sacrifice readability for pleasing color. Legibility takes precedence over everything else in presentation materials, and inappropriate color choices can interfere with basic communication. Colors don't perform the same way under all conditions, and they undergo a radical shift between the computer screen and film recorder. Pure blue on dark backgrounds is very hard to read, for instance, but blue with white type is fine. This isn't an opinion or aesthetic judgment—it's a fact of human vision and receptivity to light spectra.

Consider that your primary responsibility is to find a palette that works for your audience rather than to express every nuance of your personal taste. There will be plenty of opportunities to inject your own style within the boundaries of good design.

Proceed with Caution

Color is an area of design—whether for clothing, interior decoration or presentation graphics—that's difficult to master immediately. Beginning design classes often spend as long as a full term working in monochrome. Colors are introduced, one or two at a time, only after students have mastered value, contrast, form and composition. Some professional graphic artists maintain that if a design doesn't work in black, white and shades of gray, it can't be salvaged with colors, no matter how bold or appealing.

Your thumbnail sketches of each frame will again prove useful here. To guard against depending too heavily on color, refine your sketches in monochrome, then replace the grays with colors as the final design emerges. Maintain color consistency throughout the presentation, just as you maintain typographic and editorial consistency.

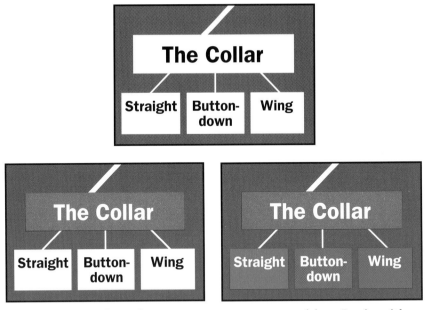

Figure 6-4: **Don't let color overpower your composition. Begin with monochromatic images, then cautiously introduce color as your design evolves.**

Before presentation graphics went desktop, more color meant more money. Traditional handcrafted graphics put the cost of color production beyond the reach of many. But now, in our delight with 256 "free" colors, we sometimes lose sight of basic design principles. It's all too easy to produce gaudy, garish neon graphics that actually detract from the content. Identify exactly how color will help get your points across, and use it to tell your story. Never allow the color scheme to take over the presentation.

THE LANGUAGE OF COLOR

The Color Wheel

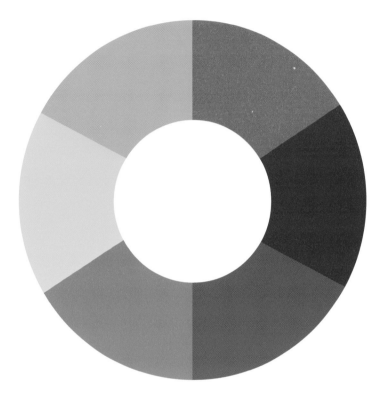

Figure 6-5: **The infinite variety of tones in the color spectrum starts here, with the primaries and secondaries arrayed as contiguous spokes in a wheel.**

You're probably familiar with this circular illustration showing the spectrum of colors and their relationships to each other. Primary and secondary colors alternate to form the wheel. We're used to thinking of red, blue and yellow as the primary colors and green, orange and purple as the secondary colors.

Complementary colors are pairs of colors arranged opposite each other on the color wheel. Each complement is a duo consisting of a primary color and a secondary color: red with green, blue with orange, yellow with purple. Placed side-by-side, pure color complements appear to buzz or vibrate.

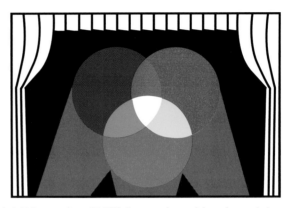

Figure 6-6: **Additive color (RGB) is produced by the mixing of light beams.**

In the world of presentation graphics, there are two different methods of mixing colors. The first mixes colors of projected light—on your computer screen, for example. The second mixes pigments like the ink on a printed page. Because they're two completely different systems, it's hard to translate what you see on the screen to "hard copy" imaged on paper or film.

The color you see on your computer screen is created by mixing red, green and blue light. Color produced with beams of light is called RGB, or *additive*, since the primary colors of light combine directly to produce the secondaries—yellow, magenta and cyan—and all the other colors you see displayed on the screen. As more colors of light are added to the combination, the image approaches white; as colors are taken away, the image approaches black. The color receptors in our eyes are sensitive to the additive primaries; we perceive the world around us by interpreting beams of light.

On the other hand, pigment—whether paint, ink, dye, chalk or crayon—is an opaque substance that absorbs light. Since each color you add to the mixture of pigments takes away part of the spectrum, this method of mixing colors is called *subtractive* color, or CYM, for the subtractive primaries, cyan, yellow and magenta. If you could mix pure cyan, magenta and yellow, you'd produce black. Combinations of two primaries produce the subtractive secondaries: blue, green and red.

Use a magnifying glass to examine the color illustrations on these pages. You'll see that they're composed of tiny dots of cyan, yellow, magenta and black. Dot patterns built of these four process colors create the illusion of an endless variety of colors.

Figure 6-7: **Subtractive (CYM) color results when pigments are mixed.**

The two methods of mixing color, with their flip-flopping primaries and secondaries, may seem confusing. Don't panic! Most of the discussion in this chapter refers to the ordinary color wheel. When you have a handle on the differences between light colors and pigment colors, you'll understand the change between what you see on the screen and what you get on the slide.

Seeing Color

Whether it's projected light or an opaque pigment, any color can be described by its properties or qualities: hue, value and saturation. Each color in the spectrum or around the color wheel represents a *hue*—red, blue, yellow, green, orange, purple and so forth. *Value* refers to the shade, or the degree to which a color approaches black or white. *Saturation* means the intensity of a given hue.

Computers & Color

Computer display color is mixed in RGB; pigments on paper or film are mixed in CYM. When you create a color frame on the screen and output it to paper or film, your printer or film recorder must translate the colors from the additive to the subtractive mode. At best, this translation causes minor shifts in color; more often, the discrepancies between screen and output colors are shocking.

Unless you're preparing an electronic presentation that will stay on the computer screen, you simply can't rely on the colors the monitor shows you. Invest in a standard color reference book like the Pantone Matching System (PMS) if your presentation software cross-references colors. Keep the Pantone swatch book right by your computer as you design your frames, so you can perform a reality check from time to time.

The surest way to examine true colors is to create your own palette slides or overheads, showing them just as they're displayed in your software. Use a projector with a built-in screen to view them as you design, or look at them on a color-corrected lightbox through a loupe.

Even palette displays can't show you how your color choices will work together as background, midground and foreground elements. It's critical to proof a sample frame on film in order to catch any problems before you invest in imaging the entire presentation. If time constraints won't allow you to proof a frame, choose a flexible palette that doesn't depend heavily on nuances of color, and be prepared for surprises, especially with the blue tones.

MAKING A PALETTE

A palette refers to a subset of the spectrum or color wheel. In computer-generated color, a palette means a group of displayable colors selected from all the possible color combinations. For instance, some programs allow you to choose a palette of 16 colors out of a possible 256.

Sequencing

When you specify a palette for your presentation, you'll also specify the order in which the colors will be used. Consult your software manual for the particular order you should follow; not all programs work with color assignment in the same way.

Start by specifying the background color. Then work through type colors, bullets, graph symbols and so forth. Some software programs call this sequenced palette a color scheme; some allow you to manually override the automatic assignments and specify a custom color for a particular element.

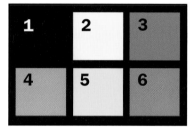

1 Background	
2 Type	
3 Bullets	
4 Graph Symbols	
5 Highlight 1	
6 Highlight 2	

Figure 6-8: **A sample color scheme**

No matter how elaborate your design, you will maintain order—and your sanity—by organizing the palette according to graphic function. When you consistently use a specific color for each type of design element, like headings, graph symbols, tags, bullets and rules, your audience will be able to associate functions or purposes with color.

Choose one or two fully saturated highlight colors for your palette and use them sparingly for small elements. When these highlights don't have to compete with other saturated elements, they're much more effective at focusing attention.

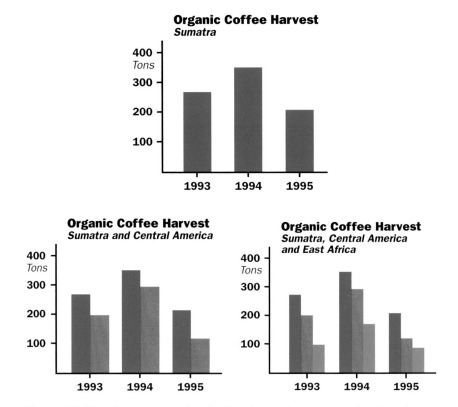

Figure 6-9: Here's an example of effective color sequencing in a bar graph.

Color sequencing is vital to the effective design of graphs and charts. Suppose you're preparing a series of bar graph frames, and each frame will show a different number of variables. You might choose a safe blue for the bars in the one-variable graph, showing organic coffee harvests in Sumatra over the last three years. In the next frame, you'll add a second variable; choose red for organic harvests in Central America, since it reads well against the blue. In the third frame, you'll add a green bar for organic harvests in East Africa. This order—blue, red and green—avoids placing blue next to green, since they can be difficult to distinguish, and it doesn't present the Christmas red-and-green combination alone.

Color Relationships

The impact of color is very much a relative thing. You have to consider a particular color in the context of its background and neighbors. Black or white grounds are the easiest to start with, but most presenters want to move into more elaborate color schemes early on. So let's look at some color-on-color guidelines.

Spectral Neighbors

Spectral neighbors are hues that sit next to each other in the color wheel. Blue and green, red and orange, yellow and green all hold hands in the rainbow. Use these pairs for shadowing or to suggest dimension.

Figure 6-10: **Use spectral neighbors to achieve subtle effects.**

The contrast between spectral neighbors is low, so avoid these pairs when your design requires a distinct visual boundary between touching elements—for example, type on a colored area or the wedges of a pie graph. Reserve them for low-contrast situations and subtle effects.

Complements

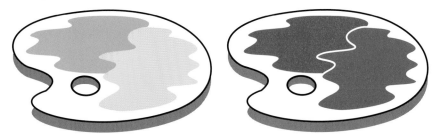

Figure 6-11: **To keep complementary vibrations low, reduce satura-tion** *(left),* **or distance the colors** *(right).*

Colors opposite one another on the color wheel are very far apart visually and, if they're fully saturated they'll actually appear to move or vibrate when placed side by side. Sometimes when saturated-color complements touch, the film recorder images a glow or halo effect between them. If you must use complements as neighboring colors, reduce the saturation of one or both, or separate them with a thin white or black line.

Triads

Figure 6-12: **Triad hues are pleasing to the eye.**

A triad is a group of three primaries, three secondaries or any other set of three hues equally spaced around the color wheel. This triangular balance can be very pleasing to the eye, especially when all three hues match in value and saturation. Blue/red/ yellow and orange/green/purple are examples of triads.

Color Contrast

As you might expect, contrasting colors differ markedly from one another, particularly in value. Black and white provide the greatest contrast. The legibility of small text and symbols depends on the degree of contrast between figure and ground. That's why most long printed documents are black type on white paper, with color used for illustrations or highlights. White on black works better for projection media, but clear white may be too bright for extended viewing. Colors help alleviate eye fatigue by reducing contrast on the screen.

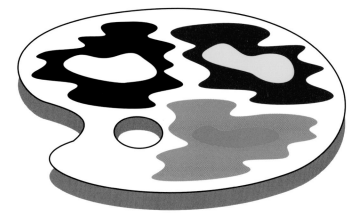

Figure 6-13: **Black elements against a white background provide the ultimate in contrast.**

Hues with low values contrast well with white or light grounds; hues with high values contrast well with black. Some low-value and high-value hues work well together. Yellow reads well on blue, for example; but cyan and orange don't combine effectively because both fall in the mid-value range.

The smaller a graphic element, the more contrast it needs. Small type requires high contrast; as the type size increases, the contrast requirements decrease. A large, bold line of type can sustain a relatively low contrast level and still read effectively.

The Misfits

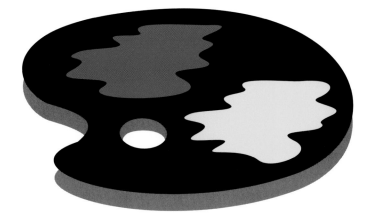

Figure 6-14: **Blue on black can produce a fuzzy-edged look—it's human physiology.**

Pure blue on a black background is a difficult combination to use successfully because of blue's position in the spectrum and the physiology of human vision. When small graphic elements like type or thin rules are displayed in blue on black, the edges appear to be fuzzy. That's because our eyes have a smaller number of blue receptors than red and green ones, and most of these blue receptors are distributed outside the focal point of the retina. It's good advice to refrain from setting small blue elements—such as type—on a black background.

Multiple Background Colors

When a foreground element stretches across several background colors, the foreground color must contrast effectively with each background. A straight, uniform line can appear alternately thicker and thinner as it crosses color boundaries. The same effects can make lines of type look distorted. Complex images with elaborate palettes can create color-on-color difficulties.

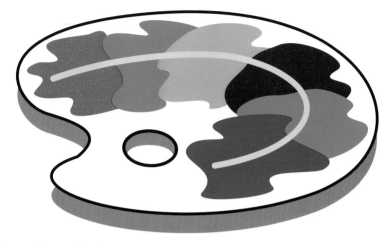

Figure 6-15: **As background colors change, the size or shape of a fore-ground element can appear distorted.**

A pie graph provides a simple example of these hazards. Suppose there are seven wedges, each colored differently. You want to place the percent value inside each wedge. From a design standpoint, your inclination is to use the same size and color of type for each wedge. As you try this, you realize that no matter which color you choose for the type, even black or white, the numbers appear to be different sizes on the variously colored wedges. What to do? You can bring the wedge colors all closer in value and saturation; you might compromise and vary the type color. You could skirt the issue by placing the percentage labels outside the pie wedges so they share a common ground, or set them inside a small, neutral-colored box or circle in each wedge.

SOME WINNING COMBINATIONS

Let's examine some sequenced color palettes that work well for various media. Slides, overheads and electronic presentations make different demands on color selections, which are influenced by lighting and viewing conditions.

Slides

Slides project best as light type and graphics on a dark background. A dark ground absorbs the blast of light from the projector and helps to set off the lighter foreground elements so they're easy to read or view. At one point, it was very popular in slide presentations to combine royal blue backgrounds with yellow and white type—safe but flat and blah, the visual correlative of elevator music.

Instead, start with a background in a deep, rich navy, forest green, charcoal gray or dark eggplant purple. Don't overlook black as a background; it's the "not there" screen color. We perceive it as no background at all, just as we see the white of the printed page as "nothing." Since it's darker than any other projected color, black will brighten all other colors by contrast, pepping up pastels and making bright colors, such as magenta and lemon yellow, appear nearly fluorescent.

The role of the background is to recede, clarifying and focusing the foreground elements. The more complicated and detailed the information in each frame, the more you need a simple, smooth background that doesn't compete for the viewer's attention.

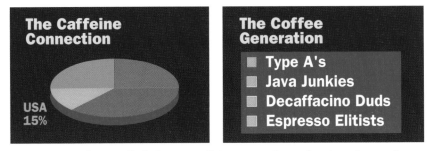

Figure 6-16: **If room lighting conditions aren't optimal, palettes for your slides should include strong dark-light contrast.**

Let's pick, for example, dark navy for our background. Foreground elements like type should stand out in the highest, lightest contrast: choose white, light yellow or light blue (more toward the cyan side of the wheel than the purple, since navy contains some red). For highlighted foreground objects—or bright but small areas of color burst—try magenta, orange, lemon yellow or bright teal.

Build the relatively large areas of midground objects, such as bar graphs or pie charts, from lower contrast colors: choose a set that looks like it belongs together, matching value and saturation levels. Good midground hues for dark navy are medium tones of purple, green, teal, gold, burgundy or gray. A set of soft pastels or heathery grayed tones would work well also, if they're a good match for the subject matter. Shift blue's spectral neighbors, green and purple, slightly away from blue and toward yellow and red, respectively. Reduce the saturation of blue's complement, orange, because the contrast between complementary colors makes each more vibrant. If you plan to position type or other graphics over midground areas, check to be sure that the foreground colors contrast well with your midground choices.

Inevitably, as we begin to fine-tune our color palette, we rely on the colors displayed on the computer screen. Stop and check these against your Pantone swatch book or sample palette slides. Dark blues are especially apt to shift during imaging. That will throw your whole color scheme off if you're not aware of the true colors. What you see is definitely not what you will get in this instance. In fact, what you see onscreen may look completely bizarre and wrong. Image a sample frame to be sure you're on the right track, and carry on. Think of the screen as the crudest of checks for your colors, just enough to show if you're in the right quadrant of the spectrum.

You'll be disappointed with your color palette if the projection setting isn't darkened adequately, and your audience won't receive the full benefit of your hard work. Do whatever you can to ensure a dark room so your slide graphics will sparkle. If you have less than ideal projection conditions, be sure your dark/light contrast is strong and your colors aren't too neighborly. Rely on the sharpness of triad groups to help compensate for poor lighting.

Overheads

Palettes for overhead transparencies are usually less elaborate than those for slide presentations. Typical overheads use bold black type—sometimes even dark-blue type—on a white background for contrast. We urge you to break out of this stereotype. While the less intense light of overhead projectors makes dark backgrounds less essential than they are for slides, they still work well, especially for detailed graphics. Mount overheads with dark backgrounds so they won't curl from the heat on the projection stage.

Figure 6-17: **Sample overhead palettes.**

When you plan to project each transparency longer than five minutes, work with saturated graphic elements against a light background. These overheads require dense foreground colors that won't wash out when projected. More subtle midground hues and brighter highlight elements make them lively and add to their over-all impact. In the sample palettes above, palettes with high- and medium-contrast colors create two engaging interpretations of the same design. The dark-blue/purple/teal combination makes a cooled-out impression; the black/gray/red set looks more digni-fied, but still interesting and appealing.

Onscreen Presentations

After all the guesswork of choosing color palettes for slides and overheads, presentations that remain computer displays are a great relief: you can see exactly what's going on. Apply the rules of color sequencing to choose background, midground, foreground and highlight colors.

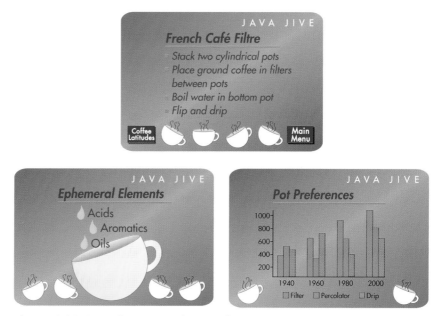

Figure 6-18: **Sample screen show palette.**

Deep, rich background colors still create good contrast, but you can afford to brighten or lighten them somewhat with electronic presentations. In fact, you may want to pick a midtone background that offers enough contrast for very dark and very light foreground elements. Important information will stand out in white type on blue-gray or teal backgrounds; reference information will be perfectly legible in dark blue. Midground shapes can be sufficiently defined with green, gold, orange and purple. Shadowing techniques can help bring them forward, out of the background.

When you project an electronic show through a video projector or overhead projection pad, you're back into the realm of slide and overhead rules. The saturation of the hues is much reduced on its way from your computer's display to the projector screen, and you must compensate by jacking the color contrast. Preview a sample frame with your projection medium, and adjust your palette for pleasing, legible color combinations.

GRADUATED COLOR

Graduated backgrounds are an appealing, simple way to add depth to presentation graphics. Audiences are attracted to the impression of process, transition and motion associated with graduated color. These backgrounds work best when each frame can be kept simple, free from a multitude of busy elements.

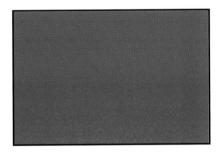

Figure 6-19: **Horizontal ramping** *(top).* **Diagonal ramping** *(bottom left).* **Radial ramping** *(bottom right).*

Graduated or ramped color refers to a special effect the computer generates that allows one color to dissolve into another without a hard break—a kind of airbrush effect. Software programs handle the specifications for graduated areas differently. Usually you choose the two end colors, and sometimes you specify the number of steps used to create the blend. Some systems allow you to control how rapidly the ramping occurs, while others offer only one automatic graduation. Color can blend horizontally, vertically, diagonally or radially—depending on your software. Choose a direction that enhances your content and overall design.

Keep your graduated backgrounds subtle and smooth by ramping from a medium tone to a dark shade of the same color, or to black. Spectral neighbors make another good combination for graduations. The heavier, darker color works best at the bottom of the frame, since we naturally see the image as a landscape and read from top to bottom. Similarly, when you graduate from side to side, place with the darker color on the right to match the way we read, from left to right.

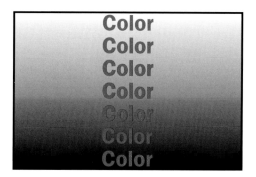

Figure 6-20: **Certain background color graduations can spell trouble with some foreground colors.**

By limiting the graduation to medium and dark values of a single hue, you will minimize the difficulties of finding effective foreground and midground colors. Take the extreme example of a white-to-black graduation, for example. What color will you use for type against such a background? Not red—it's too dark against black. Not yellow—it's no good on white. Green might be okay on white and black, but it's muddy against gray. If you graduate from medium blue to black, however, all the foreground and midground possibilities we discussed earlier open up.

Backgrounds aren't the only places graduated effects can add impact to your presentation graphics. Try placing the blend area in a corner or as a band at the top or bottom of the frame, or specify some other confined area. When the final color of the graduation matches the flat background color, they'll join seamlessly. Graduated fills for the bars of bar graphs or the slices of pie charts look smart without interfering with readability. Rules and even bullet symbols can be filled with graduated color.

Figure 6-21: **To avoid problems of contrast, ramp between similar colors or outside the text area.**

Alternatively, you might float a flat colored area on a graduated background as a tablet for your type. This technique preserves the effect of distance but saves you from color-on-color complications. Its drawback is a restricted working area within the frame.

BLACK, WHITE & GRAY

You won't always work in color, and you'll want to visualize and sketch your design ideas in black-and-white, so it's an excellent plan to develop your skill with a monochrome palette. Aside from a few technical considerations, the principles remain the same, whether your palette contains 20 colors or one. Contrast, figure/ ground definition and readability still top the list of design goals. It's just as important to design clean, crisp, uncluttered frames that contribute to your communication goals.

Figure 6-22: **You can produce a shadow effect by screening various densities of black.**

When we say "black-and-white," we mean all the shades of gray as well. Monochromatic devices like laser printers and printing presses can't actually output in continuous gray tones like a photograph, but they compensate with techniques that produce values our eyes see as gray. Screened areas of black indicate shading and shadow, built from dot patterns that appear lighter or darker according to their density.

Black Patterns

The illusion of gray can be created with various black-and-white patterns, ranging from finely spaced dots to coarse blocked or crosshatched fills. We'll focus first on dot patterns, since they're the workhorses of monochromatic design and printing.

In commercial printing, the ink density for a color tint is controlled by sandwiching a fine screen between the negative and the printing plates. As the plate is exposed, the screen stops the light where the printer doesn't want ink to print, and lets light through where tiny dots of ink are desired. With a screen of 50 percent, for example, ink coverage is about half as dense as a solid area.

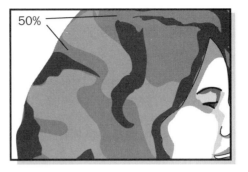

Figure 6-23: **Close-up view of a 50% screen.**

The most common screen pattern is minute round dots, though other screens are available. The size and spacing of the dots determine the value of the tint and the coarseness of the screen.

Screen density is determined by the percent of coverage, up to 100 percent for solid areas. Resolution is fixed by the number of dots per inch—typically 85 for newspapers and anywhere from 133 to 200 for offset printing.

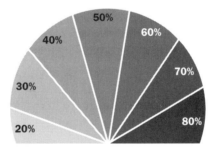

Figure 6-24: **The eye notices more change in the black-and-white spectrum between 20% and 30% than between 70% and 80%.**

Desktop laser printers incorporate these printing press techniques to produce their gray values. The resolution is fairly coarse, since the laser printer works with carbon particles rather than ink. But gray tones are still quite effective foils for the straight black and white.

It's easy to specify screen densities on the desktop. Eighty percent is very dark and 20 percent is quite light. People can't discern more than about five values of gray in the same frame. The darker screen values tend to look much closer in tone than those in the lighter range.

Ready-Made Patterns

Some software programs allow you to specify screen densities and patterns, while others simply offer sample patterns. When you pick a ready-made pattern, you probably won't know its density or resolution. Proof your frame on the laser printer and let your eye be the judge. Aim for patterns that suggest value without drawing lots of attention to themselves. You want an overall impression of gray rather than obvious stripes, hatches or checkerboards.

Figure 6-25: **Coarse patterns grab attention** *(left)*; **but coarse patterns and fine screens can spoil a good image** *(right)*.

Because coarse patterns are attention-grabbers, they're harder to incorporate into your frame design. Limit them to one or two in any particular image and, preferably, throughout the presentation. On the other end of the spectrum, extremely fine patterns can present problems for laser printers, which may have trouble imaging them evenly, especially in large areas.

Depending on the sophistication of your output equipment, screened and patterned areas can look striated, mottled or splotchy. Naturally, you want to avoid this dingy, low-budget look. Try a new toner cartridge, and have your printer professionally adjusted periodically. Design around your production limits by keeping screened areas small and patterns simple.

Type Over Screens

Screen tints don't make the best backgrounds for type and other small graphic elements, since the dots in the screen tend to clump with the type. The coarser the screen, the riskier the combination. Suppose you're designing an organization chart and you'd like to place each name in black type on a screen-filled box. If the type is fine and the screen resolution coarse, the names will look fuzzy and messy.

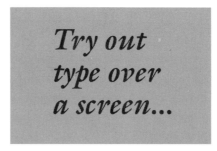

Figure 6-26: **The wrong typeface on the wrong screen (***top***). Black type on white inset (***bottom left***). White type on black (***bottom right***).**

One workaround for this difficulty is to create a white area within the box for the type, though this clutters the design with another layer of graphic elements. Perhaps white type reversed on solid black will work; plan ahead to place type away from patterns and screens. Use them to add depth through shadows and shading; their strong suit is bridging the black-to-white gap with a softer, more subtle tone.

MOVING ON

Color is great fun, and one of the most rewarding elements of designing presentation graphics on the desktop. Build your palette step by step, basing your decisions on sound color theory. Focus on reinforcing the purpose of each element with color choices. This deliberate, disciplined approach will ensure that your displays are both readable and attractive. It will also lead you to question the soundness of many ready-made palettes available in your presentation software.

Now that you've assimilated some of the most critical points of graphic design, it's time to bring them all together and start to create presentation frames. In the next chapter we'll examine text frames in detail.

TEXT FRAMES & MORE 7

We're comfortable with the familiar—so comfortable that we might as well embrace the principle and work with it, as long as we allow room for a few surprises. The majority of presentation graphics contain words and only words. But even though these text frames are the mainstay of the business presentation, they don't have to look dull. In fact, the audience's comfort level with text frames can work to your advantage, allowing you to challenge them to understand your ideas in depth. An interesting graphic design will keep your points specific, clear and connected.

Most of us enjoy making text frames because we're more familiar with words than with pictures. Remember, however, that the text frame is itself a picture, a visual entity that requires choices of color, focus, placement, balance and style. The text frame is *not* a page. Written pages must stand alone, introducing key topics, explaining and supporting particular views, and finally reviewing and clarifying the issues. In a presentation, on the other hand, you will control the pace and flow of information, using your graphics for outlining, keynoting and emphasis.

While you tell the whole story in your live presentation, your support visuals complement your words and give dimension to them. Find a visual style that reflects your verbal delivery. Don't ask people to read lots of words—they'll lose the thread of the verbal presentation. Concise wording doesn't mean oversimplified content. (People will forgive the occasional confusing graph or diagram, but they're more demanding with the written word.) Keep your concepts specific and your verbs active; stay away from generalizations and passive construction. Your audience will feel patronized by the "Dick and Jane" school of copywriting; one-syllable words alone can't tell a complex story. Aim to present the essence of the subject while avoiding information overload.

Since everybody makes lists—lists of work to accomplish, people to call, supplies to order—we're used to this telegraphic style of communication; but go beyond that and please your audience with excellent organization and with words and phrases in text frames that reinforce rather than repeat the live presentation. Not even the liveliest design can save a presenter who merely reads the visuals. When you can create outstanding text frames, you're on your way to success with presentation graphics.

OPENING TITLES

Because they're the first frames your audience will see, take advantage of the opening titles to set the visual style and engage your audience. Introduce the color palette, background treatment, underlying grid structure, alignment and typography here. The elements are fewer and simpler than the bullet lists or tables that will follow, so you're free to work out a pleasing arrangement that focuses attention on the most important elements.

Before establishing the frame design, consider the information you must include: the title of the presentation, of course; perhaps a subtitle; the speaker's name, title and affiliation; the company name and corporate logo; the name of the organization or meeting and the date; and funding agencies or other attributions. You can also introduce graphic elements that will be used throughout the show, like special rules or shapes for bullets and other highlights.

When you'd like to include lots of information up front, use more than one title frame, or build a sequence. Particularly in slide and electronic presentations, you can add or replace information quite smoothly while keeping the focus on the title itself.

Unless the speaker is especially well known, the title of the presentation is usually placed first as the featured element. Contrary to what you might imagine, the type size need not be tremendous to imply importance. What's more important is to work with a size that's easy to read, and use contrast in weight and color, as well as size, to emphasize the title. The subtitle, if any, and speaker's name and affiliation come next, followed by the company name, relevant dates, organization or seminar name, funding sources and other essential information.

Figure 7-1: **Focus attention on the title of the presentation, then add supporting information.**

To make the title of your presentation concise but at the same time interesting to your audience, you may find an explanatory subtitle helpful. Subtitles allow you to clarify a brief title, while keeping attention focused on it. A number of graphic techniques will create a subordinate position for a subtitle, without making the distinction heavy-handed—use a line, extra space or a subtle variation in typography. Without changing typeface or size, try one of these variations:

Title	Subtitle
– all-uppercase	– initial caps
– large and small caps	– small caps
– roman	– italic
– bold	– text weight
– high-contrast color	– mid-contrast color

Figure 7-2: **Make a subtitle graphically distinct from the title** *(top).* **Experiment with subtle variations in typography to further distinguish between the two levels of information** *(bottom left* **and** *bottom right).*

Of course, you may find that the contrast in length between a brief title and a long subtitle makes a smaller type size necessary. Fine. Reduce the potential for graphic overkill by changing only the size at first. If that doesn't give you enough contrast between title and subtitle, work with a second variable. Remember the choices you made in these frames so you can apply them to text frames throughout the presentation.

The opening title sequence can be adapted to close the presentation with polish and pizzazz. In one or two frames, repeat the essential information, such as the title and subtitle, speaker and date. Round out the time you've spent with this audience, bringing back all the graphic elements of the opening. Keep the tone a bit more restrained than the opening titles, signaling the audience that it's almost time to clap and stretch. Ah!

Section-Divider Frames

To introduce important new topics within your presentation, consider creating a special format for section dividers. Base these frames on your title design, notched down one step to be secondary in importance. The anticipation and excitement generated by your opening titles will spill over to the section-divider frames. Your audience will recognize a section divider as a road sign in the flow of information, and appreciate the signals you're sending to aid understanding and provide continuity.

Figure 7-3: **Section dividers should build on the title frame design.**

While separate section dividers work easily for slides and electronic presentations, they can add fuss and bother to overheads. If you're preparing an overhead presentation and plan to launch directly into the next topic without spending much time on a transition, you might incorporate the section heading into the first text frame of that section.

Running heads are helpful guides, providing continuity throughout a complex presentation. The running head identifies the section topic in a small line of time near the top of each frame in that section. It integrates the set of frames and reminds the viewer of the presentation's larger structure.

Adapt the section divider format to present a pithy quote or an authoritative claim. A humorous quote will add sparkle to your presentation; a provocative citation will add spice. You don't want your presentation to be top-heavy with loads of information. Pace yourself through a long presentation with changes in density of information as well as changes in your vocal tone and intensity. Your audience will appreciate both the accent and the pattern.

HOW TO USE LISTS

The best lists are the kind of notes each member of the audience would write if they really understood the material: tight summaries of each idea. Use lists when your material lends itself to itemizing groups of things like names, procedures, sequences or features.

Bullet Lists

The essential ingredients of good bulleted text frames are excellent organization and consistent presentation of concepts. These frames help members of the audience key into the speaker's points, orienting them to the subject matter at a glance. For this reason, bullet lists are effective only if they're brief and clear. If they're overwhelming in detail or length, they'll distract from the presentation.

Figure 7-4: **Bullet lists condense and emphasize key points.**

The speaker's job goes beyond the condensed, telegraphic style of bulleted points; a speaker should never turn to the screen and read the list. In the same vein, the audience should never have to tune out the speaker in order to decipher the graphics. Ideally, the speaker, audience and graphics will harmonize: that's when we communicate our ideas most directly.

Headings

The headings for bullet lists should be lively and focused; when possible, include an active verb that supports the topic. Steer clear of clichéd phrases and tired lines. Write each frame heading in a particular group using a similar style, consistent in construction; make each a short phrase, a single word or a brief sentence.

You might be tempted to put a colon at the end of the heading, but the format of the frame will clarify the relationship between the heading and the bulleted entries. Avoid punctuation, since it can interfere with the effectiveness of the design.

Consider breaking ideas into headings and subheads to help maintain consistency without sacrificing content. Visually distinguish these headings and subheads as you did in the opening titles.

Bullet Entries

Reduce each item in a bullet list to a few key words or a tight phrase. Don't worry about complete sentences or the traditional outline format, but do keep points on the same frame grammatically consistent, using the same type of phrasing or structure. Work for this kind of consistency from frame to frame, as well.

Move repetitive words or phrases to the heading or subhead. For example, when listing regional reports (see below), pull the word "Reports" from each entry and use it in the heading.

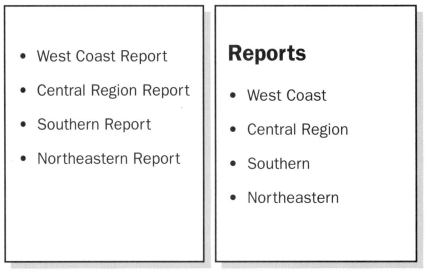

Figure 7-5: **To avoid repetition, pull out recurring words or phrases and use them as headings.**

Condensed language will help you keep each entry on a single line, for a more streamlined visual effect. When you come across an idea that simply won't be cut to less than two lines, work it into your format gracefully by setting less space between the two lines of the entry than between bulleted items. "Hang indent" the second line so it begins right under the type on the first line. Choose the spot where you'll break the line to match the content or phrasing, rather than running the type to the maximum line length on the first line with a few leftover words on the second.

It's important to separate the last line of one item from the first line of the next bullet point. Otherwise, the visual effect will be confusing, even when bullets signal the beginning of a new idea. Make the extra effort to use wisely the space between lines of type and between bullet points. The resulting graphic sophistication will more than repay your fine-tuning.

Figure 7-6: **Extra line spacing between bulleted groups helps distinguish them visually.**

How many bullet entries can each frame hold effectively? That depends on the complexity of the ideas presented and the format of the entries—whether they're one-word quips lightly passed over or full phrases considered in some depth. In general, though, you should consider breaking topic headings with more than four or five bullet points into two or more frames. Group the points logically so the frame breaks follow your content. You might even keep the same heading for this series of frames and write different subheads to indicate the organization within the broader topic.

Bullet entries rarely need punctuation, either within the line or at the end. In fact, the discrete quality of the phrasing and line breaks creates its own rhythm, and commas, semicolons or periods distract from the open flow of information.

Bullet Symbols

The bullet symbols themselves make interesting graphic elements. Traditional printer's bullets—dots, squares, arrows or pointing hands—serve to set off individual entries. Each has a distinct personality that contributes to the overall frame design. Squares, for instance, are sharp and bold; dots more subtle; right-facing triangles imply motion. Check marks indicate checklists. Long em dashes make excellent bullets for secondary points.

The Zapf Dingbats font provides a wide variety of ready-made bullet shapes. Set these shapes several points smaller than the text type, to keep the bullets from overwhelming the frame. Foreground colors will emphasize the sequence of bullets. Variations of standard shapes, like square bullets with a graduated fill, can be extremely effective additions to text frames.

For a special presentation, create your own bullets with simple shapes that reflect the subject matter. Slight variations of the standard symbols work more effectively than complicated drawings. When you make your own bullets, remember that whimsical shapes can become tiring and dull when used frame after frame.

Numbers might be considered a particular kind of bullet symbol with a special quality: they prioritize and rank the bullet entries. When you choose numbers, be sure the points are part of an ordered sequence, related by time or hierarchy of importance. Consider also that numbers can imply such an order, even when you don't intend it. A whole series of numbered frames can grow tedious and overbearing, so be sure to take the context into account when you opt for numbers.

Subentries

When the concepts under discussion are complex, bullet lists may work best with subentries that break out more detailed information about a particular point. Limit the layers of information in each frame to two—or three at the very most. Otherwise, your audience may become tangled in the structure of the frame and lose the anchoring connection.

On any particular frame, subentries should be the exception rather than the rule. When many points need further clarification, don't try to squeeze lots of levels into one frame. Instead, devote an entire frame to a major point, plus three or four subentries of detailed information you plan to emphasize in your presentation. If necessary, you can then return to the overview frame and pick up with the next major point.

Visually distinguish subentries by indenting them under the principal entry and choosing a secondary size or weight of type, or a subsidiary bullet shape or color. We find that em dashes work quite well as bullets for subentries.

Summaries

Summary frames take the audience in the opposite direction from detail frames, providing an overview of the major topics in the presentation as a whole, or in any portion of the program. Use them right after section divider frames to orient the audience, or following a segment to give your viewers a quick review of the points you've made on that topic. You might even label them "Summary" or "Overview" to distinguish them from other bullet lists and to allow the audience to reflect on the overall shape of the material you're presenting.

Build Sequences

To keep your audience following the flow of information through your presentation, you may want to build your bullet lists over a sequence of frames, revealing your points one by one. This method encourages the viewers to focus on the current point, and prevents them from reading ahead to your next points (and getting confused). Builds work very well with slides and electronic presentations, since the cost of extra frames is low or nonexistent and the changes between frames are smooth.

Figure 7-7: **Try different variations of build sequences (there are many to choose from), but stick with one variation at a time.**

Because they're more dynamic, build sequences help keep your audience involved visually with the screen. On the first frame, viewers will see only the heading and subhead, and possibly the first bullet item. As each new point is added, it's highlighted to focus the viewers' attention on it. All previous points are low-lighted for contrast. Highlight and lowlight through brighter and duller color combinations, boldface and roman type weights, larger and smaller typefaces, or different bullet symbols. Experiment to find the contrast that works best for your frames, but keep it fairly subtle. Your audience will recognize the new information quite readily—you don't need to use your loudest voice.

When all the points for a particular topic have been added, your bullet frame is complete. This full frame provides a good opportunity for review; it might also serve as the first frame of the sequence if the presenter will refer to the bullet points during the introduction of the topic.

Variations on the standard build sequence are legion. You might start with an overview frame, then keep the entire list onscreen and move through the bullet points, highlighting just the entry under consideration at the moment.

Detail-reveal build sequences incorporate subentries within the flow of the series by allowing the highlighted bullet to have subentries, but dropping the sublists as new points are highlighted. The final frame in a detail-reveal build recaps all the major points with no subentries at all.

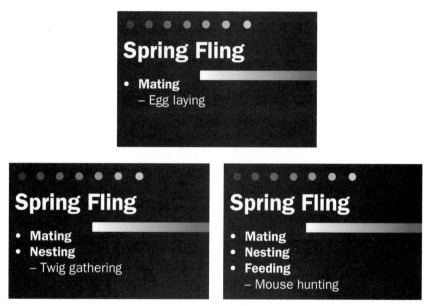

Figure 7-8: **The detail-reveal technique is an uncomplicated way to add depth and interest without crowding the frame.**

HOW TO USE TABLES

The calendar is a fine example of a table—a multicolumn list that presents a matrix of items and subitems arranged in two directions. Tables make great organizing tools for comparing many separate but related bits of data. Each entry represents a meeting point of the two variables represented by the two directions. Entries can be words, numbers or both.

When graphs aren't specific enough and verbal descriptions are too cumbersome, tables offer elegant solutions for showing exact numeric values. They can be quite visually appealing and provocative. Design tables by envisioning the motion you want your audience to follow—across a column, down a row or hopping from one entry to another.

● ● ● ● ● ● ● ●

Up Till All Hours

Sightings:	Night	Day
Jan–Mar	42	18
Apr–Jun	36	13
July–Sep	21	16
Oct–Dec	32	24

Figure 7-9: **Tables are an efficient format for organizing many separate but related bits of data.**

Separate the vertical columns of a table with enough space to keep the entries from running together (about an em is enough), and resist the temptation to create a gridwork of vertical and horizontal lines that isolate the bits of data, working against the connections and comparisons you'd like to create. Allow plenty of room between horizontal rows to open up the grid. Thin horizontal rules or subtle horizontal bands of color can help the viewer follow the information across categories, working with the natural motion of left to right. Or if a particular column holds the key to your ideas, try highlighting it with a vertical band of color.

As a rule, columns of words or short phrases should be set flush-left; columns of numbers should be placed flush-right or aligned by decimal points. Of course, you'll find exceptions, such as the flush-right/flush-left combination for a two-column text table that enhances readability by keeping related entries on adjacent rows close to one another.

Some tables are matrices of yes/no answers or small symbols that indicate a particular response to the two variables in the row and column labels. This condensed presentation allows you to convey a large amount of information in a relatively small space. Remember to break it into bite-sized chunks for your audience, who may have trouble following very dense information.

Decimal Points

When your figures include decimal points, help your audience read and compare the quantities by aligning columns to the decimal and carrying out all values to the same number of places right of the decimal point. When all your values are whole numbers, don't bother with decimal points. All those extra zeros might seem impressive, but they're more likely to be confusing and misleading. Follow the clutter reduction principle and opt for clarity.

Feast or Famine

Per Day:	Mice	Rabbits
Jan–Mar	10.3	.8
Apr–Jun	8.9	1.4
July–Sep	21.6	2.3
Oct–Dec	15.4	1.9

Figure 7-10: **Align decimal values on the decimal point for clarity in comparisons.**

Column & Row Labels

Labels for vertical columns can follow the alignment of the column below, or they can be centered over the column when that defines the column more clearly. If you have a column of figures with a noticeably ragged left edge, flush-right column labels will look just right. On the other hand, a thin column of checks or visual symbols calls for a label centered above it.

Typographic choices for labels should reflect the type size and style used in the body of the table, with subtle differences to set them apart slightly. Boldface column labels over lightweight type provide a good solution; so do thin rules between the labels and entries. When your table is successful, your viewers will have no trouble distinguishing labels from entries, and they will be able to move between entries with ease.

The Nest Egg

Species	**Eggs**	**Survival**
Snowy	1	1.2%
Barn	2	1.3%
Screech	2	1.9%
Horned	1	1.2%

The Nest Egg

Species	Eggs	Survival
Snowy	1	1.2%
Barn	2	1.3%
Screech	2	1.9%
Horned	1	1.2%

Figure 7-11: **A well-designed table helps your viewers distinguish each entry without difficulty.**

Long, complex horizontal rows with many entries require extra line spacing between them, to help them hold together as a unit. When space is tight, thin horizontal rules can accomplish the same purpose with just a bit more clutter. Experiment also with low-contrast, alternating background bands like the paper accountants use to assist in line tracking. Only a subtle shift is needed, and the light touch keeps attention focused on the entries themselves.

ILLUSTRATED TEXT FRAMES

Occasionally you'll find you'd like to combine text in the same frame with a graph or diagram. A classic combination image shows both a graph and a table to demonstrate relationships while providing exact data values. Both parts of the frame contribute significantly to the viewer's understanding, and neither would work as effectively alone.

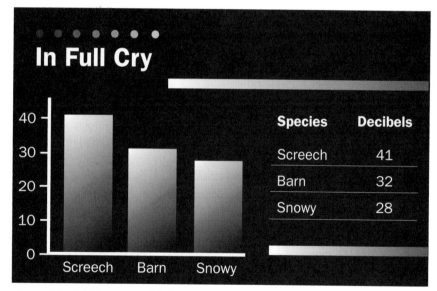

Figure 7-12: **When combining text and illustrations, explore several ways of visualizing your message before deciding on a final form.**

Pause to reflect before automatically including a graph or illustration in text frame. Simply because they're visually interesting, these elements may draw attention from the point on which you want to focus. Illustrations alone won't tell your story—or you wouldn't have felt obliged to include the table. Is the effort to link the two worthwhile? Will communication really be enhanced by the graph, or will a simple text frame table be more effective? Presenters sometimes assume that they should always graph numbers; actually, there are many instances when a table can make the point more strongly. Evaluate your message and explore several ways to visualize it before deciding on the final graphic form.

QUESTION FRAMES

Because they help with technical issues of lighting and continuity, question frames tend to be more useful with slides and electronic presentations than with overheads. When the speaker plans to pause and ask for questions, a simple text frame can signal the event. It provides a neutral background for the question-and-answer format, and avoids the awkwardness of displaying a frame on one topic while you're talking about another. The audience sees that the speaker expects questions, and feels encouraged to speak up; question frames are a formal invitation to participate.

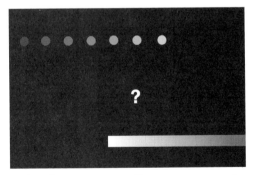

Figure 7-13: **Question frames neutralize your screen to allow for discussion with your audience.**

Follow the graphic rules you've established for the rest of your presentation. One small question mark or the word "Questions" will certainly convey the point. An assortment of question marks

in different sizes, colors and typefaces is overkill. When you anticipate several question-and-answer sessions during the course of a
presentation, you can use the same design each time.

BLANK FRAMES

Sometimes there will be a part of your presentation for which no
text or graphic is required, or even appropriate. If this visual break
is long, you'll probably want to turn up the house lights and re-
establish personal contact; but for a short break, you can use blank
slides or a blank computer screen. That way, the audience won't
keep staring at the last slide of an old topic while new points are
introduced.

Figure 7-14: **Use place-holding blank frames during short periods of
your spoken presentation that require no accompanying visuals.**

Design blank frames to match the presentation's overall design.
A combination of graphic elements already familiar from previous
frames will make a relaxing, non-distracting "place-holder" frame.
If your background color was black anyhow, try some defining
elements such as rules or a box to avoid an all-black screen (or
readers may think there's been a power failure). Conservatively
and sensibly designed, blank frames can help pace the presentation.

MOVING ON

Distilling your message to its very essence will help you create simple, effective text frames. They quickly communicate the key ideas or points you want your audience to absorb, freeing them to understand the speaker's more detailed presentation.

Just as text frames provide the appropriate format for the written word, graphs and diagrams give shape to the relationships between numbers. In Chapter 8 we'll examine the various kinds of graphs and see how effective design choices are made.

USING GRAPHS

Graphs give physical form to abstract concepts; they show relationships, comparisons and change. Their strong suit is the representation of numbers and quantities. By translating the conceptual into visual equivalents, graphs make your ideas easily accessible for your audience.

You can create your own graphs with sophisticated drawing programs, or save time by using automatic rendering software. Whatever production technique you choose, make sure you understand the data completely. What are the variables? What sort of comparison do they evoke? Are there any unexpected values? Next, be certain you're clear about the conclusions you're asking the audience to derive. Are you demonstrating relative size, change over time or typical values? Will one event predict another? Let each graph support one particular point; then focus attention on the crucial segment of the visual interpretation.

Most software for presentation and financial analysis includes automatic charting and graphing features that organize and automatically plot data into a wide variety of graph formats. Producing this kind of visual interpretation is easy, but many design decisions seem to be taken out of your control. In many cases, these are merely program defaults that you can modify and customize. To regain power over the frame design, it's essential that you have a clear visual concept sketched out. That way, rather than meekly following predetermined decisions, you'll be able to ask the program to do specific things instead of generating bland, generic graphics.

By all means, take advantage of the automatic charting features for their terrific production capabilities—who wants to figure all those angles for a pie chart, for instance? But direct the charting genie for the colors, size and position of the pie. Decide where labels will work most effectively, how big they should be and what typeface will read best. Tie the pie chart frame to the rest of the presentation by using the same background, grid framework and heading style.

GRAPHING TERMINOLOGY

In relation to graphing, the term *data* means counted or measured information. To be graphed usefully, data should vary over some regular interval of space or time, from group to group, or in some other way. Population density represents the kind of data that varies over space; population growth changes through time; and total population by age group shifts by proportional relationships. Often, it's interesting to track a particular category of data to show how it depends on a related factor. For example, data points may show how bird populations change in relation to food supply.

Many graphing terms relate to the process of data collection. Each measurement or value is called an *observation*; each observation becomes one plotted point on a graph. A *variable* refers to the set of observations for each activity; a *plotted variable* means a collection of points used to shape a trend line, set of bars or other graphing symbols.

The *range* of the data is the extent of spread between minimum and maximum values. This range determines the optimum graph size, shape and scale, allowing room to plot the values in the data set. *Units* give the terms of measurement for the data—dollars, percentage points or millimeters, for instance. A *scale* of units with appropriate reference values gives meaning to each axis of a graph. The *grid* is formed by the intersection of the two scales.

Scale

To represent quantities, time or space, graphs must be drawn to one or more scales. Normal scales use direct relationships: when one inch on a graph represents $1,000, then two inches equal $2,000, four inches $4,000 and so on. Logarithmic scales, on the other hand, compress or expand time, quantities or other values according to a progression based on a mathematical logarithm.

Graphs with one scale usually answer the simple question "Which is biggest?" You can plot more complex, two-variable graphs with two scales: one along the horizontal axis, the other along the vertical axis. Graphing convention leads us to expect time-related data on the horizontal and a second variable, such as quantity, along the vertical. To chart annual rainfall by month, for example, the months are typically scaled from left to right and inches of rain increase from bottom to top.

DEFINE YOUR PURPOSE

To choose the best graph format, focus on the core relationship or pattern you want to depict in each frame. For example, when you plan to show your audience past trends as indicators of future activity, the ideal graph will emphasize the time-related aspects of the data. The two variables of a time-series graph will plot variables like employment figures or revenue against the appropriate units of time. Keep the same horizontal and vertical scales from frame to frame when you're building a comparative series, so the audience can count on a constant frame of reference.

Relationships between the values associated with different places or things at a given point in time also make simple and elegant visual stories. You might want to focus on productivity by shop and by individual employee performance. To detail this information verbally might well require several boring or confusing minutes; instead, you can make it crystal clear in a frame or two.

Often you'll find that the ideas you want to illustrate in a graph are based on interdependent values. Are you showing how market share and budgetary allocations influence total sales activity and profit outcome? How the size of a house relates to household income? Whether plant growth and inches of rainfall or years of education and amount of fat in the diet influence each other? These sets of interdependent relationships require careful consideration to make the best format choice.

TYPES OF GRAPHS

Compare one quantifiable aspect of places or things at a particular moment with single-scale *horizontal bar graphs*, the simplest format for information graphics. Typically, these graphs are scaled only along the horizontal axis; the vertical distance between bars is not scaled but, like the thickness of the bars themselves, the amount used is an arbitrary decision based on design consider-ations. Because these graphs don't include a scale of time, it's never appropriate to connect the bars with a trend line; allow your viewers to draw their own conclusions from the clear evidence.

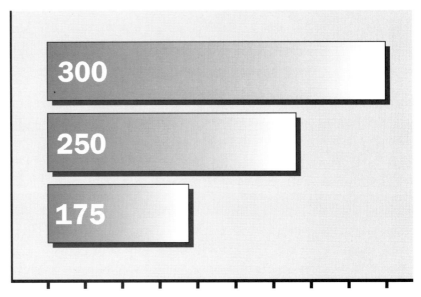

Figure 8-1: Single-scale bar graphs visualize comparisons at a particular moment in time.

Time-related *vertical bar graphs* show the activity of one or several things through a particular time period. Single bars or sets of bars, some taller and some shorter according to the values on the Y axis, are spaced at distinct intervals through time. This horizontal scaling isn't very noticeable when observations were made each month, quarter or year; but when data is missing for any period, a gap in the graph for the missing period indicates the passage of time without an observation.

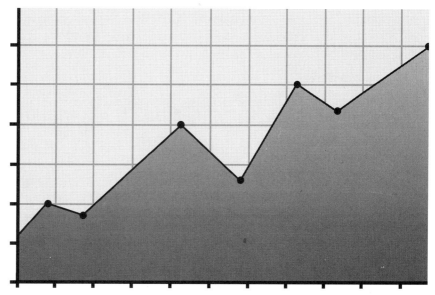

Figure 8-2: Line graphs link observations to show trends; area graphs imply volume.

Line graphs start with points plotted relative to scales on the horizontal and vertical axes; each point marks a known occurrence. Connecting these data points with a straight line gives a representation of what probably occurred between observations. Usually line graphs indicate rate, the relationship between change (scaled on the vertical axis) and time (scaled on the horizontal axis). While bar graphs are limited in the number of data points they can portray effectively, line graphs can accommodate any number of data points. Choose a line graph to show changes in quantities that vary continuously through time; choose a bar graph to represent countable things like production units.

Building *area graphs* is like building line graphs, with one addition: the space between the horizontal axis and the plotted line is filled in. This fill implies volume, so you should use area charts to present information that measures magnitude.

Pie graphs show proportions in relation to a whole. Each wedge represents a percentage of the total. Viewers comprehend pie graphs quickly and easily, provided a reasonable number of components are being compared. Pie graphs are best at giving rough impressions of proportions; but unless each wedge is labeled legibly with its amount or percentage, it's impossible to make proper comparisons. It's possible to use other shapes, but the circle continues to be the most popular and universally understood.

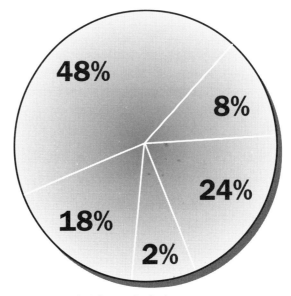

Figure 8-3: Pie graphs divide a whole into component parts for reviewing relationships.

ANATOMY OF A GRAPH

Four distinct elements are used to build any type of graph: the graph window, reference values, data symbols and text.

The Graph Window

Technically, the graph window is that portion of the Cartesian plane on which you render your data. It is defined by the *origin* and *extent* of the frame necessary to plot the data. The origin is the starting point of the information, the conjunction of the lowest positive values on both the vertical and horizontal axes. Typically, the origin is found at the lower left corner of the graph window, although negative quantities can affect the placement of the axes within the graph window. The extent refers to the end of the graph window, the highest and longest space that must be opened in order to display the data. The extent is usually found at the upper right corner of the graph window, although negative values may open an area to the left and/or below the origin.

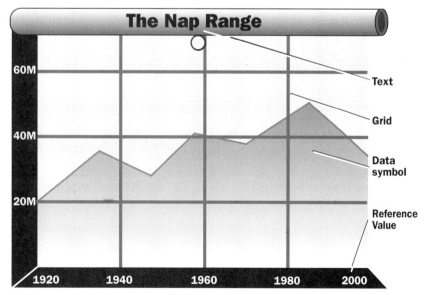

Figure 8-4: The graph window opens information for view.

Set the origin and extent within the graph window to accommodate the range and reference values of your data. Design graph frames to allow a generous graph window size so the data symbols can be large and prominent without distortion. Look to the data itself to determine the scale and shape of the graph window. The graph symbols should nearly fill the window. Avoid extents that overrun the data and create large, empty spaces that dwarf the symbols. Make an exception to this guideline, however, when you're preparing a series of graphs comparing the same variables. Then use the frame with the largest range of data to draw a standard graph window, keeping the scales consistent from frame to frame to give comparisons a standard context.

Color: In addition to size and shape, the color of the graph window is an important design decision. Keep the color contrast low between the background and the graph window. Consider slightly lighter or darker shades of the same color, or choose a midtone gray or neutral for the window. If you graduate the background, try graduating the window in the opposite direction.

The Window Grid

Any graph depends on a grid within the graph window to present the scale and reference value labels that give meaning to the visual treatment. The grid orients viewers to the starting point for observation counts or measures and makes clear the numeric progression from that point. In most cases the starting point reference is zero, but it can be another appropriate value.

Be sure to make the starting point for your observation values obvious to your audience. To avoid distorting the data, it's vital to include the full progression from the reference value to the plotted observations, even when the reference value is zero. Suppose your data ranges from $6,000 to $9,000. If you start the vertical scale at $3,000 to save room, the bar representing $9,000 will be twice as big as the $6,000 bar—quite misleading.

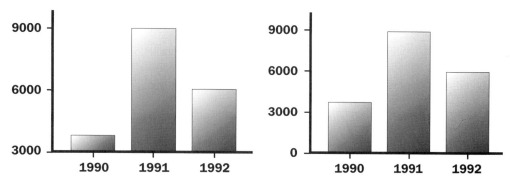

Figure 8-5: When the reference values don't include the starting point (e.g., zero on a numeric scale), the column sizes can be misleading, as illustrated at left. Correct proportions are represented with the full scale, at right.

Sometimes very important increments can be emphasized on the graph window grid. "Break-even level," for instance, may deserve a special bright grid line since it's an essential reference.

There are many ways to handle the grid itself: graph-paper squares with supplementary ticks to horizontal lines, tick marks only, vertical scale only, or no marks at all. When you decide not to indicate the grid at all, it's often helpful to place the observation values next to the plotted points—but use this technique only with the right audience and data, in cases where individual values are more important than a comparative scale.

Thin horizontal grid lines can help the viewers read data points in formats like line graphs, where it's awkward to label observations with exact quantities. When time is important, light vertical grid lines orient viewers to the critical moments.

Generally, graphs in scientific or formal presentations use tick marks to avoid cluttering the graph window. When the graph window and background offer enough contrast, you don't even need to draw the horizontal and vertical axes—place tick marks right on the edge of the window. Some people prefer a lightly drawn complete grid. Consider using a low-contrast pair of colors for grid lines and window background. Clear results count more than following some hard-and-fast rule.

Reference Values

Your viewers will expect scale values to break at familiar incre-ments, divisible by 2, 5, 10, 25, 50 or 100. For very large scales, re-duce the bulk of the figures by representing values in thousands, tens of thousands, millions and so forth. Note this near the refer-ence values—never in the heading where it may not be noticed or understood.

The conventions for labeling time increments in graphs have been refined over the years by practical considerations. If you're pressed for room, there's no need to include all four digits for each year in annual data; for most graphs, include the four digits of the first observation year and only the last two digits for subse-quent years. Abbreviate months to save space. When you're using familiar time increments, there's no need to spell out "Time," "Years" or "Months" under the horizontal axis.

Data Symbols

Symbolized data forms the main part of a graph. Points, bars, pie wedges, lines and graphic symbols illuminate statistics and clarify their relationships. The graph window, grid, reference values, notes and scales are all "support staff," helping viewers make sense of the data symbols.

The lines connecting plotted points show what probably oc-curred between observations. The points show what we actually know; the line interpolates what we suppose about a trend through time. The line should be quite bold, with sufficient con-trast in width and color to pop it out of the graph window back-ground.

Many presenters distinguish between magnitude and rate; they use bars and areas to imply magnitude, reserving lines for rate over time. Areas tend to be large presences in the graph window, so the bright colors necessary for a thin line can be overwhelming. Tone down the palette slightly toward the background values for area graphs.

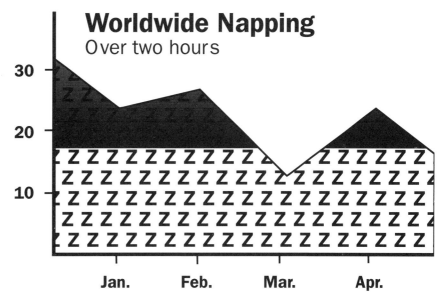

Figure 8-6: As data symbols, bars and areas represent volume, with considerable presence and impact.

Whether bars are oriented horizontally in single-scale graphs or vertically in time-related graphs, they are linear symbols that should change size only in one direction. In other words, your bars can grow longer or taller but no thicker or thinner. Think through the entire presentation before you start with very thick or very thin bars. How practical are they for all the bar graphs you'll be making? What would you communicate with a radical change in bar thickness from one frame to another?

The one-dimension change rule is easy to remember for simple bars, but it's equally true for more complex pictorial symbols. Stack small symbols instead of increasing symbol size; otherwise, you will inadvertently imply a shift in volume.

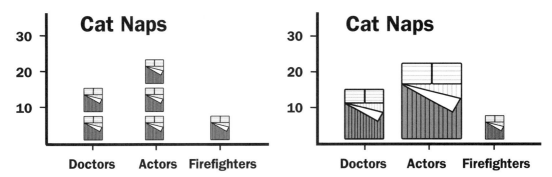

Figure 8-7: Stack symbols to show growth along one scale. When you increase size (as on the right), you enlarge the symbol in both directions and misrepresent volume.

While bar graphs compare measurements, pie graphs show the component parts of the whole. When you tilt a pie for a three-dimensional look, be sure the data supports the idea of volume. Avoid radical tilts that foreshorten the circle and distort the proportions.

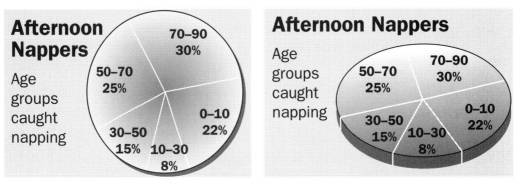

Figure 8-8: Tilting pie graphs can distort relational information, making smaller wedges seem more important because of their position in the foreground.

As you design the graphs in your presentation, remember to maintain consistency from frame to frame by using the same color palette and keeping the same placement of headings, subheadings and the graph window. Bring the data symbols to the front of the visual field. Use strong color contrast to make bars, points, lines or pie wedges bold enough to stand out from the background. In electronic screen shows, motion effects can focus attention on the data symbols, but be sure to allow your audience time to become oriented to the context before beginning the motion. Take care that the window grid recedes to the midground or background, explaining but never competing for attention with the core symbols.

Text Annotation

Graphs wouldn't make much sense without titles, labels, scale indicators and other annotation. A great heading will encapsulate the idea behind the graph in a way that the audience finds interesting. Every graph needs some text to identify exactly what is illustrated. If your audience will want to know where the information came from, include your source. But avoid overload; the more you add to a graph, the more you require of your audience.

TIME-RELATED GRAPHING

The information most of us deal with usually falls into the category of time-series graphs, with variables counted or measured as time passes. The two major families of time-series graphs are line graphs and vertical bar graphs.

Line Graphs

The typical line graph subject is rate, the measurement of quantity over a particular period of time. Line graphs "fill in the gaps" between plotted observation points to illustrate trends. You can symbolize individual observation points emphatically or subtly, depending on your message. When you draw a line between the points, you imply that the quantity measured was continuous throughout the time period. The jagged trend line clearly shows the intervals between measurements.

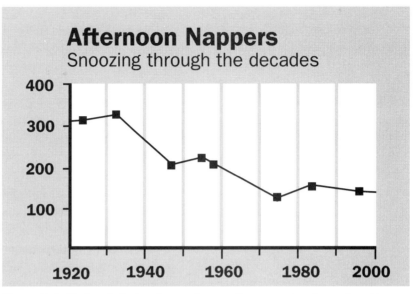

Figure 8-9: **Plot points to show observations made at varying time increments.**

When observations have been made at uneven time intervals, or at intervals not consistent with the time increments on your horizontal scale, it's conventional to plot them as clearly marked points in addition to trend lines. The line by itself is adequate, unless you're making a special point about the time intervals. In either case, be sure to make clear exactly when the measurements were made.

Sometimes your point may be served best by plotting individual observation points, then showing a curve by drawing a trend line through those points. Rather than connecting individual points, this curve illustrates the relationship between points as a flow. Because it gives a sense of pattern rather than precise measurements, it's helpful to combine with a table that provides more detailed information. When data are missing, a dashed or straight line will indicate your interpolation.

Motion effects can make line graphs more interesting to the audience when the line grows from left to right. Emphasize the individual data points by pausing at each observation. You may even pop up the data points first, left to right or high to low, depending on your message; then draw the trend line to connect them.

Area Graphs

While line graphs concentrate the viewer's attention on a single stroke, area graphs demonstrate volume by filling in the area from the baseline of the horizontal axis to a trend line. Areas are flat, bold and graphic, eliminating many of the design difficulties associated with lines. Lightly marked grids on the graph window help differentiate the area from the background.

If areas are impressive, three-dimensional areas are even more striking. Use these mountain-range images selectively to emphasize volume even further. We see the "tops" of the area blocks, so it's usually less confusing to keep them narrow. That way, the value of a particular plotted data point can be read much more easily against the vertical scale.

Vertical Bar Graphs

Vertical bar or column graphs give us another way to visualize time series; they represent a count of the same group or groups at various moments. Each observation in the series is marked by a bar that rises or falls from the horizontal axis. The contrasting bar heights show the difference between values over a period of time. The upward energy of vertical bars rising skyward lends an optimistic outlook to the graph. Electronic screen shows allow you to reinforce this motion by growing the bars from the horizontal axis. Grow all the bars at once, or add them gradually to follow your content.

Bars work well for counts of production units, orders and returns, intensities and concentrations, or populations. Where exact figures are important, they can be included at the top of the bars themselves, or below the horizontal axis. The time intervals can be days, weeks, months, quarters, years, decades or centuries—just spread them evenly across the horizontal axis with a bar or cluster of bars at each interval.

In contrast to line graphs that can display a nearly unlimited number of data points, bar graphs work well with data sets with a discrete number of observations. As a rule of thumb, show five or fewer observations with bars rather than a trend line.

Too many bars will make comparison difficult. Unless pertinent information is only revealed with the more detailed treatment, it's easier for the audience to grasp four quarterly bars than twelve monthly bars. Use bar graphs with many columns as overview frames, then follow with detail frames that show sections of the overview.

Three-dimensional effects, drop shadows and bars shaped like pyramids or octagons look intriguing at first. Accuracy is the major difficulty in working with these unusual bars. Sometimes adding depth makes it hard to tell what part of the bar represents the top, so it's impossible to read individual values against the reference values. Visual comparisons can be distorted by pointed shapes like pyramids that are squat when small and needle-like when tall.

Time-Series Combinations

Think of points, lines, areas and bars as the basics of time-series representation. Variations and combinations of the two—such as multiple lines, multiple areas or multiple lines and bars together—convey more complex information and relationships. Audiences see certain patterns more readily in combination graphs than by following single-subject graphs presented in a series. For instance, how did monthly projected sales compare with real sales over the past year? Two lines will tell the story.

The more information you pack into a single frame, or the more complex and multifaceted the comparisons, the more vital it becomes to be absolutely clear about the message of the frame and the information essential to convey that message. Spin off secondary ideas into separate frames so you can limit your combination frames to a particular point your audience will follow with ease.

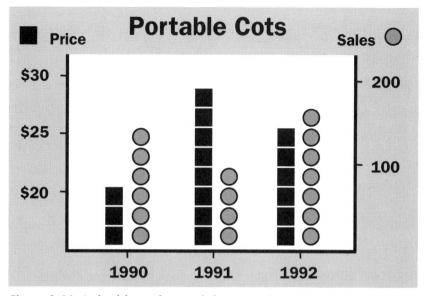

Figure 8-10: **A double-scale graph lets you show the relationship between two types of information over a period of time.**

A look at your data will help you determine whether you can chart it clearly. How tangled and entwined are your lines? Can you adjust the vertical scale to pull them apart slightly? A distinctive, bright color will help separate them visually. Label each line close to the right edge of the graph window, and align the labels to keep the frame as clean as possible.

Multiple area graphs work only when smaller areas can be placed in front of larger areas. When the trend line of an area dips behind the area in front, the information is lost to view. Label areas within the graph window whevever possible. Use legends for line and area graphs only as a last resort, since they take up space you could use for the graph window; also, they require the viewer to take another interpretive step.

Clustered bar graphs generally do require a legend to identify the elements, so if your presentation will include this format, design a space that can be used for a legend without interfering with the audience's focus on the graph symbols—to the left or right of the graph window, for example.

To further enhance and develop your message, build a combination graph over a series of individual frames. Start with your first and most basic line or set of bars; then add layers of information over the course of several slides or transparency overlays. When you're working with an electronic screen show, animate each line or set of bars to display separately. By the time the image is complete, your audience will already understand your message and you won't find yourself trying to decipher a celtic knot of lines and bars for them.

Most combination graphs show data collected over the same time period, using the same vertical scale of units. Occasionally it's useful to compare the trends or general shapes of data collected about two different kinds of units. In such cases, keep the time values constant and draw a double-scale graph, using two vertical scales. A graph that demonstrates the relationship between product price and the number of products sold requires this kind of double scale for a pair of variables measured in dollars and product units.

Double-scale graphs require clear, concise labels and scale indicators to help the audience identify the variables quickly. Label the scale for one variable on the usual vertical axis at the left side of the graph window, and create a second vertical axis on the right for the second variable scale. Link data symbols to the correct scale with color, shape, texture or other graphic device.

As your graphs grow more complex, attend closely to annotation and scale identifiers. Are they absolutely clear? Can viewers make the right connections quickly and easily? Keep your language terse and make every word contribute to the meaning.

COMPARING COMPONENT PARTS

When the parts of a whole are presented successfully, the audience grasps their relative importance intuitively. Any shape can be divided proportionally into component parts, but circles are the traditional favorites. The wedges cut from a pie graph make sense to us, as long as they're not too small. Squares and rectangles can be divided, but audiences don't recognize them immediately as parts of a whole. There's also the chance that viewers might interpret them as area or bar graphs.

Budgets are excellent subjects for this type of representation: visualize total revenues as the entire pie, with each expenditure category a separate wedge.

Pie Graphs

With a simple, flexible structure, pie graphs make interesting and elegant charts. Be sure your data supports this format, however— pies work only when the parts add up to a whole. They're scaled with only one variable, starting at zero and going around the circle that represents 360 degrees, 100% or some other appropriate whole unit. To determine wedge sizes, convert each observation's value to a percentage or fraction of the total value, then take that portion of 360 degrees.

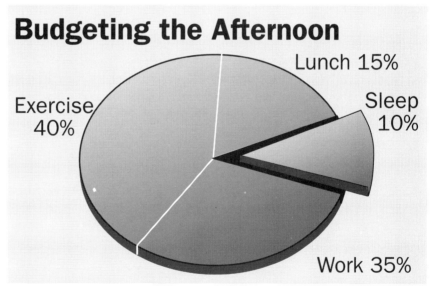

Figure 8-11: **The pie graph gives us an immediate, intuitive sense of the proportions in a whole.**

Pie graphs work best with relatively few slices—more than seven components can be confusing for the viewer and difficult for the designer to label. In fact, labeling is a challenge and often a frustration in creating a pie graph; sometimes it takes a lot of work to position and size labels for maximum clarity. If any wedge is small, as usually happens, labeling inside the pie won't work. With more than four or five wedges, labels look too scattered and diffuse when they're positioned next to the wedges outside the pie.

One solution to the labeling dilemma is to create a callout list to the right of the pie, aligned flush-left. Connect each label with the appropriate wedge by drawing a thin line, jointed if necessary but never crossing another line. A small dot on the end of the line will anchor it to the wedge. Labels, values and percentages can all be included in the callout list when they enhance the content. A row of small bullet-like squares, colored to correspond with the appropriate pie wedge, makes a nice addition to the callout list, but avoid a true legend if you can find an alternative. The main idea is to allow your audience to read the chart at a glance.

The conventional way to organize pie segments is from small to large, starting at the top (12 o'clock) or the right (3 o'clock). In a graph with only two observations, center the smaller segment at 3 o'clock. Handle the color palette with care. Draw pies directly on the background of the frame—no graph window is necessary—but position them where you've designed the window to fall on other frames in the presentation. The simplest color combination includes a high-contrast color for the focal wedge and a medium-contrast color for the remainder of the pie. White labels and wedge outlines look clean and crisp. If you find it advantageous to color each wedge differently, work with a palette of similarly subdued hues, saving the bright colors for emphasis.

Direct attention to a slice you'd particularly like to emphasize by choosing a high-contrast color or by exploding it out of the pie. Electronic shows may allow you to animate the piece out of the pie. If your presentation includes reference to each pie slice in turn, consider exploding and highlighting each with animation or through a series of frames.

Designers enjoy working with the pie shape because the form is simple and flexible enough to allow shadowing, tilting and adding a third dimension. These design treatments definitely add to the visual appeal, but they can distort the relative sizes of the wedges. After making any of these design choices, be sure your graph still expresses the relative values you started with. Sometimes rotating the pie helps solve these perceptual difficulties.

Pies aren't the ideal format for comparing components of two or more wholes. It's difficult for us to compare the size of wedges in different pies unless they are extremely simple. In that case, let the second and any other pies follow the order of the first wedges, even if they're no longer organized by size. For more complex information, try divided bars, a series of clustered bars or a table to communicate comparisons between groups more effectively.

Divided Bar Graphs

Because it can be more precise than a pie, a divided bar graph is a good alternative for comparing parts of a whole. In this format it's easier to compare the components in two or more wholes over time, and it's possible to compare the relative size of the wholes as well. Labels fit nicely inside the bars. Although it may take a little longer than it does with pie graphs for the audience to make the comparisons, divided bars can display certain types of information extremely well.

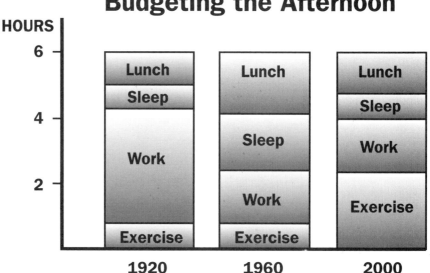

Figure 8-12: Use divided bar graphs to demonstrate changes in component makeup.

You might be tempted to divide the bars into more components than you'd use in a pie graph—but resist the urge. Give your audience only the information they will be able to absorb during the time they're viewing the frame. Build or animate the bars, division by division, to demonstrate the relationships between them.

COMPARING PLACES OR THINGS

To show relationships between people, products, regions or companies at a moment frozen in time, bring the horizontal bar graph into action. Because this visual comparison uses a scale only along the horizontal axis, you're free to organize observations vertically in any order that reinforces your point.

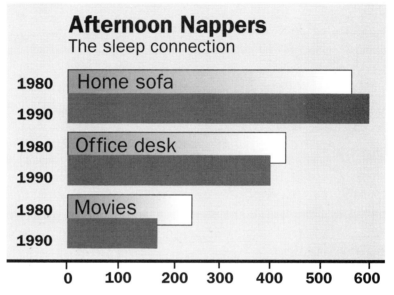

Figure 8-13: **Horizontal bars answer the question "Which is bigger?"**

Traditionally, observations are ranked by size with the largest bar at the top. If another order would work best with your material, however, that should certainly override convention. When you ask the audience to compare information in two or more horizontal bar graphs, remember to keep your observations in the same order on each frame.

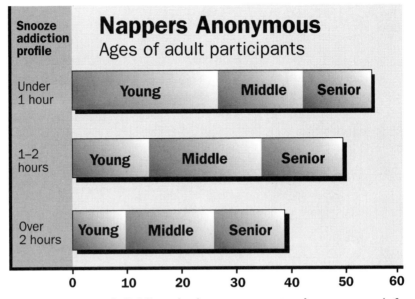

Figure 8-14: **By subdividing the bars, you can track even more information.**

Horizontal bar charts emphasize the observation with the longest bar—it's second nature for us to look for the "winner," the first bar in the group across the finish line. Structure your live presentation to take this inclination into account and highlight with color or position other bars you'd like the audience to notice.

Because they start simply, horizontal bar graphs lend themselves to elaboration. Show total volume with some additional detail by subdividing each bar. To direct attention toward specific values or attributes, pair or group the bars.

Pairs of Bars

The population pyramid is a great format to use for organizing demographic information into a specialized form of the paired horizontal bar graph.

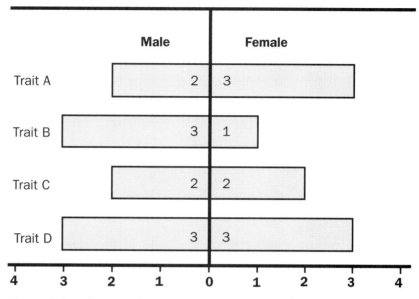

Figure 8-15: **The population pyramid changes in paired sets of demographic information.**

Place zero at the middle of the graph; then draw one scale to the left of zero to reference the number of males and a second scale to the right of zero for the female count. The scales should be mirror images, using the same values and increments. Each bar represents an age group. Unlike the comparison of places and things, bars in population pyramids join flush at zero, since this type of data is continuous.

Try this model to represent other paired values, flipping one to the left and the other to the right. Sometimes the butterfly configuration helps the audience understand the data more intuitively than grouping the variables as pairs of bars along a single scale to the right of zero. The longer, shorter structure may also fit better in your available space. Choose the structure that works best with your data and audience.

Animated effects create interesting patterns with butterfly graphs, growing the bars from the central vertical axis, either one set at a time or all together. Or if you'll be talking about all the female variables first, draw the right side up just as you would a regular horizontal bar chart. When you're ready to move into the male variables, draw up the left side of the graph.

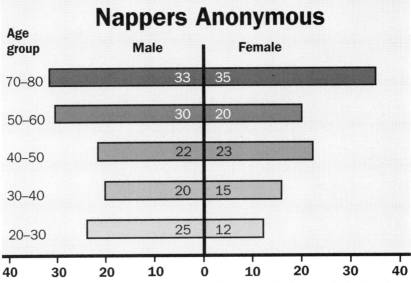

Figure 8-16: The population pyramid's butterfly format is helpful when the relationship between sets of information is critical.

Deviation Bars

Bars to the right or left of the reference axis will indicate the area of standard deviation, emphasizing divergences from the expected value. Because position says it all, it's not necessary to color-code observations to the right or left of the reference value.

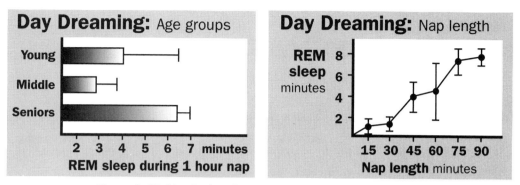

Figure 8-17: Vertical or horizontal deviation bars define the area in which you expect statistical values to fall.

With particular types of information, it's appropriate to use deviation symbols horizontally, as sliding or floating bars. They indicate the beginning and end of each observation, like the visualization of a time line.

DISTRIBUTION & CORRELATION

Graphs can show more than a set of observations or a trend: they also demonstrate what's typical or exceptional about an event. Statisticians apply precise mathematical measurements to determine the parameters of data sets, and they use specific graph forms to express them. You may find that you need to incorporate statistical analysis in your presentation; here's a guide to handling such data accurately.

Frequency Distributions

Statistical studies start with raw data, which must be organized for analysis. One method of arranging data is by dividing it into groups that are easy to compare and reveal interesting relationships.

The *frequency* of a variable is the number of times it occurs. The *frequency distribution* measures size (quantity or magnitude). A classic example of frequency distribution can be seen in a graph of student test scores. Let's say the perfect score for the test is 50 points. Some of the students taking the test scored between 40 and 50 points; some scored between 30 and 40 points, and so on. The number of students scoring within a given point range represents the frequency of occurrence.

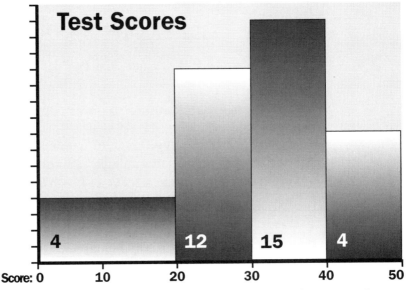

Figure 8-18: **A histogram organizes data into bins for comparison.**

Chart a frequency data graph as a *histogram*. The shape of the histogram reveals the distribution of measurements along the horizontal scale, which is divided into bins. The height of each bar shows the number of measurements that fall into a particular bin. The normal curve, or bell curve, is a good example of the histogram. The curve of a normal distribution of test scores confirms what we suspected: most of us are average, a few are slightly above or below average, and even fewer are far above or far below average.

Unlike the bars in time-series graphs, the rectangular bins in histograms are scaled in two dimensions. The width of each rectangle represents the class interval (the 10 points between 40 and 50, for example), while the height of each rectangle represents the number of occurrences. If class intervals aren't equal, rectangle widths must be varied accordingly, and adjustments to height made to preserve accuracy. The bin symbols are areal rather than linear.

The bin drawn for the first class (scores ranging from 0 to 20) must be twice the width of the 10-unit classes. Also the height of the bin must be half of what it would be if the width weren't doubled. This accurately represents the data: four students scoring between 0 and 20. If the height hadn't been cut in half, the histogram would have shown eight students in this bin.

Because histogram data is continuous, the bins are drawn flush to each other and to the sides of the graph. Time-series bars, by contrast, are separated by space.

Until you've made several presentations that incorporate frequency data, you may not feel totally confident about how to visualize the information . Ask the person who made the study or passed the data along to look over your sketches before you go into final production.

Correlations

We know that some activities are linked to each other by virtue of cause and effect. The degree to which one event can be predicted from another can be visualized in a graph. When linked pairs of variables are part of your story, make it clear to the audience how one variable increases as the other decreases, or vice versa.

Scattergrams

A scattergram shows how two data sets correlate. As in time-series graphing, points are plotted in reference to two scales. Each observation in a scattergram, however, is independent of the others, so the points are never linked as they would be in a line graph. The pattern of plotted points alone reveals the nature of the correlation, defining a positive, negative or absent relationship between the variables. This pattern can be built in a screen show by adding several sprinkles of dots.

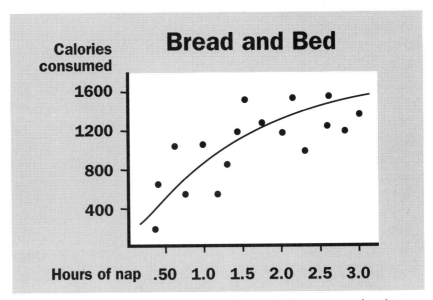

Figure 8-19: **A regression line drawn through the scattered points helps to define the trend.**

Scattergrams are often presented with a regression line. The slope and position of this line are calculated from the data to represent the trend of the data set. Make the regression line a different color from the plotted points. Draw it on the screen or build it into a sequence of frames after you've presented the points. Include a regression line only when it's statistically derived. If you don't have precise numerical values for plotting the line, don't estimate—just leave it out.

A background grid is rarely helpful in scattergrams. Instead, use tick marks along the axes to leave the data symbol field as clear as possible. Size and color the point symbols so they're readily visible on the background of the graph window.

Beware: The fact that two variables tend to increase or decrease simultaneously doesn't necessarily prove cause and effect. Perhaps the two variables are driven by a third, without which your graph will present an invalid conclusion.

Frequency graphs and scattergrams are not only tricky to construct, they're tricky to interpret. Not all audiences will respond positively to them. Ask yourself whether the folks out there will relate to these graphic forms. Would a table or a verbal explanation make the information easier to understand? As strongly as we believe in visual presentations, we still urge you not to use graphics to create complex images that might be over your viewers' heads. When your viewers have a scientific background, such forms are fine, but for general viewing it's usually safer to stay with other types of visual representation.

MOVING ON

It's vital to choose the right graph for the information you want to communicate in each frame. Keep that information tightly defined so the graph can do its job. Integrate the graph frames with the title sequences and text frames, so they're all part of the same story.

The next chapter deals with another form of visualization—one that's ideal for showing nonnumeric relationships and processes. Diagrams can be simple or complex, but they're indispensable for explaining certain concepts to your audience.

9
USING DIAGRAMS

Frequently, a key point in your presentation will benefit from a visual interpretation that is neither statistical (like a graph) nor strictly representational (like a traditional illustration). Time sequences, processes, plans and even some abstract concepts become much easier to understand when their structures and relationships to other components are shown in a diagram.

While graphs show relationships between quantities, diagrams unfold relationships among parts of a whole that aren't necessarily quantitative. When you want to communicate the exact amount of difference between one element and another—people in the city drink four times as much full-strength coffee as decaf, for instance—use a graph with reference values and a grid. But when your goal is to show simply that people drink a whole lot more full-strength coffee than decaf, and the scale of difference isn't very important, use a diagram.

Each diagram is unique, and there are few hard-and-fast rules. We can, however, visualize concepts using common elements.

LINKS & NODES

You can construct many types of diagrams using links and nodes as building blocks. Think of nodes as the entities that remain the same: people in an organization, occurrences that happen over time, activities that must be accomplished. Then consider the links that show the process and flow between nodes: the hierarchy of people in an organization, transitions from one status to another, or branches of a decision tree.

Begin visualizing your diagram by organizing the nodes. The links will follow, since they're more flexible. Sort the nodes into like and unlike groups—this can help add dimension to the structure. Try to reduce these groups to about four categories. When you draw your diagram, these categories can be differentiated by shape, color, size or position.

Figure 9-1: **Contrast helps to distinguish nodes from links.**

Since all the links between nodes won't indicate the same relationships, categorize them as well. When movement is a factor, for instance, separate the one-way from the round-trip and use different arrowhead shapes for each. Links can be coded by color or varied in width to imply different types of relationships. Dashed or dotted lines often show intermittent or partial links. Translate the vital characteristics of a link to visual terms whenever possible. Occasionally the special circumstances required for creating a link will have to be explained in a note or key.

The Pattern

Freed from quantitative restrictions, the layout of a link-and-node diagram gives you a great deal of freedom to visualize patterns of ideas in the way that will be most helpful for your audience. In most cases, the arrangement of the nodes is up to you. Don't confine yourself to any particular preconceived structure at this point; sketch and let the natural shape of the diagram emerge. As you experiment with paper and pencil, work out an arrangement of nodes that reduces the number of links that cross one another, since those are the points where the risk of confusion is greatest.

Design

After you've organized the links and nodes into an elegant two-dimensional relationship, you'll want to incorporate this pattern into the overall design of your presentation frames. Consider setting up an overall grid structure to align the pieces, positioning nodes across the frame at the grid's invisible guidelines. This approach makes it easy to incorporate the diagram into the presentation's structure for the heading, subhead and other consistent elements of each frame. On the other hand, diagrams sometimes work best when the designer relies on symmetry and centering to give them a balanced structure, and then positions them in the presentation frame.

Contrast will help your viewers distinguish between links and nodes. Regular, rectangular nodes are set off to advantage by curving links; heavy nodes call for lighter links; nodes drawn free-form need geometric links.

Flow

Make your diagrams accessible and easy to read; in a presentation, the audience must grasp the important ideas in a limited time, so representations that take a lot of time to decipher really don't help illuminate the content. Instead, try to break down complex systems into component parts, addressing each section separately; then show how they all fit together in a summary frame.

Work with the direction and motion your audience will find natural. We usually expect time-related diagrams, for instance, to read from left to right. Occasionally they'll work from top to bottom, when the content is consistent with this organization of events, but they're almost never successful right-to-left or bottom-to-top.

Authority typically flows from top to bottom, and this structure makes the hierarchy clear. Left-to-right might be acceptable as well, again depending on the context. When you're constructing an organizational diagram, be sure to put the big cheeses where they belong.

Since order and time are major factors in most sequenced information, a big part of your job is to visualize them clearly. Step-by-step instructions and other sequential diagrams should flow from left to right or top to bottom, illustrating the organizing factors. When you must show a long left-to-right sequence in two or more rows, connect the series visually with a device such as a ribbon wrapping from row to row.

Labels

Continuing the theme of clarity and immediacy of perception, it's best to label a diagram as directly as you possibly can. Place the type right on the nodes and alongside the links rather than in a legend. Making the labels fit comfortably and legibly should be a design priority. When the diagram is too complex to allow all the labels to fit, find an alternative method—build step by step, for instance, labeling each node and link as it appears.

For labels, select type that contrasts well with the type you use throughout the program for headings and subheads. Weight, size or typeface changes will provide the separation you need. The consistent application of a type style within the diagram will help hold it together as a single unit.

In some diagrams, the label itself can represent the node, without a border or box of any kind. Carefully composed labels allow the type to do all the work; links connect the labels. You might want to allow a rectangle of open space around the label, a kind of implied node box that's the same color as the diagram background. Or you might try pulling the node area out of the background just a bit more with a drop shadow or three-dimensional shadow, keeping the face of the node box the same color as the background.

Builds & Motion

Showing development and movement between points is what diagrams do best. That's why they're particularly good candidates for motion media or sequential unfurling through a set of frames. As you plan each diagram, think of it as a series of small steps in a certain direction. Adding these steps one at a time, either with a series of static frames or an animated motion sequence, focuses attention on the particular information at hand while revealing the overall pattern.

Motion allows you to differentiate further between links and nodes. For instance, you might animate the linking lines to draw across the screen in the proper direction, then pop up the nodes.

It can be tedious to make each node represent one step; alternative or simultaneous occurrences can easily draw up together. Pause between steps if necessary, or complete the diagram in one smooth movement to give the audience the entire picture.

PROCESS DIAGRAMS

A particularly satisfying type of visual representation, the process diagram tells a story with a beginning, middle and end. Process brings together raw materials, acts to transform them, and results in a product or conclusion. It involves nodes and sequences, conditional branches, relationships, functions and changes. When clearly conceptualized and rendered, process diagrams are a kind of universal language for how things work. That's why we're able to read the processes in pictograms from cultures far removed from our own in time or space.

Imagine a very mundane activity: cooking an egg and toast for breakfast. You need eggs, butter and bread as raw materials. Your tools are a heat source, a pan, a toaster, a plate and a knife. Certain steps must take place in the correct order: heat and butter a pan, break an egg into it, allow the heat to cause chemical changes to the protein of the egg, turn the egg over, and transfer it to a plate. The result is a fried egg.

If you want to make toast at the same time the egg is cooking, the process is elevated to a higher level of complexity. Butter becomes a shared resource that supplies both the frying pan and the toast; the plate receives both finished products. The simultaneous activities of this process require a different approach than one we would use for a single set of steps. Build frames or use motion to move out from the central raw ingredients and down each chain of events. Position and timing are critical.

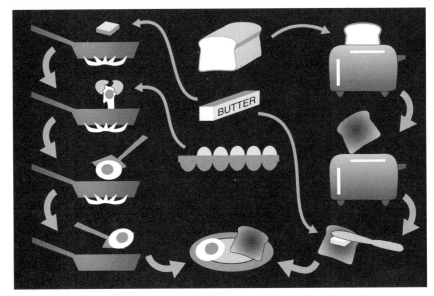

Figure 9-2: **If you can diagram the process of making breakfast, you're ready to tackle more profound subjects.**

The construction of a building is also a process that can be diagrammed. Wall supports must be up before the roof can go on; certain materials must be on-site before the plumbing system can be installed. Because it involves many more steps than cooking breakfast, you'll have to decide on the level of detail you want to show. It's perfectly possible to present an overview frame, then delve into the particulars of certain phases in follow-up frames.

Diagrams give us a new way to understand activities, one that's more concentrated than a narrative description. They're handy tools for planning and organization, revealing the gaps in our systems. The order of activities, availability of materials and supply of specialized skills are so essential to many projects that special graphic forms have been devised to handle them: PERT charts, critical path diagrams and Gantt charts.

PERT Charts

The PERT (Program Evaluation Review Technique) chart is a management tool for planning processes and checking to be sure they're on track. Especially valuable when a slew of activities must be accomplished in a certain order, a PERT chart shows the correct sequence and the length of time necessary for each task. Unlike garden-variety flow diagrams, links are drawn to scale so that tasks requiring more time are shown as longer lines.

Adapting the typical PERT chart as a presentation graphic will involve simplification and streamlining. Working charts of big projects are complex and detailed; extract the main points and clarify the underlying concepts. Visualize what the audience needs to know to follow the presentation. When details are necessary, separate facets of the chart into individual frames so viewers aren't overwhelmed. Screen shows that allow you to layer information behind "hot buttons" that can be clicked for details about particular topics are most effective with highly structured and detailed information like this.

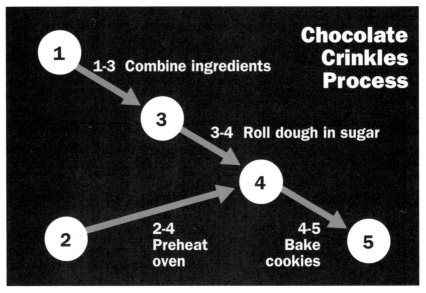

Figure 9-3: A good PERT chart presents a complex process in short, simple phrases and complementary graphic elements.

Critical Path Diagrams

Another tool for project management, the Critical Path Method (CPM) diagram displays a succession of project activities arranged from start to completion along a "critical path." Arranged like beads on a string, these activities add up to a total time span; if certain activities are scheduled simultaneously, however, the time frame can be shortened dramatically.

The critical path project schedule often takes a graphic form like a Gantt chart—a cross between a horizontal bar graph and a time line—with the path highlighted. Bar length reflects time required for each activity; links between show the optimal order.

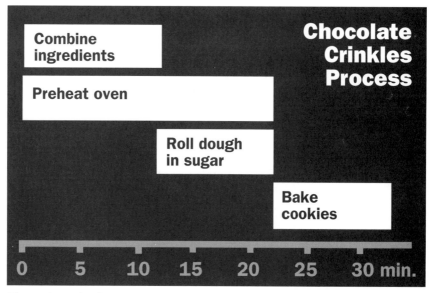

Figure 9-4: The bars in this critical path diagram serve a dual purpose.

Gantt Charts

Like PERT charts, Gantt charts are usually created for management activities, not for presentation graphics. Your first step will be to simplify and generalize the material. If one streamlined chart doesn't present the project in sufficient depth, divide the entire length of time into portions the audience will understand intuitively—months, quarters, years or decades. Don't ask the audience to study a single labyrinthine image. Perhaps you'll find it best to open with a simplified version of the big picture, follow with a series of closely focused detail frames, then close with a return to the overview. Motion will help you focus attention on particular steps, changing graphic factors such as color or size as you move the audience through the process that's represented.

Other Processes

Process diagrams are extremely flexible forms of graphic representation—they work well for routing plans, communication networks, decision structures and logic. Even when the systems they represent are quite complex, the frames illustrating them need not be confusing. Use bold, clear areas of foreground, midground and background just as you would in any effective presentation graphic. Abstract and simplify to telegraph your points to the audience. Add elaboration in your live presentation or through layers of frames for members of the audience who are interested in the details.

Specialized diagrams for project management (PERT, Gantt, etc.) aside, process diagrams are highly individualized in design and layout. Remember that it's the structure and relationships you're focusing on, not individual nodes or links. Use the graphic latitude of diagrams to show others your own understanding of the elements in context. Size, color, form and placement will be your tools in generating outstanding process images.

This flexibility makes diagramming a truly satisfying experience. Without worrying about exact statistical values, you can put your personal mark of creativity on the frame. Explore different layouts, figure/ground techniques and three-dimensional methods. Work in series whenever possible, and use motion to enliven the frame. As long as you keep your message foremost, you can let your imagination be your guide.

ORGANIZATION DIAGRAMMING

Organization diagrams are pleasantly straightforward. Corporations, institutions and government agencies use organizational diagrams, or "org charts," to show the relative positions, roles and responsibilities of individuals and departments—who talks to whom and in what capacity. Organization diagrams are invaluable management tools; they can be especially helpful in orienting new employees or in troubleshooting communication problems.

Names, titles, key roles and hierarchies are all examined in this type of diagram. Fringe and core groups or figures are revealed. Would the wave of restructuring sweeping corporate America be possible without the workhorse org chart?

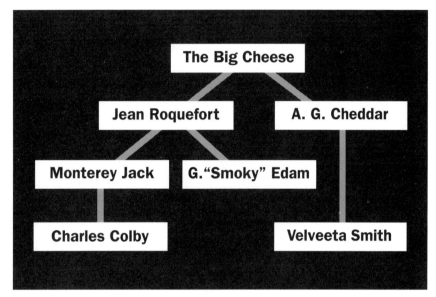

Figure 9-5: The nodes represent individuals' departments or positions; the links track the chain of command.

Organization diagrams are pleasantly straightforward. People or departments become nodes and the flow of authority or communication among them becomes a network of links. But don't let your audience sink into the lethargy of familiarity—turn the diagram on its head to show that communication also works from the bottom up, or establish lateral links to show a team network rather than a structure of bosses and worker bees. Use a traditional structure to demonstrate the unexpected!

TIME LINES

Audiences like to feel they're oriented to the context of the presentation, so at some point, either at the opening or during another opportunity for an overview, many presentations include a historical perspective of the subject at hand. Time lines are the perfect vehicle for bringing the audience up to date by showing them what has happened so far, pointing out the significant dates, inventions, discoveries and the like. They set the stage for future events, providing a structure based on relative timing. They demonstrate the long-term or short-range nature of the subject.

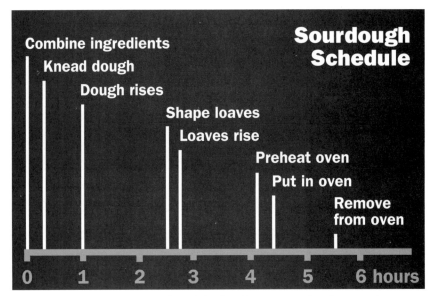

Figure 9-6: **A time line works with the time part of a time-series graph.**

Line and vertical bar graphs use a form of time line as their horizontal axis, integrated with another variable that's scaled on the vertical axis. The standard time line is really the time part of a time-series graph, freed from the vertical dimension.

Show the time line in a variety of ways, depending on the amount of detail and the number of events you want to include. Remember that you're working with symbols scaled to time; even when there are long stretches during which nothing relevant seems to have happened, you must include these "blank" periods to represent the passage of time. Often the fact that time elapsed between events is itself significant.

When activities bunch up and you're pressed for space, it's misleading to expand time. To fit a lot of activities into a short length of time, try using vertically staggered labels, callout lines with "elbow" joints to create parallel angles, arrows, or (as a last resort) a legend relating events or categories to colors or patterns on the time line bars. Consider dividing the frame into a series of several frames that cover shorter periods, or "zoom in" on one particular segment in a follow-up frame.

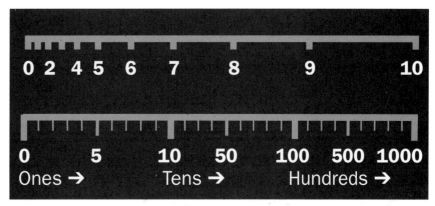

Figure 9-7: **Use a scale that accommodates the contents without creating distortions.** *Top*: **Logarithmic scale;** *bottom*: **logical progression.**

Your scale can make a big difference, so pick it carefully and label it clearly. Unusual scales help solve some visual problems. Logarithms work well for events packed closely together at one end and spread apart at the other. If mathematical logarithms scare you off, try marking time with a logical progression of linear scales to fit your story, combining tens/thousands/millions or ones/tens/hundreds. If you devise your own scale, be sure to mark the diagram so it's indicated clearly and viewers will have no trouble understanding your time scheme.

EXPLODED DIAGRAMS

If you could take a photograph of something flying apart (like the famous print of the splash of a milk drop), component parts would appear in their separate forms. To make an exploded diagram, imagine this bursting apart, freed from gravity. This technique allows you to show details that would otherwise be hidden or obscured.

Explode only the parts that are relevant to your story, allowing the others to stay together as the remainder of the whole. Suppose you're creating graphics to show the next generation of home coffee-roasting equipment. You want to detail one aspect of the equipment—say the safety features—and show how it fits into the rest of the unit. Draw the assembly and explode the thermostat and circuit breaker.

Figure 9-8: **An exploded diagram exposes hidden details.**

Be sure to include guidelines or arrows to show how the exploded parts fit with each other and back into the whole assembly. These guides can be lightly screened or dashed, and should be consistent with the perspective of the entire drawing.

Exploded diagrams are actually a kind of illustration, and they are almost always rendered as three-dimensional objects. For best results, it's important to be familiar with perspective drawing. Parallel projection is the most common as well as the easiest technique for most people. One-point perspective, where all depth vanishes to a single point (think of looking down a railroad track), is slightly harder to draw, but it looks more realistic. Two-point perspective (where depth vanishes to two spots) looks even more realistic. Experiment with the sketch sheets in Appendix C to determine the best technique for your exploded diagram.

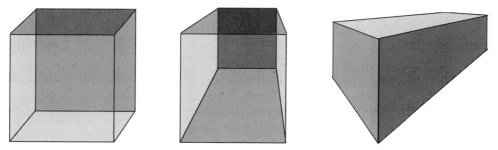

Figure 9-9: **Parallel projection (***left***); one-point perspective (***center***); two-point perspective (***right***).**

FLOOR PLANS, MAPS & OTHER SCALE DRAWINGS

Some points can be made most precisely by demonstrating relative size, proportion or location. Draw these illustrations to a particular scale, and maintain the scale strictly in all portions of the image. You can loosen up a bit with inserts and details, but set them off in clearly separate areas of the frame with a second scale. Alternatively, follow the complete image with a detail or reduction frame. When changing scales between frames, zooming in or pulling out, be sure to indicate the difference to the audience.

When you're showing the scale in presentation media, you must show a particular length and its equivalent value, rather than stating that "one inch equals 100 miles." Remember that when your frames are projected or displayed on another monitor, your original inch would be tremendously distorted, so stick with relative comparisons.

Figure 9-10: **Show two different scales by insetting a detail box.**

Product illustrations should be drawn to scale in order to maintain fair representation. Chocolate chip cookies pictured with chips three times larger than actual size make us feel cheated. We expect the real thing to look like the picture in the presentation, with the same relationship between chocolate chips and cookie dough.

Floor plans are a particular type of scale drawing that show the scene of a crime, the layout of a building, the room arrangement of a model home or other such spatial information. We usually represent floor plans from a bird's-eye view, as if we could remove the roof and look straight down into the interior. Elaborate floor plans may include perspective drawings of the walls, the type of foreshortened perspective you might remember from the Clue™ game.

If you're lecturing on fire escape routes and safety exit locations, or if you're orienting new employees to production areas, you'll want to include a fairly detailed floor plan in your presentation to represent the physical context. Floor plans allow us to enter a space imaginatively and follow the speaker through doors, past windows and into corridors.

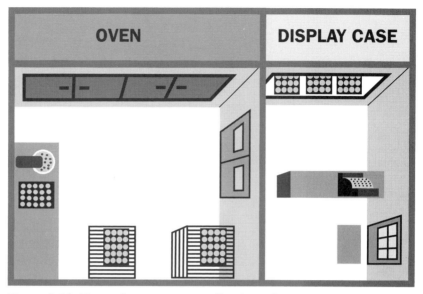

Figure 9-11: **Floor plans are most effective when they provide a sense of scale and place.**

Like floor plans, location maps are two-dimensional representations of the physical world, seen from above. Their strong suit is situating a particular building or feature of the landscape, like a company headquarters or sales office. The reference elements will make or break a successful location map. Provide enough familiar features to give the viewer a sense of both scale and place. Consider how well the audience knows the area. Scout the location for interesting landmarks to give your map flair and individual immediacy. Include a north arrow and a simple scale for reference.

Statistical and thematic maps are great ways to present activities observed by geographical site. They're content-driven graphics, showing the prevalence, intensity or density of target activities; they're only possible when you have the right data to interpret. On location maps the symbols represent tangible things, while on thematic maps they represent abstract factors and forces that cannot be seen on the ground.

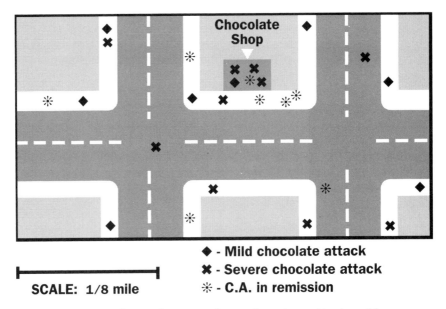

Figure 9-12: **This thematic map relates chocolate attacks with proximity to the Chocolate Shop.**

Mapping Symbols

Maps translate data into spatial patterns. The data is represented by various symbols, which can be particularly effective for election returns, cultural patterns, demographics and production activities.

When you're working with data collected at discrete locations, try a dot map. A colored dot can represent each occurrence or group of occurrences, just like the colored pushpins on the giant wall maps at the Pentagon. The result is something like a scattergram, scaled to place rather than other variables.

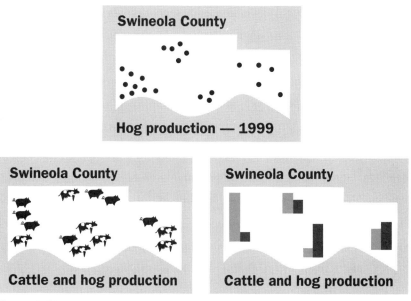

Figure 9-13: Dots, icons and bars add different dimensions to the data represented in these maps.

Suppose you're mapping hog production. One dot can equal one hog, or you can scale the data so that each dot represents 100 or 1,000 hogs, depending on your overall numbers. You might replace the dots with symbols if you want to show both hog and cow production, and you could color the dots or symbols to show particular breeds. Scaled bars or columns like those on vertical bar graphs work well to show relative quantities; locate the bar bases to correspond with the site they represent.

If your data was collected by region, use shade, color or pattern to show statistical intensity. Group values into four or five ranges and assign a visual code to each range.

Suppose you're the new marketing manager for Piece-A-Pizza. You want to make a map that will help you convince your vice-president that your proposed marketing plan will target the right geographical areas. The only sales figures you can find were collected state by state.

First you group the sales values into high, medium and low ranges. You assign each range a color, remembering that cool colors recede and warm colors come forward: try blue for low sales, green for medium and orange for high. Color each state to match the sales figures. Your audience will find it easy to pick up the geographic patterns that emerge from the map; they'll have a new vision of their sales effort and you'll have demonstrated your knack for knowing what's going on. It's all in the interpretation—and the more visual, the more convincing.

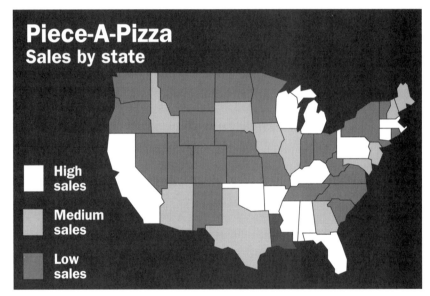

Figure 9-14: Color coding works well for geographic maps.

MOVING ON

Diagrams are wonderful devices for communicating priority or procedure, where things are or how they work. Especially when your information is highly abstract, your audience will benefit from a visualization of the relationships you want to draw between the concepts. Concentrate on structure and flow to distill a topic to its bare bones. When you devote time to this type of graphic, the payback goes beyond helping an audience understand the ideas and information you're presenting. You're also giving them a framework for remembering the concepts and incorporating them into their daily practice.

Throughout the overview of presentation graphic design and conceptualization, we've suggested ways you can use motion media techniques to clarify your message. Now we'll turn to consider the basics of multimedia as it's emerging on the desktop.

MOVING INTO MULTIMEDIA

Multimedia is the new golden glow, pushing us on-ward, beyond desktop publishing, beyond desktop presentations, into the stratosphere where communica-tion is instantaneous, and where nobody but nobody would dare nod off during the show.

LOVE AT FIRST SIGHT—AND SOUND

You've probably experienced it, too. We've all fallen head-over-heels in love with innovative technology at some point, infatuated by the incredible possibilities we can imagine.

And it is an alluring dream. What could be more exciting than combining desktop computers and everything they can do—from simple text frames to graphs, diagrams, illustrations, animation and 3D modeling—with the strength and versatility of conven-tional video and audio segments. Explore any topic by mixing many different approaches; sound, graphics, video images and text work together to engage the audience. Who could resist a presenter armed with such a marvelous display? And if that's not enough, you can add interactivity, providing access to layer after layer of detail behind each concept.

Figure 10-1: Multimedia is the djinn on the desktop that will summon illustrations, video clips, animated sequences, sound, text and interactive information.

Gradually, gradually, multimedia is coming down to earth with software packages that really work, hardware that's affordable and a learning curve that's less than astronomical. It's just about to land in your backyard, so get ready!

Growing the Seeds of Change

Multimedia's strong suit is showing transformation and change. Multimedia motion effects can accomplish effortlessly the visual unfolding of information that we try to generate with build sequences and series of frames in static media. Demonstrating the development of an idea, showing change over time or following the transformation of one process into another—multimedia gives you a splendid tool for these jobs.

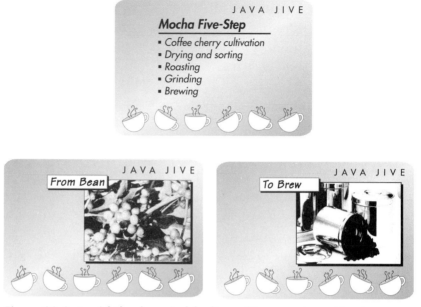

Figure 10-2: **Avoid the frenzied feeling of too much motion by planning occasional straightforward still images like the frame at lower right.**

Motion on the screen really does grab viewers' attention. Their involvement will be at a very high level—initially. While you might think you'll need to keep everything in motion to maintain that interest level, the concept of contrast works here, too. For the full effect to redound to your advantage, the audience needs the periodic relief provided by intermediary frames that don't razzle and dazzle. Give them some breathers that allow your points to soak in.

Live presenters need excellent multimedia support, not competition. Use motion video, especially videotape "movie clips" sparingly, since they pull attention away from the presenter. Audio effects can be great boons in small doses. Try using them for sound effects that reflect the motion on the screen, as an occasional "second voice" to make your points, or to build instant credibility when respected authorities speak. Low-key music can help pace your visuals and highlight important points.

Upping the Ante

Multimedia applications make wonderful sales presentations, product announcements, training and educational programs, reference materials and display modules. They stand alone or give a speaker strong support. When they're successful they work like magic, and only you will know how much effort it took to make the magic work.

You still need to follow all the planning and design steps you'd go through to produce a conventional presentation. It's vital to identify your points, then organize, prioritize, emphasize and summarize. Because multimedia effects are so engaging and seductive, they can take an audience right off the track if you're not extremely well focused. Know exactly what role each element should play, and keep your presentation tuned to your basic objectives.

Figure 10-3: **Computer displays look best with clear, uncomplicated shapes and simple but shapely sans-serif type.**

Design multimedia presentations with the limitations of computer displays in mind. Avoid thin horizontal lines that can look wavy on the monitor, and use clear, uncomplicated shapes in your graphics. Simple, bold typefaces work best. Slight drop shadows often bring the type forward, out of the background. You don't have to worry about the headache of color shift since the computer screen is your ultimate display medium, but choose your color palette carefully to avoid strong spectral opposites. Place vital elements slightly away from the edges of the screen, in case other monitors scan the image differently.

Complications in Paradise

Multimedia motion effects, audio segments and video clips increase the technical complexity of your project because they make strong demands on your system's capabilities for storage and speed. Consider, for instance, that the standard rate of video display refresh is thirty frames per second. Each frame must be stored and then accessed smoothly—multimedia gobbles disk space.

The development of more efficient compression schemes along with more affordable storage systems that provide faster access are some of the breakthroughs propelling multimedia onto the desktop. Nevertheless, plan your production in terms of available memory space. And remember that the promised "instant access" to information is tempered by the rate of transfer from storage your system provides, and the speed of your computer's processor. Storage and speed become both production and presentation issues.

Multimedia software is a matrix that can require additional interface cards, software, and recording and playback equipment. When memory needs exceed the space available on your hard disk for storing your production tools and various pieces of the program as you refine it, you might consider investigating laser disk and CD-ROM players. Be sure you have an efficient backup mechanism so you won't lose all that work! Catalog your current system, taking stock of the multimedia options open to you now; then list the hardware you'll need to create shows with elements like video clips and digital audio editing.

Figure 10-4: **Good design and planning can present complex layering of content information without visual confusion.**

Complexity creates a major design challenge as well: you want to provide rich content in the presentation while maintaining a sophisticated but uncomplicated face. Especially with interactive shows, viewers need a clear idea of where they are at all times, with the options at each stage clearly presented. Make sure plenty of choices are available and that each choice leads to interesting and varied new terrain. Such richness must be planned carefully and implemented cleverly to make best use of storage and overcome speed limitations.

MULTI*WHICH*?

One of the difficulties in defining and discussing multimedia is the fact that different multimedia software programs allow you to work with different types of source materials, assembling them into a string of sound and images held together by transition effects. Some multimedia software works only with frames created in that particular software, while some acts as a glue to integrate imported frames and sequences. Consider a wide range of possibilities as raw material for the program, but be sure to check your hardware and software limitations.

Hear Ye

Audio material for your multimedia mill includes recorded music (with permission, of course), voice-overs and sound effects, in addition to tracks produced on traditional multichannel analog

mixers. Keyboard synthesizers and other electronic sound genera-
tors may interface directly with the computer; the material can
then be edited and manipulated digitally. Pull audio from a
videotape, with or without the image for the sequence.

Vision of Delight

The visual elements of multimedia are manifold, and each software program accepts its own set of file formats for them. Learn
the nuances of your software; some programs only animate
frames you build inside the program, for instance, while others
start with imported frames. Potential visual elements, raw material for your multimedia program, include frames with text and/
or graphics, animated sequences, frame or screen grabs and full
motion video clips. Remember that multimedia effects alone can't
tie disparate frames together—you must implement an overall
plan for color, typography and frame layout.

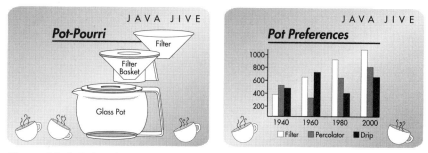

Figure 10-5: **Bring images created in your favorite drawing, charting
and presentation software packages to the multimedia party.**

Images generated in draw, paint, charting or other presentation
programs make excellent multimedia frames. Import text frames,
charts, graphs, diagrams and illustrations. Even when your multimedia software includes features for creating these frames within
the program, you might be more comfortable using more familiar
or sophisticated programs. Imaging software specifically for 3-D
illustrations, for instance, can be particularly appealing. To save
time and aggravation, modify and use again the frames and art
you've already created.

Animated sequences can be produced in special animation programs, as screen show effects from other presentation programs, imported as prepared animation clips, or generated in the multimedia program itself. A series of static images can be linked by transition devices like dissolves, creating the illusion of animation.

Frame grabbers pull individual frames from video input, in the form of either a live camera or a VCR. They isolate one static image—a single frame. Screen grabbers can also take a snapshot of a screen in a program that you can't import in some other way. They're particularly handy for demo disk support. Within the multimedia program, you can add motion graphics over the grabbed frame, or create the effect of motion by grabbing four or five frames in a sequence, then cross-fading between them.

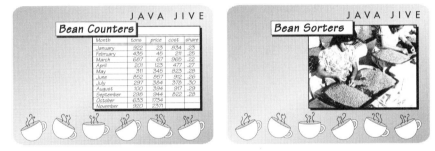

Figure 10-6: **Grab a single frame from another program (*left*), or import a brief video clip into a window in the multimedia shell (*right*).**

Full-motion video clips can also be placed into the multimedia framework from either a live camera or a videotape recorder. They usually require an additional video card in your computer system. These sequences are very memory-intensive; beware of grainy screens or jerky motion—clues that the system has made some compromises to keep the file size within manageable limits. The smaller the video window on the screen, the less memory it will require. Try a window about half the screen size, designed to work well with the background elements. Does the video sequence still communicate the right message? On the other hand, excellent video quality can be found in multimedia programs that access conventionally edited video clips stored on laser disks.

MIXING IT UP IN PRODUCTION

Bring all your source frames and sequences—from simple line graphs to animated cartoons and full-motion video clips—as raw materials into the multimedia module, where you'll integrate your resources into a dynamic, coherent presentation. Multimedia software places visual and audio events on a timeline, creating the structure of the program. It allows you to fine-tune the relationship between these beads on a string, using animated effects and transition devices like wipes and fades.

Without careful planning, the complexity of this assembly process and the number of individual events can be overwhelming. Even when you're tightly organized, you'll find that working on several levels at once is challenging, as you move between creating source materials and composing the full presentation. You'll keep a lot cooler if you can stay flexible and give yourself time to experiment and revise.

Combined Resources

During multimedia production you can combine images from several different sources—place a video sequence in a graphics frame, for instance, or superimpose a diagram over a screen grab. Use this technique to add headings and text areas with background bars to frames that come from many different sources, generating consistency in typeface, size and color. As an extreme example of what some multimedia programs can do, imagine a computer screen with an interesting graphic background; one by one, four boxes slide onto the left edge of the screen, a live video clip playing in each one; the animated boxes continue their journey across the frame and slide off the right edge.

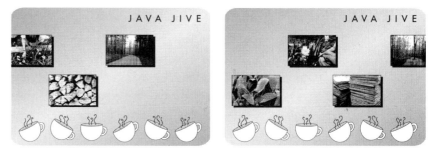

Figure 10-7: Processing speed, memory and storage are limiting factors, but it's possible to combine video clips with screen animation—and any number of other effects.

Transition Devices

The most basic way of adding multi-image motion effects to a series of frames—either static, animated, or full-motion video—is to make wise use of the transition devices that link individual screens. The motion of the transition, wiping across the screen, catches the eye and is easy to specify.

Dissolve one screen into another—and just change one element so that it appears to be moving. Fade out an image to black, or fade in from black to the image. Cross-fade by placing a nearly identical second copy right over a particular object. Vary the two images only by the color of an element, working from black-and-white to full color, for instance.

For a sharper effect, quick-cut from one frame to another. Wipe one image off the screen and another on, specifying direction and speed—down or across the screen, diagonally over the image area or out from the center. Close a section with a set of venetian blinds. Or shrink an image to the upper right corner and off the screen, revealing the new image beneath it.

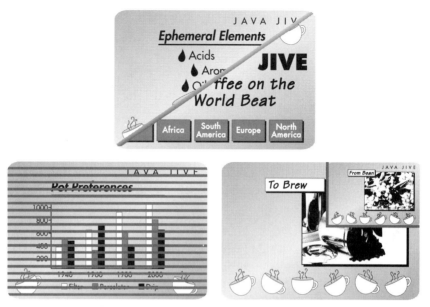

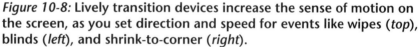

Figure 10-8: Lively transition devices increase the sense of motion on the screen, as you set direction and speed for events like wipes (*top*), blinds (*left*), and shrink-to-corner (*right*).

During transitions, strange things can happen to color. To save on file size, many onscreen presentations use 8-bit indexed color that allows 256 colors to be displayed at once. Different images may have different groups of 256 associated with them, and when two of these images share the screen during a transition effect like a wipe, the colors in the second image are drawn up incorrectly until the transition is complete—then they pop into the proper colors quite noticeably. If this shift makes your transitions markedly odd, try working with the colors in the two images to bring them into a common palette.

Animation & Pseudo-Animation

Multimedia programs allow presenters to make their points by moving objects around on the screen, growing the columns of a bar graph or the lines of a line graph, popping up bullet points or sliding a text frame onto the monitor. Depending on the software, you might prepare the sequence in a program dedicated to animation, or create it right in the multimedia program itself. Many presentation packages allow you to create simple animation, defining a line along which an object will move at a particular rate. Some have auto-animate features that put motion into standard formats like graphs and text frames.

For the *effect* of animation without true frame-by-frame animated artwork, try creating a beginning and end frame, then using a transformation or blend tool to generate a series of intermediate frames. When the sequence is run together quickly with fast dissolves between the frames, the motion effect can be quite convincing.

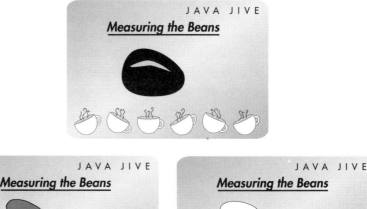

Figure 10-9: When time is short, use intermediate "blend" steps with cross-fade transitions to fake an animated transformation.

Another interesting and rather amazing animated effect can be created by making an object and rotating it in a 3-D software program. As you rotate it, save a series of frames. When you link these frames into a fast-paced sequence with transition devices between them, the object really seems to float in space.

Motion Clips

Many multimedia programs include a set of motion clips, just as drawing programs include a library of electronic clip art. These clips create effects that can be lots of fun when you're in a hurry, adding a little sparkle to the frame. The sparkle may then dissolve into another clip, such as a star shower. Just as you wouldn't use clip art indiscriminately, be sure to keep motion clips for exactly the right situation, where they won't seem clichéd or tacked on without any real purpose.

Sounding Board

Depending on their sophistication, many multimedia programs offer tools for audio processing and editing. MIDI, the common digital language in computer software applications, accepts input from units like keyboard synthesizers and drum machines.

The multimedia software can then act as a digital processing workstation for audio elements, synthesizing music and effects and mixing them with a taped voice track if necessary. The computer offers digital audio functions for multichannel equalizing, time scaling to stretch or compress audio over time, and special effects like echo reverb. It links the digital audio to the visuals in the presentation, running the sound as a concurrent event with the pictures for perfect synchronization.

INVITING INTERACTIVITY

While we usually organize presentations to move from point A to point Z, that kind of restrictive, two-dimensional structure isn't always appropriate. We all know most topics are denser and more complex than we're able to show as a chain of beads. At best we're compromising between the full range of our knowledge and the level of interest we expect in our audience.

Interactive presentations open up the possibilities of layering information so details are available to those who are interested. When a speaker is asked to elaborate on a particular aspect of the presentation, visual support is ready at the click of the mouse on a "hot button," an area of the screen the designer defines as a way to access a topic. As they're needed, further layers of specific information can be defined and accessed through hot buttons.

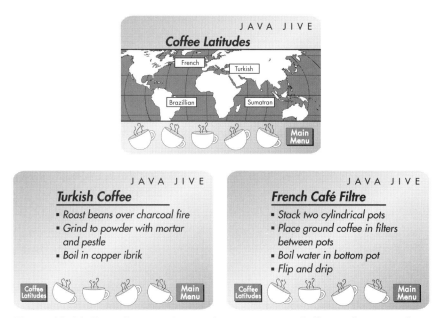

Figure 10-10: Keep interactive pathways easy to follow when moving forward through the material and when retracing steps to review a point.

Alternate paths through a network of ideas and information allow people to choose their own pathways through the material presented. There may be many roads to a screen or sequence of screens that explains a particular subject. The computer offers immediate access to text, graphics, audio and video segments, whether the audience is a single person working at a touch screen display or a group of distributors learning about the latest product line.

All this information, presented with motion effects, transition, and audio and video clips, adds up to a lot of disk space. Consider using CD-ROM technology to hold it, or working with a system that combines a laser disk for video and digital audio segments with the programming data that enables navigation and interactivity on disk.

Make sure you design interactive screens so the viewers always realize where they are in the structure, and help them find their way to the next topic they want to visit. Include a way to escape from the current screen, including a return to the last branching point and a return to the main menu where they can quit the program.

MULTIPRESENTING

The most important consideration in presenting with multimedia support is securing the appropriate equipment on-site. Many software companies offer a run-time version of their multimedia programs, so completed presentations can be displayed without loading the entire software package. But you'll want to be sure the graphic display and audio system in the playback location will accommodate your show.

As the program components grow more complex, your ultimate presentation site must be able to match them. If you've brought it on floppy disk or removable cartridge, move the file onto the hard disk. Make sure you have enough disk space and speed for your motion sequences to play correctly. Be prepared to ad lib in case things slow down.

Technical hitches can destroy the whole high-tech effect and dissolve hours and hours of work into embarrassing waits and stumbles. Even though you have rehearsed your program countless times in advance, arrange for a run-through on-site to go over it one more time, so you can become familiar with the room and the equipment.

MOVING ON

The multimedia dream—using your desktop computer to combine all types of visual and audio sources into one cohesive presentation—is becoming more practical every day. Planning and excellent design will make the most of this emerging format. Produce multimedia programs that play to the strengths of motion and transformation; use them to show change and development.

As you implement your presentation tools and skills, you'll want to be aware of the most common pitfalls in presentation design so you can avoid them. In Chapter 11 we'll identify design mistakes, and offer a wide range of solutions.

DESIGN CRIMES & HOW TO PREVENT THEM

11

I t's ironic, but the most common mistakes in presentation design reflect a bit (or a wallop) too much enthusiasm about all the graphic bells and whistles the new desktop systems make so readily available to us. But forewarned is forearmed: if you're mindful of the pitfalls, you won't walk straight into the most common traps that weaken the design and the effectiveness of your presentation.

In communications, form really will follow function when you are very clear about the function. The opposite, however, is rarely true: function and meaning are more often distorted than clarified by a pre-existing form. So concentrate first on drafting frames that "read right."

A truly functional design enhances your message, making it easy to understand. It radiates integrity and credibility. And it's strong on practical matters—economical to produce and easy for the speaker to handle. Direct your efforts toward meeting function, and the form will begin to emerge. Then apply basic design guidelines to this nascent form, and your visual organization will reflect the content beautifully.

Unfortunately, the natural inclinations of first-time designers often get in the way of achieving the desired results. Inexperienced designers assume that the dynamic frames they've admired in others' presentations are the result of tricks and elaborate use of presentation design tools. But experience always sends us back toward the simplest, most elegant design that solves a clearly defined communication challenge.

Beginners tend to repeat the same design mistakes—dead giveaways of less sophisticated desktop presenters. So here are some common pitfalls, the minefields of presentation graphics. If you can recognize and avoid them, you'll be miles ahead.

TYPE

Size & Weight Problems

When they're just starting to specify type sizes and weights, beginning designers tend to use type that's too big and heavy for page graphics and type that's too small and light for presentation graphics. These choices make a page look coarse and the frame seem wimpy. Pick up a magazine you find especially exciting visually. Look through it, concentrating entirely on typography to get an idea of the upper limits of size and boldness of weights.

Projected and screen graphics, on the other hand, need a somewhat heavier texture to look and read best. Frames that appear overbearing as handouts can be exactly right on the screen. Start with medium or bold type weights. Don't fill up the entire screen with type, but experiment with headings that generate impact and text type that's large enough to read without effort but small enough to allow a phrase to fit on a single line. Remember that each presentation frame should make one key point. The coarseness of the type should serve that "in your face" objective.

Stacked Characters

The 52 members of the uppercase and lowercase alphabets work together most naturally in a horizontal, left-to-right orientation. Any other scheme—for example, stacked letters that require the reader to assume a distorted posture in order to make out the words—creates an obstacle. Regardless of the configuration—

uppercase or lowercase, centered or flush-left—stacked type looks odd and disappointing after the extra time and work you put into creating it.

If you're tempted to stack letters to make the best use of available space when you're designing a graph, remember some alternative, better solutions. Rotate an ordinary line of type 90 degrees to read like the spine of a book. Or use horizontally aligned headings over vertical graph elements. These methods keep the letters in the proper relationship to one another so that the words are quickly recognizable.

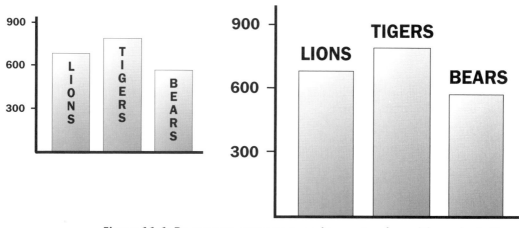

Figure 11-1: **Be sure to arrange type in a natural, positive orientation that leads the eye through the graphic.**

Distorted Baselines

It's not easy for our eyes to follow lines of type on a screen; in many ways the page is a more comfortable reading medium. Special effects that might look great in a brochure can be disastrous in presentation graphics—for example, curved or wavy lines of type following curved or wavy chart lines. This may seem like a clever device, but to the viewer it just seems odd. Lines of type set on a diagonal may strike you as zippy and upbeat at first, but reading them soon becomes tedious. Let lines of type play "straight" to inventive graphics.

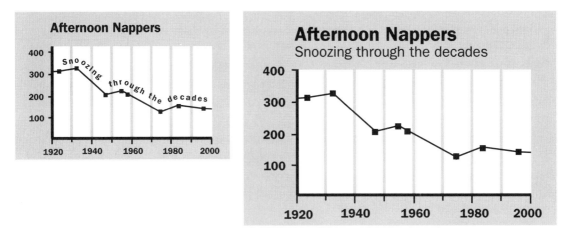

Figure 11-2: **Your software program may allow you to make unusual type placements, but type reads better when you keep it serious and practical.**

Type is meant to be read. In your presentation frame you've ruthlessly cut all but the most essential words. Now you can't afford to risk losing any of them. Whenever you veer from the left-to-right, linear orientation that readers normally expect, you decrease legibility.

On the other hand, sometimes the risk is acceptable as the best solution to a difficult problem. Long column labels in a table, for instance, may fit much more felicitously when angled at 30 or 40 degrees, creating a table with much better overall proportions. Just be sure you gain more than you lose with tricks like this.

LAYOUT

Before the advent of desktop computers, complex graphics meant expensive graphics. Skill, time and budget constraints kept presenters from cluttering their graphics with lots of extra visual elements. Now we have to exercise restraint in the opposite direction: it's so easy to add them, we put graphics in jail behind the bars of competing boxes and rules.

Because we're taught in school to underline or highlight important information in a textbook, we're inclined to add a line or border around part of an image to direct attention there. And, of course, we know that several parts of the image are very important, so we build layers of imprisoning lines.

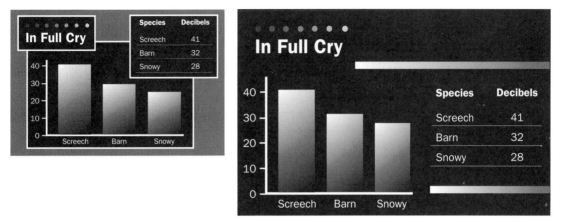

Figure 11-3: **The more graphic elements boxed into a frame, the less attention each one commands.**

Surprise! Rather than emphasizing the message, boxes and borders can weaken the effect. The lines often create a distraction and limit legibility. Open space, on the other hand, concentrates interest and draws the eye to an element within it. When you're tempted to underline, box or border, try increasing the space around it instead.

BACKGROUND DESIGN

Desktop presentation programs can generate wonderful, rich backgrounds in solid or graduated tones. Don't be afraid to let these backgrounds show. Give the graphic elements plenty of breathing room to project an aura of calm and self-assurance. When a frame begins to look too crowded and dense for the medium, split it into two or more images.

Don't feel pressured to decorate the space that's left after you've presented the core message. A clean, uncomplicated presentation style is much more professional and effective than one that's cluttered with a lot of clip art and foreign matter.

COLOR

When used effectively, color is more interesting, exciting and inviting than monochrome images. Most of us prefer full-color materials, although the nitty-gritty honesty and integrity of black-and-white fits some messages to a T. And given the choice between low-quality, fuzzy color and high-quality, sharp black-and-white, we may do well to opt for the latter.

Because color is a powerful design element, with negative as well as positive implications, it must be handled with a careful eye and restrained hand. Build a palette that works well together, not just in hue but in value and saturation as well.

Black & Blue

Human eyes have trouble with any but the lightest blue elements on a very dark background. That's because of the way our retinas receive blue light. Blue text on black looks fuzzy and out of focus.

Of course, blue continues to be a favorite presentation color—so long as it's not used for elements that require close focus against a black background. Use fully or partially saturated blues for backgrounds or for foreground elements on a light background.

Speak, Don't Scream

We've all fallen prey to the idea that using lots of bright, vivid colors will make our frames more attractive, interesting and memorable. Oops—another assumption bites the dust of the projection room.

Neon images that scream for attention just confuse and tire our eyes. Four to six colors generally make a fairly complete palette. Of these, only one or two should be fully saturated foreground colors that draw viewers toward the key point of the frame.

Try it and see—frames built with a palette of black, white, grays, warm neutrals and a couple of bright colors for small elements will actually look richer and warmer than the fluorescent combinations you may be tempted to choose. Each bright color needs to be offset with a much larger area of dark, deep color—a background from which it can emerge most strongly.

MULTIMEDIA

Don't allow your enthusiasm for animated effects and transitions to turn motion into mania. Animation should serve to engage the viewer in a process that underlines the content. Instead, many multimedia novices pull out all the stops: fancy transitions between every frame; animated titles, text and graphs in the same frame; blinks and spins.

Motion Sickness

With all this motion going on, the frame never stops vibrating with energy and effects. Unfortunately, the audience stops vibrating to the message and begins to tune into the technology itself. You want people to wonder, "What exactly does this imply for our town?" rather than, "How in the world did he do that?"

Save major transition effects like blinds and long wipes to signal important divisions in the content of the presentation, perhaps with the section divider frames. Between frames and sequences in the same area, use subtler effects such as dissolves and fades.

You can animate the line of a line graph, explode the wedge of a pie graph that represents a vital segment, or introduce the bars of a clustered bar chart set by set. But remember that competing effects cancel each other out, so focus attention on the most important elements. Make sure the underlying structure—the frame without any motion effect—is sound. Then trace the connections you want your audience to draw, visualizing the process for them.

ALIGNMENT

Working with a grid structure and the three alignment possibilities—flush-left, centered and flush-right—every frame offers a wide range of placement options for text and design elements. It's important to establish an alignment plan and rules that will work for the entire presentation. Odd-numbered grid divisions (three, five, seven) help create open space and dynamic asymmetrical balance, and are a good place to start the alignment process.

Stuck in the Middle

For some reason, beginning presenters often assume all text and graphics should be centered within the frame. Nothing could be farther from the truth! Symmetry is not magical—it's static.

Figure 11-4: **Use the grid structure instead of centered alignment to create a balanced effect.**

Centering creates a good many design difficulties. It divides the available open space into two equal units that have much less impact than a single more expansive area. It requires readers to find a new starting point for each line, instead of returning to a common left margin. When a heading is centered in the frame, it may not be visually centered over another element like a bullet list where most of the copy is toward the left of the text block.

Centered text works well only in extremely formal situations like wedding invitations, where the words and phrasing are quite familiar to us. Anchoring text and headings flush-left on a vertical grid line makes it easy for readers to follow the content. Allow areas of open space to balance areas with text and graphics in a more vigorous configuration.

Justifying Justification

Caution! Justified alignment of text rarely enhances a presentation frame. If properly written, presentation copy is just too short to fill a justified line without extremely large gaps. And since presentation copy should never be hyphenated, the mechanical approach of justified copy must give way to the more organic flush-left, centered or flush-right approach. In fact, since a flush-left alignment works so well and is so readable, you could make it standard for headings and text in all your presentation work.

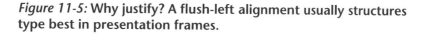

Figure 11-5: **Why justify? A flush-left alignment usually structures type best in presentation frames.**

This doesn't mean that all lines of type in every frame should start at the same left edge, huddled over toward the far left of the screen. On the contrary, use the underlying grid to "hang" blocks of type and open up the space in the frame (see Figure 11-4).

EMPHASIS

Every presentation frame should feature a key element, even if it's just a name on a title slide. How can you help your audience identify immediately the most important information? Try the double whammy of color and open space.

Color With Caution

Choose it carefully and color will create emphasis. Highlight the information you want to feature and lowlight the secondary details. Remember the art teacher who told his students, "If you can't make it good, make it big. If you can't make it big, make it red." Sometimes nothing beats a small red arrow aimed right at the featured point.

Typographers also speak of another kind of color—the "color" of type, meaning the level of gray in a particular block. Generate contrasting levels of emphasis by using two fonts of a single typeface, and thereby create two "colors" in the same frame: roman with bold italic, or extra bold with medium italic.

Don't Overemphasize the Point

Size is another natural way we draw attention in daily life—the giant "SALE" banners grab customers on their way by the department store. Many people assume that big elements represent big concepts and ideas.

Figure 11-6: **Overkill can defeat your best intentions.**

But it's easy to go beyond emphasis. Work your way up in size by trying out several intermediate sizes. Or increase type weight in one or two steps. Wise designers find that they rarely have to increase both size and weight to draw attention to the points they're trying to make.

Capital Restraint

Back in typewriter days, the only ways to emphasize were underlining and capitalizing. Many people still assume that setting words or phrases in all-caps will make them more important.

The truth is that words set in all-uppercase type are usually less attractive and definitely harder to read. With so many other, more effective options at our disposal, we don't have to run the risk that viewers will fail to recognize important ideas set in caps. Alternative colors, type size and type weight can distinguish levels of importance quite effectively.

Helvetica and similar sans-serif faces that do a good job in presentation work were designed to be used in lowercase with initial capitals for graceful, elegant words. But Helvetica in all-uppercase can look stiff, awkward and amateurish. Use it only when the type size for elements like diagram or graph labels would be too small to be legible in initial caps and lowercase, or when words and numbers regularly appear together in the same lines of type throughout the presentation.

CLICHÉS

Clichés can be seen as well as heard. You're probably aware of verbal clichés, but visual references can get old and worn out as well.

Graphic designs and styles used over and over are as boring as phrases you've heard time and again. You probably have been exposed to visual tics—design elements used compulsively to fill an open space that would have been fine silent and uncluttered.

Jigsaw puzzles to show how the pieces fit together to explain the "big picture," keys that unlock one's potential, boats sailing into the wind and meeting each difficulty with skill and aplomb—they're not bad ideas, they've just been done too many times before.

Punctuation Marks !$?

Because they're such common shorthand symbols, cliché punctuation marks can slip into your presentation if you're not vigilant about avoiding such devices. Dollar signs, question marks and exclamation points are fine used as legitimate punctuation, but they're not strong visual symbols.

Dollar signs must be the worst offender. Remember the two moneybags marked with dollar signs, sitting on a balance scale? So does your audience. Images like this have lost their impact, so don't rely on them to replace creative thinking.

The profile of a face with a halo of question marks is a classic graphic cliché. A scattering of question marks across the frame in different typefaces, sizes and colors is another. When you pose a question, use a question mark—but leave it at that, okay?!?

MOVING ON

Allow these examples to guide you around some of the most common trouble spots in desktop presentation design. If you can avoid them, your work will take on real polish and sophistication.

With design basics and graphic style firmly in hand, let's consider some settings where presentations are made frequently. Chapter 12 examines nine situations with typical presentation environments and audiences, and explores strategies suitable for each situation.

SAMPLE SCENARIOS 12

As you plan your presentation, keep one eye looking ahead to the environment you'll find around you when you stand up to deliver the goods. While your main concern should always center on the content, don't forget the practical considerations your setting will impose. From the boardroom to the banquet hall, each place requires the right match of medium and equipment, structure and tone.

Some environments offer better room design than others, with classroom or lecture hall arrangements that direct attention toward the speaker. When you have the luxury of choosing your own presentation site, look for comfortable seating, excellent acoustics with a clear sound system, controlled lighting, and a booth or similarly isolated area with audiovisual display or projection equipment already installed or readily available.

To help you imagine the environmental challenges you'll face, in this chapter we review some typical presentation scenarios, from the most casual to the most formal. In each case we've offered pointers for choosing media and equipment as well as adapting content and design to the location. Remember to identify objectives, audience characteristics and your budget before launching a full presentation plan.

PEER GROUP MEETINGS

Meetings with coworkers are usually small, casual confabs. Many company conference rooms are outfitted with overhead projectors and screens; indeed, transparencies make an excellent choice in this situation. The ideal presentation length for new material is 20 to 30 minutes; if you're just updating and reviewing work to date, keep your time to 10 or 15 minutes.

Figure 12-1: **Overhead transparencies prove ideal for the casual atmosphere of peer group meetings.**

Media

In your choice of media, demonstrate to your peers that you've been using your time wisely—accomplishing the tasks and objectives assigned to your group, rather than making fancy presentation graphics.

With this type of in-house show, most people find black-and-white overheads right on target. They're flexible and fast, allowing speedy turnaround with the production processes at hand—just your desktop computer and laser printer supplied with transparency film.

If you're lucky enough to have access to a color laser printer, consider whether a full-color palette will add clarity to your graphs and diagrams. With little additional effort or expense, you may be able to add greatly to the impact of your materials. If you're limited to black-and-white, but still feel your audience will need help focusing on critical information, add one highlight color by hand with special overhead film markers. Keep the style of this highlighting loose and casual—a simple marker stroke to underscore or a brushy squiggle to fill an area. That will keep your frames interesting and vital rather than fussy and messy.

Handouts can be very helpful for folks who'd like to take notes at the meeting or use your organization to jog their memories about the material presented. It should be easy as pie to make paper laser prints from your monochrome presentation files. Proof color frames first on paper in black-and-white to see how the software translates colors to shades of gray; then if you need to adjust the palette for tones that aren't differentiated sufficiently, create a second file.

Since overheads and page graphics have similar requirements for density of information in each frame, it's a simple matter to create handouts from your overhead files. Try reducing the image size to 80% when printing handouts; this keeps the paper versions from looking too bold and overwhelming.

Content & Design

Go ahead and compromise when you're creating peer graphics—it's expected that your materials will reflect more the sense of a working draft than a polished, perfect final version. People rarely look for an elaborate show at a weekly meeting or brown bag lunch, and they may be suspicious of work that's not basic and straightforward. Find the balance for your particular group that results in effective communication and a feeling of collaborative effort.

You can count on a high level of audience commitment to the material. Focus, therefore, on the content by using excellent organization, conceptualization and legibility. The group you're addressing already knows a lot about the subject and won't tolerate oversimplification. Instead, show them what they already know in a new visual way, calling attention to your original thoughts and conclusions to add spice and pique their interest.

Corporate culture presents one trap in the arena of peer graphics. Some corporations are in a real rut: meeting preparation means a stack of overheads. Since everybody wants to appear organized and ready, the whole group suffers through many tedious and visually obscure overhead presentations. Even when you're truly well prepared with graphics that will enlighten and inform, your jaded audience may be predisposed to tune out.

It may take a little thought, but you need not be defeated by such expectations. The trick is to break out of the mold while also fulfilling the dictates of corporate culture. Capture attention by turning off the overhead projector—it's suddenly quieter and less mechanical in the room. Relate a brief anecdote that summarizes your message, or tell a good on-target joke, or read a letter from a customer. In other words, engage your audience using material that wouldn't benefit from visual backup anyway. Then turn on the machine and run through the overheads you've prepared.

Another good technique for re-establishing interest in your presentation—though it only works a few times with the same audience—is to bring an object into the conference room with you. Make it something unusual for that environment—a boot or bucket or measuring cup—and keep it close to you and in full view of your audience while you're making your presentation. Near the conclusion, turn from your overheads and use the object to make an important point about your material by analogy or metaphor. Don't dilute the impact with an introduction like, "I'm sure you've been wondering why I have this loaf of bread here with me." Take it for granted that they have certainly wondered, and paid better attention because of it. Reward them for their interest by giving them a new and interesting connection with the material—they won't soon forget the bucket that bailed them out of the red ink.

SCIENTIFIC & PROFESSIONAL CONFERENCE PRESENTATIONS

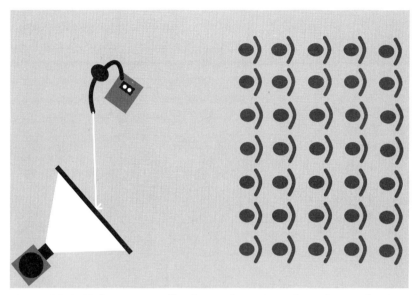

Figure 12-2: **Slides are usually the preferred medium for professional group meetings, for image clarity and ease of presentation.**

With higher expectations of visual sophistication, larger audiences, longer preparation times and much more at stake, graphics that support presentations at professional meetings are a horse of a different color. They deserve as much attention to detail and polish as you can afford to give them.

You're still addressing your peers, so you retain the advantage of a common body of knowledge, a certain familiarity with the subject matter and inherent interest in your material. Your audience is a definite plus: these are the folks who will really get excited about what you have to say.

On the other hand, the settings for professional meetings rank among the worst ever for making presentations. Believe it or not, the facilities can make you pine for the comforts and luxuries of your company's conference rooms. Hotel or convention center meeting rooms are often makeshift and downright inadequate for addressing a large audience and displaying your graphics. Projection equipment can be Neanderthal—a dim slide projector teetering on a stack of boxes at the far end of the room (which was the dining room just an hour ago). Lighting and acoustics are often poor. When the speaker turns in a particular direction, the sound system tends to comment with a shrill whistle of feedback. Seating arrangements can be a disaster. You'll cringe when you think about all the work you put into graphics that can't possibly be seen to their best advantage in such an environment.

To add insult to injury, you may be scheduled at an awkward time of day. The very presentation that could "make your career" might take place at 8 in the morning, when your audience is just waking up and drifting in well after the time you're scheduled to begin. Or, worse yet, you may be slotted for 4 o'clock in the afternoon, when everyone's been to at least one presentation too many. This decrease in audience commitment and high distraction level, combined with a poor setting, creates an interesting design challenge, to say the least.

Fortunately, a little planning will go a long way toward making the situation bearable. Consider that part of the effort you're expending to prepare the entire presentation will be devoted to organizing the equipment you'll need. Your overall frame design can help to maintain legibility and impact under adverse circumstances. Decide when it will be appropriate to be entertaining, when it will be advantageous to be forceful. In this situation, forewarned is the only way to be forearmed.

Media

Traditionally, slides are the medium of choice for large professional and scientific meetings. In some sectors, such as the computer industry, however, there is an increasing movement toward electronic presentations, projected on large screens either through video or overhead projection pads. Unless you're specifically asked to use this medium, overhead projection often isn't appropriate for this setting, where rooms can be large and seating haphazard. Overheads just don't have the necessary flexibility in position and image size.

It's important to find out the degree to which the room can—and will—be darkened for projection. Ask, and keep on asking until you find the person who can answer your questions. Make sure that any lights striking the screen can be turned all the way off. Request in writing the lighting plan you want. Recruit a friend to dim the lights during the presentation and bring them up again for questions and answers.

Sometimes, however, conference organizers don't assign rooms for each presentation until a day or two before the event. Then you will have to play it safe and design for the worst case. When you arrive at the conference site and receive your presentation room assignment, schedule a time to check out all the equipment as well as the sound and lighting controls with one of the audiovisual technicians the facility provides. Run through your graphics to see how they look from the back of the room. Then be sure to arrive at the room well before your start time to make any necessary last-minute adjustments.

Plan to advance slides fairly rapidly in order to hold interest. For a thirty-minute presentation, tell your story with thirty or forty slides, each one clear and straightforward. Pace the frames evenly and smoothly—don't allow any one image to remain on the screen while you talk on and on, and don't rush through a whole sequence as if it were there by mistake.

Glass mounts will keep your slides sharp from edge to edge and prevent the film chip from warping with the heat of the projector. When projectors have been grinding through presentations all day, this is especially important. Carry your slides to the meeting in a covered carousel tray, so you know they're clean and loaded correctly. Then you won't risk the embarrassment of showing a slide backward or out of sequence.

Content & Design

To orient viewers whose attention may have been distracted momentarily by an old colleague in the next seat, include plenty of road signs—subtitles, section markers and review frames—in your visuals. Small running headings at the top of the frame can give late arrivers instant orientation to the content and visual organization. Work with overviews and detail frames to keep moving forward through complex information.

For a scientific or academic audience, cite the sources of all your facts and figures; name names on the graphics and you won't have to be bothered in your speech. Be sure graphs and diagrams are clear and to the point. Flashy or extraneous elements won't cut it with this audience. Let the content carry the presentation.

Design to overcome difficulties of projection and lighting by using lots of contrast between foreground and background, little subtleties of detail, and bold areas of color and typography. Make sure all your essential points are presented clearly. Consider using more frames than you might under ordinary circumstances, to restate and emphasize key concepts.

Equipment

When you're projecting slides in a large room, request a special high-intensity bulb for the projector. Ordinary bulbs just aren't bright enough for most conference settings, and they grow duller with age. They throw an unpleasantly dim image on the screen that can make an audience sleepy. To make sure your graphics stay snappy and sharp, send plenty of light through the lens.

Remote control advance units and lavalier microphones need plenty of extension cable so you can move around a bit. Ask for a laser or light pointer, if it's practical for the setting, so you can interact with the graphics.

Sometimes conference organizers set up two screens side by side, with dual projectors. If your subject lends itself to pairs of slides displayed simultaneously—a photograph next to a diagram or explanatory text, for instance—you may want to take advantage of this option. It's more complicated to advance two projectors, so make speaker's notes that show what will be onscreen at any given moment. The easiest approach is to advance both projectors together rather than staggering them, although with practice and considerable familiarity with the order of the images you may find it convenient to flip back and forth. Just be careful not to let the sequences get out of order; it can be quite a tangle to unscramble—and in front of all those people, too.

SALES SHOWS

Each of us is the audience for a slew of sales pitches every day. Bombarded by elaborate sales techniques in packaging, billboards, magazines, newspapers, direct mail, radio and television advertising, we've become a bit blasé about all the attention directed at our pocketbooks. If we want others to pay attention to our particular sales presentation, we must consider what they'll tolerate and what they expect from the situation.

It's no secret that sales and marketing materials tend to be elaborate, and presentation materials are no exception. Pull out all the stops in a sales show, and nobody will criticize you for going overboard. Color, special transition effects, multimedia, 3-D, sound, motion—they're all tools for your consideration. The hard part is to match them to your audience, creating precisely the right tone and impact. While we're no fans of lackluster, austere sales presentations, glitz merely for the sake of throwing around high-budget technology doesn't pass muster, either. The more elaborate your presentation, the better designed it must be. Tie your presentation technique to your message. Be innovative, but be skillful about it.

Media

Electronic presentations have eclipsed slides as the slickest sales medium. People are truly impressed with computer-generated motion graphics and delighted with interactive systems that are user-friendly and foolproof. Elegant transitions between frames and animated sequences keep audiences tuned into the live presentation. "Touch" screen displays allow the viewer to take control of the situation, accessing levels of information and even short video clips or longer video sequences stored on laser disks.

Most people are becoming experienced media viewers and are conversant with a wide range of electronically generated video techniques from television, so they also demand polish and sophistication in electronic or multimedia presentations. That means you will have to work hard to learn, design and produce interesting desktop versions of broadcast video effects.

You'll want to leave more than copies of visuals from the show with your audience after a sales presentation. Brochures, including color reproductions of visual elements used in the presentation, help to tie the two together. Focus on a common theme, in content and design, for the print and presentation materials.

Content & Design

Compared with a scientific presentation, a sales show allows you more flexibility in the way you display facts and figures. As long as you're scrupulously honest and correct in your interpretation, with solid data to back you up, you need not factor statistics down to the last decimal. It isn't mandatory to list sources and references—but you must be sure they're valid. Your audience will expect a broad-brush, expansive approach in a sales pitch, and they'll probably meet it with some good-humored skepticism.

Polish is essential; there's no room for amateurism in the sales arena. Potential buyers won't forgive bumbles and flubs. Your show must be as good as you claim your product is. Any slip-up in the graphics will be translated into skepticism about the quality of the wares you're promoting. Test the presentation on sample audiences. Make sure you have an airtight design, impeccable proofreading and smooth technical execution. Practice till you really are perfect, and till you're sure your show is running perfectly, too.

TRAVELING SHOWS

For sales or training, internal corporate updates or customer communication, traveling shows are in a class of their own. Designed to practically run themselves, these briefcase-or-smaller presentations are sent or carried from place to place.

Imagine that you work as a representative of an insurance company that has begun to offer a new corporate health care plan. To explain the benefits of the new plan to small groups of employees at each customer corporation, you arrange a series of informal lunchroom meetings at their sites. Your graphics include photographs of service facilities, graphs of expense figures, diagrams of the reimbursement process, and lists of benefits and facility locations.

Media

You have a choice among three media formats for your presentation: a table-top flip book, a self-contained portable slide display unit or a laptop computer. You'll probably have most direct contact with your audience if you use a flip book, which will stay quietly in the background. Your own skills will assume most of the communication burden. Some audiences will appreciate this person-to-person contact much more than a flashy display.

Self-contained slide projectors are available with tape playback capabilities for a synchronized audio track. In addition to narration and/or musical background, the cassette is programmed with an inaudible signal that advances the slides. These small boxes work well in daylight, and they can go out on their own with a simple set of instructions. Even when you use them merely to project slides, however, presenting all the accompanying material live, the audience will focus on the visuals. Make sure, therefore, that they carry the full range of information you want to convey.

Laptop computers are becoming more and more powerful, with a wide range of graphic capabilities. Even more than slide units, computers tend to steal the show. Design your laptop presentation graphics with the display screen firmly in mind. Make sure your audience will be able to read the screen, since the displays are legible only at particular angles, limiting the size of the audience severely. What kind of memory and screen refresh rate does the laptop provide? Will elaborate visual effects run effectively? Will animation become slow as molasses (and just as tedious)?

Sometimes you'll have the luxury of communicating with people who have computer systems compatible with your own—other branches of your corporation or campuses of your university. Then all you need to travel with, or to send them, is a floppy disk. Most presentation software offers a runtime version that allows you to load and run a complete show without installing the program itself. For instant viewing, send the file over the modem.

Printed materials help summarize and reinforce the key points of any traveling show. They can also expand the material that's presented in the program, with details, questions and answers and the name of a person to contact for more information.

Content & Design

High on your list of design considerations for a traveling show will be media management. For example, most self-contained slide projectors have square screens. Laptop computer displays limit an audience's size and viewing position. Orient images to take advantage of the entire presentation screen, but keep important information centrally located where your audience will be most likely to see it.

While a slide can stay on the screen easily for a minute during a live presentation, full of personal energy, the rise and fall of the voice and engaging gestures, 60 seconds is an eternity to watch the same image and listen to a tape. To avoid glazed eyes in your audience, plan a tighter pace for both content and graphics when you replace a speaker with a taped soundtrack.

Rely on 80-slide carousel trays for traveling shows, to be sure your images will drop into the slide projector properly. (Carousel trays that hold 140 slides can't accommodate glass mounts, and they're apt to jam on slightly warped or travel-damaged plastic and cardboard mounts as well.) Prepare setup instructions for shows that travel alone, and be sure to revise them as necessary. Check the slides each time they return for missing or out-of-sequence images, and make sure the audio track and projector are in good working order.

The leaves of a table-top flip book should turn smoothly. A spiral binding allows a clean flip; easel-backed three-ring binders make excellent supports. Design the pages to be read from a distance of 8 to 10 feet. Page tabs can help you find the right section in longer books, and nonglare plastic sleeves protect pages. To avoid bulkiness with longer presentations, use both sides of the page or sleeve. After you've flipped through the graphics for the first half of the show, turn the whole book over and run through the second half.

COURTROOM EXHIBITS

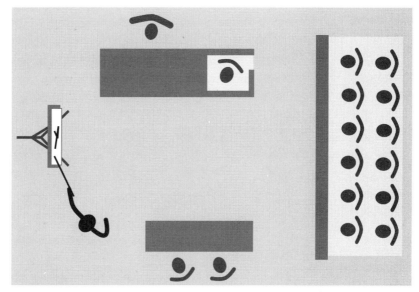

Figure 12-3: **Large, centrally located posters serve well in a courtroom-style seating arrangement.**

Graphics specially designed for use in legal proceedings require special production considerations. Rendering techniques depend on the case being tried, the number of graphics, the layout of the courtroom, the flexibility of the judge and the personal style of the attorney with whom you're working.

Media

It's hard to find the perfect medium for courtrooms—the viewing area is fragmented, with different vantage points for judge, jury, witnesses, attorneys and spectators. There's no single position that will allow everybody to focus easily on a single video display or projection screen.

Slides cause trouble because courtrooms are typically difficult to darken; both video and projection media cause disruption for the occasional chart or graph. The judge may object on the basis that the equipment draws the jury's attention away from the facts of the case. When video is already part of the proceedings—video depositions and day-in-the-life-of videos are increasingly common in courtrooms—video presentation graphics are more viable. Handouts may raise an objection from the opposing counsel or be excluded by the judge.

That leaves posters as the medium of choice for most legal exhibits. Make them very large, mount them on foam-core board, and set them on a very sturdy easel. Use overlays to build a complex image. Some attorneys like to have a single base graphic, like a scale drawing or floor plan, covered with removable clear acetate layers that can be marked up by various witnesses as the hearing proceeds. This allows the witnesses to make a visual record of their testimony.

Content & Design

Rely on the attorney to give you directions about subject matter and its treatment. Needless to say, the utmost accuracy in representation is mandatory. If your work is challenged by the other side, it may not be allowed into the proceedings. A successful design, however, isn't entirely cut-and-dried. Size labels and headings and position them for utmost clarity. Pay attention to small details like callout lines and legends.

When the budget permits, create your graphics in a high-resolution drawing program and image them on 4 x 5 film with a PostScript film recorder. Enlargements printed from these films should maintain their clarity even at very large sizes. Because you're printing a positive from a positive, you'll pick up contrast, so avoid white and very light colors and don't expect much detail in dark areas.

View your job as a neat piece of technical work, creating excellent graphics that convey the information as clearly as possible, stand well on the easel and make a point to the judge and jury. In some cases, you may even have to make graphics that accommodate all kinds of requirements—posters that fit under an airplane seat, for instance (hint: hinge the backing board to allow folding).

FINANCIAL REPORTS

Money is one subject we all have to handle with care. Presenting financial information is serious stuff to the people you'd least like to offend. Imagine a dark pin-stripe suit with carefully cut lapels, a starched white shirt and a power tie. Think neat, conservative, confident. No funny business allowed when money talks.

Media

Financial data is presented in countless settings, running the gamut of media choices from overheads at informal departmental meetings to intricately sequenced multi-image shows at Fortune 500 annual stockholders' meetings. Money speaks all these languages.

Whatever presentation medium works for the message, audience and situation, most viewers prefer to have personal copies of the financial information. Nobody likes to make a mistake about money, so we all want to check our facts. The scope of these handouts will depend on the audience—a single sheet of paper may suffice for the departmental meeting, while the stockholders require an elaborately designed and printed annual report. Plan to include data in tabular form as well as graphs and diagrams, so people can refer to exact figures during and after the presentation. The sophistication of the handouts should match the quality of the presentation graphics.

Content & Design

The most important advice about designing financial presentations: stay sober. To convey confidence in the facts and figures laboriously collected and analyzed, follow the established rules of presentation graphics. Choose several weights of a simple, strong typeface. Make sure that the lowercase l and the uppercase O can be distinguished from the numerals one and zero.

Limit your palette to a few well-behaved color choices. Save the hot pink for another topic on another day. Some financial wizards go so far as to ban red from their graphics—it's the color of loss.

Follow the rules for making graphs and diagrams. Keep them simple, so they convey power and truth. This isn't the place to embellish or experiment with effects. Show profits above the horizontal axis and losses below; make sure your labels are elegantly positioned and clearly legible. There's no need to turn your graphs inside out or flip them on their sides just for the sake of visual interest. Even when you're reporting gargantuan profits, keep your feet on the ground.

BOARDROOM GRAPHICS

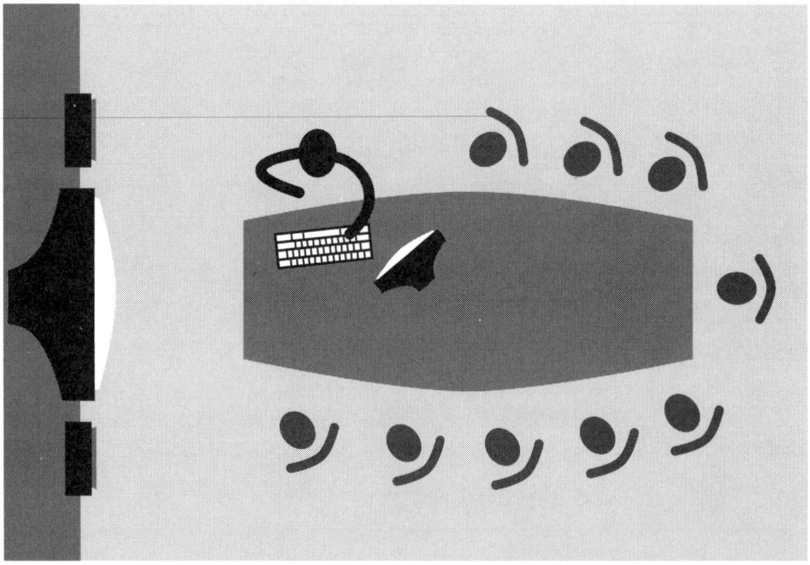

Figure 12-4: **Presentations on sophisticated interactive computer systems are in order for board meetings.**

Since companies tend to invest in the latest and most effective audiovisual equipment for their boardrooms, these exalted chambers are usually quite well turned out for presentations as polished as those at a professional conference and as current as those in a working peer group. Fast, powerful desktop computers with large-screen, high-resolution displays run presentation software that can link with spreadsheet programs for automatic updating.

Media

These desktop systems are generally purchased to interface with compatible systems throughout the organization so you can create a presentation and bring it to a meeting on floppy disk. Up-to-the-minute displays of financial status, current productivity rates, order backlogs and sales activities can be examined and varied endlessly. Define hot buttons to call up background data that support certain aspects of a graphic.

Because these presentation materials often serve as the basis for discussion, planning and brainstorming sessions, it's ideal to have access to revisions online, generating "what if" scenarios with ease. This quick-response, real-time approach allows presenters to adapt a standard graphic format and maintain high standards of design, even as they work with new data.

If the particular boardroom you've been assigned lacks such conveniences, don't despair. The combination of desktop computer, projection pad and overhead projector will produce a perfectly passable display, albeit limited in motion capabilities. You'll be able to make the same projections and create on-the-spot alternatives when asked to gaze into your crystal ball.

Content & Design

Familiarize yourself with the sophisticated bells and whistles surrounding the boardroom setup. You'll be presenting to the board of directors or top management, so you'll want to be conversant with their sophisticated equipment. Chances are it will run exactly the same presentation software you regularly use, but draw up the screens more quickly and display them more grandly.

Whether the graphics are projected onto a video screen or shown on a large monitor, the images will never resolve as finely as they will on a film recorder. Work with simple typefaces, in generous type sizes. Limit the amount of material in each frame, and use motion to reinforce the sense of growth or accent the particular comparison that's your focus. Obvious transition effects (shades, wipes, and so forth) will signal the end of one line of inquiry and the beginning of a new type of information.

Practice in the boardroom before your presentation. Learn what you can expect of the equipment, and work with your materials long enough to feel comfortable with them in this situation. Presenting to the board is an opportunity to demonstrate your understanding of the concepts and your expertise in solving problems. Make the equipment your ally, a familiar tool that can picture the future for you.

INSTRUCTION AND TRAINING MATERIALS

Some companies dedicate rooms to training activities; others set up temporary classrooms as needed. In either case, you're probably safe making some general assumptions about an instructional setting. Audience size rarely exceeds 20 or 30 people for seminars and 8 or 10 for longer sessions. The room probably has an overhead projector and some way to control the lighting. Participants most likely sit at tables or chair-desks with a surface for writing. The material may require a presentation of a few hours or several days. You may be joined by other presenters in the longer sessions, each of you communicating your own areas of expertise.

Media

Overhead projection pads that translate electronic images from the computer to the screen are wonderful machines for instructional settings. You can create full-color frames in any quantity that supports the material best, and update them instantly without the expense of re-imaging overhead transparencies or slides. You can face your students, communicate directly with them and answer their questions. You may even create a new graphic by changing a quantity in an existing frame. This kind of lively exchange helps generate discussion and reinforces learning.

While it's certainly not practical to distribute paper copies of each graphic in the presentation, it will help organize the material for the students if you prepare some note-style handouts based on the most important concepts. These handouts needn't be elaborate or expensively produced—they're working papers designed to encourage participants to take notes and aid them in retaining the information that's been presented. Presentation frames concentrate your message in key words or phrases, but the materials you give out will make more sense to the students if you write them in complete statements. Be sure to include essential graphs and illustrations from the presentation to follow through with the visual interpretation of the information.

Interactive video programs offer a great solution for teaching a body of material to many people in different locations who can't get away from their regular work at the same time for a seminar or course. These computer-based programs lead students through data and concepts, allowing them to make choices and solve problems. Laser disks can be created that will play out a number of scenarios in graphic detail. Video clips, digital audio sequences and touch screens enhance the program. Creating an interactive program requires a substantial initial investment in time and energy, but it can bring important information to people with time and location constraints. For people who are willing to learn as their schedules permit, well-designed and engaging interactive video can be the vehicle for a truly creative meeting of the minds.

Content & Design

The tone of training materials should be warm, informal and encouraging to put participants at ease and make learning easier. A little humor and a friendly approach will help make the educational experience more enjoyable. Avoid rigid and geometric sans-serif typefaces. Set your type in lowercase with a first initial cap—but avoid caps on the rest of the line. Flush-left alignment helps to lead the eyes through the information.

Projecting the graphics directly from your computer file will encourage you to keep the information up to date. It's expensive to re-image slides or overheads but it only takes a few minutes to re-vise a computer file. Design a style that will accommodate later changes, one that's flexible and elegantly simple. Share style templates with anyone who will teach part of the class so they can make their own graphics without reinventing the wheel. Suggest that the training department as a whole adopt a style for all presentation materials that includes a color palette, type choices for headings, subheads, text and labels, and an underlying grid structure for the placement of each element.

Finally, choose a design you can live with—because you'll probably be living with it for a long time. Don't saddle yourself with peculiar colors or ornaments that seemed great last year but haven't endured the test of time. When you evaluate your frame design, imagine that you've just finished your 200th frame in this format. Will you still be enthusiastic about the design?

MOVING ON

Each presentation situation is unique, but all shows can be evaluated according to common qualities and requirements. Be observant and learn from others' successes and failures. Remember that place, time and audience play large roles in determining whether a presentation design is effective. As experience increases your awareness of what goes into presentation graphics, you'll understand that while there's no one perfect solution for any meeting or program, some options are more viable than others.

In the next chapter, we'll conclude our study of presentation design with a few words of advice on polishing your show to make it as effective and professional as possible.

13

A FINAL GLANCE

To round out our exploration of effective presentation design, let's take a brief look at some of the final preparation stages. The true strengths and weaknesses of your show may emerge late in the game, giving you an opportunity to congratulate yourself when your presentation magically comes together to meet or exceed your original objectives—or prompting you to rethink and revise frames that miss the mark.

Whether it's color, typeface, word choice or the entire frame, whether it's related to design or media selection, every element of a presentation should contribute to the communication of your message. If one aspect doesn't help your audience understand the content, change it. Instead of asking yourself again whether a color or graphic treatment enhances the appearance of the frame, determine exactly how it improves communication. When you can justify every aspect of your presentation, you've achieved your goal—elegant simplicity.

RHYTHM & PACE

Presentations can range from a few minutes to several days. The longer the time period, the more you'll need to work at holding the viewers' attention. Vary your format and sequencing to avoid monotony and that awful feeling of boredom.

The rhythm of the presentation graphics is determined by the sequencing of frames in relation to the speaker's pace. Your goal is to achieve an evenly measured presentation that the audience can follow comfortably. But don't let your frames click by with the hypnotic regularity of telephone poles in Kansas—follow the natural moments of tension and relaxation in the material.

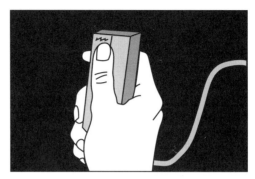

Figure 13-1: **Sequence your frames in rhythm with the speaker's pace.**

As you plan your presentation, estimate the number of frames you'll need. Review your content outline with visual sequencing in mind. Slides and electronic screens can contain less material, so they should change more rapidly than overheads. The average display time for any slide frame shouldn't exceed one minute. With transition effects and motion, screen shows are even faster. A half-hour presentation requires 30 to 50 frames, more if you plan to create a number of build sequences.

Denser in content, overheads require more reading time and so they can be given more display time. Count on 15 to 20 overheads for a half-hour, and more if you're able to break up the information into smaller units.

Production Strategy

To guarantee smooth transitions and sequences, as well as visual consistency, it's best to render a single presentation from start to finish, in the order it will be shown. That way you won't run the risk of using a term or concept you haven't introduced, or leaving something out entirely. Of course, you'll have sketches for the more complex frames, so you won't come to a particular section of the presentation and find you must revise the overall frame design to accommodate that information. You probably won't be able to produce the entire show in one session. But work forward, roughing in the frames that rely on last-minute information with place-holder figures.

Design the transitions between frames to be smooth and easy for the viewers; don't distract them with abrupt changes in color, layout or subject matter. Strive to unfold information visually, using techniques that allow the audience to follow the construction of a final image, such as build sequences with text frames and diagrams.

Work from the simple toward the more complex. Avoid repeating information unless you're intentionally reviewing it. Ideally, the end of one frame links tightly to the beginning of the next without leaving a gap in your story.

PROOFREADING

To avoid some very embarrassing moments in front of an audience, proofread your work. Then ask a couple of other careful readers to proof it again. Misspellings, dropped text and inconsistencies can be eliminated by this last check before you go into final production and imaging. Don't rely solely on a spell-check program—actually read the words on your graphics—all of them. And since the whole point of proofing is to catch errors, allow time to correct mistakes.

Figure 13-2: **Take a close look at your work, checking each stage for production errors.**

You can save yourself from other goofs by checking at each step. Review content for mistakes or omissions. Proof for production errors like misspellings or incorrect figures. Make sure your graphs make sense visually—you may have entered an incorrect number in the worksheet. And finally, run through the show for presentation errors like upside-down or backward frames. You'll be glad you did.

Proofread onscreen one last time. Run through the program with your software's electronic show features to double-check sequencing and continuity. Then you're sure to have it right!

BACK TO THE DRAWING BOARD

In addition to fixing errors, it's not unusual to decide you'd like to make minor revisions to content or layout. Somehow, when a show starts to appear in its final form it's easier to think of ways to improve wording, organization or design. Because we all want to make the best presentations we can, good planning takes this step into consideration. Seize this opportunity to fine-tune the whole program, adding supplementary frames to clarify certain points or splitting frames that are too complex.

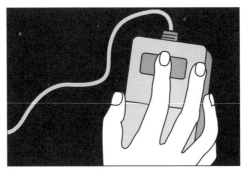

Figure 13-3: **Even when you think you're finished, you'll catch small points you'll want to improve—it's only natural.**

Information is always fluid, changing even as we struggle to interpret it. Because data is revised, job titles change and continuing research alters many a conclusion, leave a cushion of production time to incorporate updates in the final frames.

PARTING THOUGHTS

Before you wrap up the project, pause for a moment to be sure the presentation you created hasn't strayed too far from your original concepts. Does it meet your objectives? Will it speak to your particular audience? If it has departed from the first plan, see whether the change is for the better. If not, revise the graphics to reflect your initial ideas more clearly.

Design and layout are tools to support your message, not to bury it in a blaze of color and dazzling graphic effects. Imagine yourself as part of the audience. What story do the images tell? Is that the one you want to convey?

If you can answer "yes" to the following questions, consider yourself in good shape:

❑ Can viewers in the back row read the material without straining?

❑ Does the density of the content on each frame fit the medium?

❑ Are the frame changes well paced?

❑ Is the color contrast appropriate to the type size?

❑ Are the viewers' eyes directed through the graphic frame, moving first to the most important information?

❑ Have all distractions from the essential communication process been removed?

❑ Are the images integrated into the overall graphic design?

To produce an outstanding presentation, you must combine design skill, clearly stated objectives, and empathy with your audience. Evidence of these qualities will be apparent from the thumbnail-sketch stage to the final product. The result will reward you richly: a presentation that interprets ideas and information visually, allowing your audience to understand and remember them. You're doing all this because you want other people to see what's important here. You'll know when you succeed: the light will come on in their eyes.

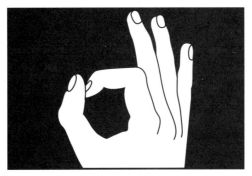

Figure 13-4: It's a wrap—way to go!

STORYBOARD SHEETS

To unfold your presentation visually, sketch each frame in sequence with the speaker's lines written next to the frame. Choose the storyboard that matches your medium; each is rendered in the correct proportions. Keep these pencil drawings rough and easy, with double lines or hash marks to represent type size and line length.

Check the consistency of head, subhead, artwork, text and bullet list positions from frame to frame. How many graphs and diagrams are you planning? How do they relate to the text frames? Will the audience follow the visual flow of the presentation? What about variety? Have you paced the visuals evenly with the presenter's content? Should you insert section-marker frames to signal a change in topics?

Refine the design and layout; resequence, insert and delete frames as necessary.

Slide

Speaker

Video/Computer

Speaker

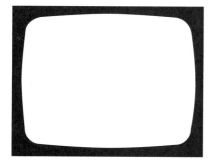

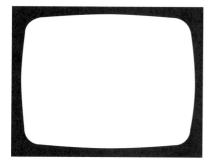

Overhead

Speaker

B

GRID SKETCH SHEETS

When you've drawn small, rough thumbnail sketches you like, try refining one on a sketch sheet to define the overall layout grid for your presentation graphics. The screened grid blocks will be useful in transferring the sketch to the screen in the correct proportions. Choose the sketch sheet that matches your medium; each is rendered in the correct proportions.

Be sure you mark the important layout grid lines on your sketch: left and right verticals for starting points; center vertical if you're centering text; baseline or top line horizontals to position heads, subheads, text and bullet lists; and reference points for placement of charts, diagrams and illustrations.

Under the sketch, note any special production details—color choices, typeface and size, three-dimensional treatment, drop shadows or reference to existing artwork.

Slide Graphic Sketch Sheet

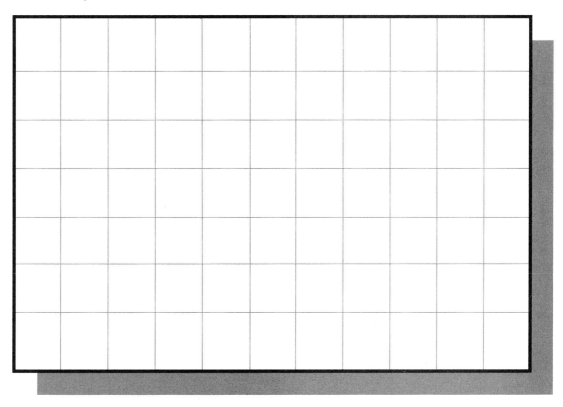

Production Notes:

Computer/Video Graphic Sketch Sheet

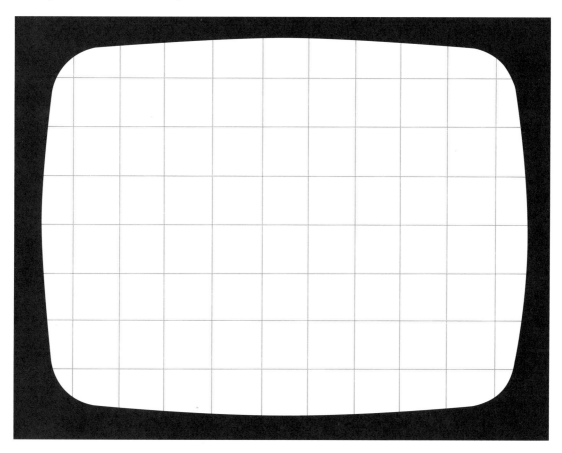

Production Notes:

Overhead Graphic Sketch Sheet

Production Notes:

CREATING THREE-DIMENSIONAL OBJECTS

The illusion of three dimensions can make a graphic come to life. With the bold, clear colors and sharp edges available in computer-generated art, even the simplest methods can produce three-dimensional effects that add impact to your design. But, a word of caution: limit these effects to the focal point of your graphic. Applied too widely, this device diffuses viewer attention and becomes counterproductive.

Shadow

The easiest way to add depth to your graphic is with a simple shadow (see Chapter 4). Remember, you're creating the illusion of a shadow, so it must be darker than the background. Shadows don't work well against a black background. Usually you'll want to keep the shadow darker than the primary object, also. One exception: a black object might cast a gray shadow. Watch out for shadows that interfere with the interpretation of graphs and charts. For instance, your audience should never be left wondering whether a bar chart indicates the value represented by the bar or the value represented by the shadow.

More complex shadows—from shaded to oblique "tombstone" effects—are effective in certain designs. But be sure they enhance understanding of the basic information before you launch into a time-consuming rendering.

Shading

Many presentation graphics packages offer graduated "fills" that ramp vertically, horizontally, diagonally or radially (see Chapter 6). These effects can be subtle and clear or overwhelming and distracting. Try shading with two tones of the same color, to show dimension without screaming for attention. Or drop a simple shadow behind a shaded object to increase the illusion of space.

Parallel Projection

While true perspective drawing can be quite complex, a simple geometric projection might offer just the effect you seek with less time and effort. The two types of parallel projection, oblique and axonometric, are shown below.

Oblique projection

In *oblique projection*, keep the front of the figure parallel to the picture surface, as if it met the paper or screen straight-on. Draw the other sides at a consistent angle and proportion. For instance, in the cube on the left, opposite sides are parallel. The sides can be drawn at any angle to the front, as long as you hold the same angle throughout the figure.

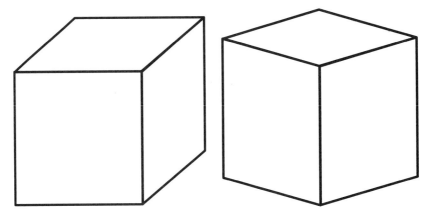

Figure C-1: **Parallel projection: oblique (*left*); isometric axonometric (*right*).**

Axonometric projection

If you want to set all sides at an angle to the picture surface, as if the object were tilted up or down, *isometric projection* is the easiest of the *axonometric projections*. If you could reach in and rotate the oblique cube (shown on the left in Figure C-1), you'd create the isometric cube shown on the right: the sides are the same length and the angles remain constant.

Perspective Drawing

True perspective drawing (see Chapter 4) gives the impression that objects recede into the distance as they get farther away from the viewer. Parallel projection suggests that objects are three-dimensional, but it can't show the effects of distance.

You probably remember one-point perspective in the railroad-track image of lines converging at a single vanishing point. On a box drawn in one-point perspective, horizontal and vertical lines are parallel. Angles and diagonal lines follow the imaginary vanishing-line grid (page 289).

In two-point perspective, the figure recedes toward two vanishing points. Only the vertical edges of a box are parallel (page 291).

Three-point perspective creates a figure without any parallel edges, as all sides are drawn in reference to three vanishing points. This type of perspective will be of limited value in creating high-impact presentation graphics because the shapes of some objects will be distorted. Carefully weigh the time required against potential value when you're tempted to move into this rendering technique.

Use the following perspective sketch sheets to plan objects drawn in one-, two- or three-point perspective. It may be helpful to refer to the illustrated cubes when deciding how to place objects against the grids.

One-Point Perspective
SKETCH SHEET

ILLUSTRATION SHEET

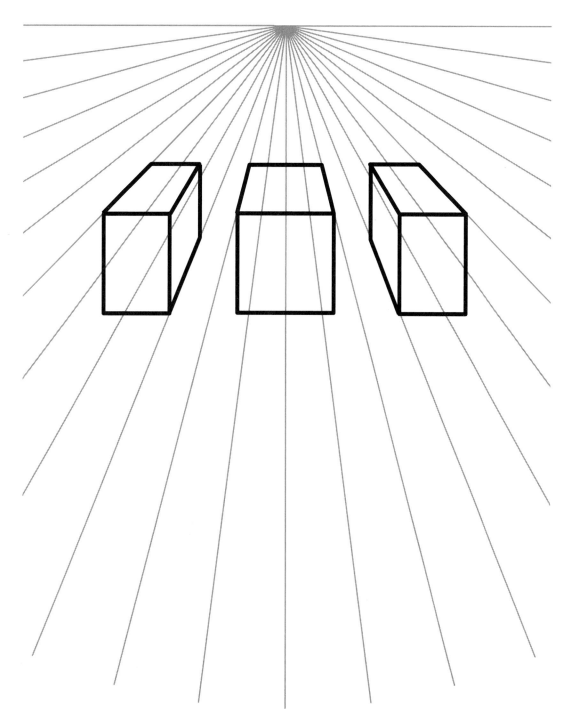

Two-Point Perspective
SKETCH SHEET

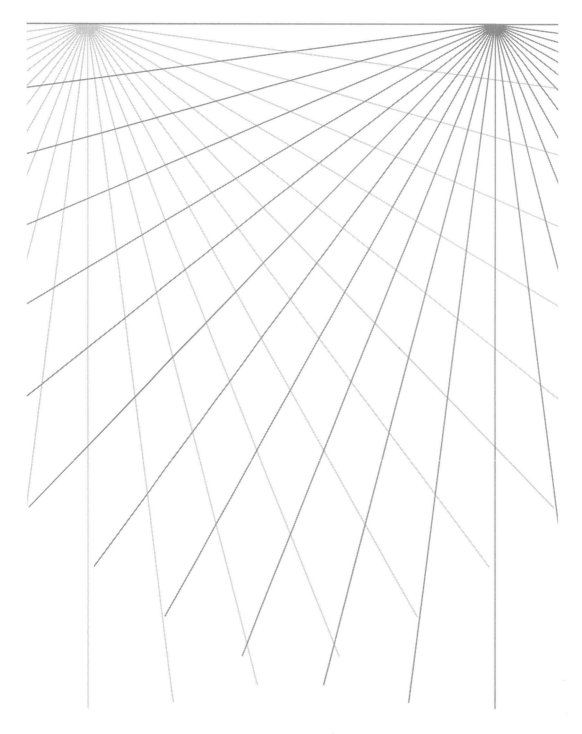

ILLUSTRATION SHEET

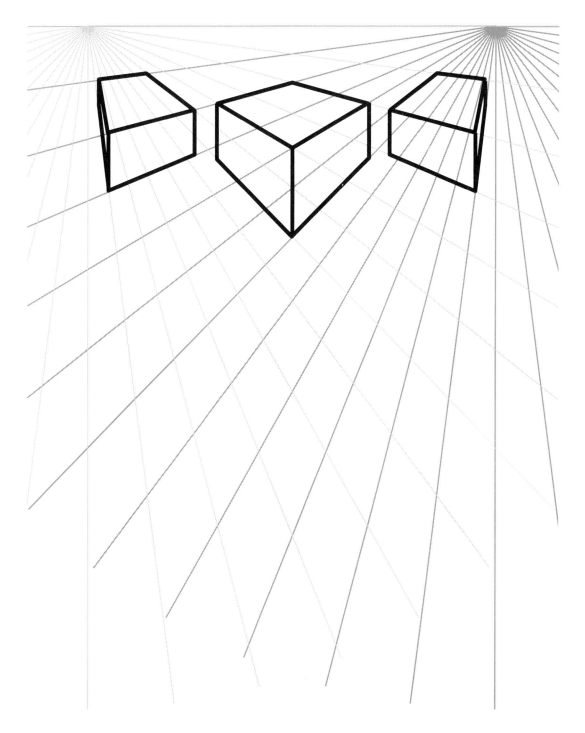

Three-Point Perspective
SKETCH SHEET

ILLUSTRATION SHEET

RESOURCE LIST

ADOBE SYSTEMS 1585 Charleston Rd.
Mountain View, CA 94039-7900
(800)833-6687
(415)961-4400 (in CA)
Typefaces for PostScript-compatible printers and clip-art
software packages; Adobe Illustrator drawing program;
Premier multimedia software; Adobe Photoshop image
manipulation software; Adobe Type Manager screen and
printer font management utility

ADVANCED COMPUTER PRODUCTS 1310 Edinger Ave.
Santa Ana, CA 92705
(800)366-3227
(714)558-8813 (in CA)
Memory chips and computer components and peripherals

ADVANCED GRAPHICS SOFTWARE 58225 Avenida Encinas, Ste. 105
Carlsbad, CA 92008-4404
(619)931-1919
SlideWrite Plus for DOS and Windows

ADVENT COMPUTER PRODUCTS 449 Santa Fe Dr., #213
Encinitas, CA 92024
(619)942-8456
Neotech image-grabber

ALDUS 411 First Ave. S.
Seattle, WA 98104-2871
(206)622-5500
(800)685-3540 (24-hr. literature line)
(206)628-2320 (customer support)
PageMaker desktop publishing programs; Aldus Persuasion presentation software; graphics illustration package; Photostyler image editing program (for the PC)

ANALYTICAL SOFTWARE 10939 McCree Rd.
Dallas, TX 75238
(214)340-2564
Boardroom Graphics business graphics program

APPLE COMPUTER 20525 Mariani Ave.
Cupertino, CA 95014-2094
(408)996-1010
Hardware: Macintosh computers; Macintosh Computers with CD Rom; Macintosh PowerBooks; LaserWriter Printers; Apple Color Printer; Apple OneScanner; Apple Color OneScanner; Software: System 7.1; Video software: QuickTime (enables integration of multimedia); Apple Font Pack (43 TrueType fonts); HyperCard; ColorSync (enables color matching)

APPLICATION TECHNIQUES 10 Lomar Park Dr.
Pepperell, MA 01463
(800)433-5201 (orders only)
(508)433-5201
Pizazz and Pizazz Plus CGA, EGA and VGA print enhancement and capture utility; PictureEze (a Windows graphic file conversion utility); WinDings (an information management tool)

APPLIED OPTICAL MEDIA CORP. 1450 Boot Road, Bldg. 400
West Chester, PA 19380
(215)429-3701
FAX: (215)429-3810
Art and audio clips: Mediasource Library

ARKWRIGHT 538 Main St.
Fiskeville, RI 02023
(800)942-5900
(401)821-1000 (in RI)
Transparency films for computer output devices; all copiers, color copiers & infrared thermal printers

ART MACHINE 594 Broadway, #307
New York, NY 10012
(800)842-6417
(212)431-4400
Dealer and systems integrator for PC and Mac computers

ARTIST GRAPHICS 2675 Patton Rd.
P.O. Box 64750
St. Paul, MN 55113
(800)627-8478
(612)631-7800
High-resolution graphics boards

ASYMETRIX CORP. 110 110th Ave. NE #717
Bellevue, WA 98004
(206)637-1500
FAX: (206)454-0672
Multimedia software: Multimedia Make Your Point

ATI TECHNOLOGIES 3761 Victoria Park Ave.
Scarborough, Ontario M1W 3S2
Canada
(416)756-0718
Graphics display boards

AUTODESK INC. 11911 North Creek Pkwy S.
Bothell, WA 98011
(800)228-3601
FAX: (206)483-6969
Animation and multimedia software: Autodesk Multimedia
Explorer

AUTODESK RETAIL PRODUCTS 11911 North Creek Pkwy. S.
Bothell, WA 98011
(800)228-3601
(206)487-2233
Generic 2-D and 3-D CAD software packages

AZTEK 15 Marconi
Irvine, CA 92718
(714)770-8406
ARTCENTER network imaging system; AZartist software;
AZTEK Picture Pump (drives color digital film recorders);
Spectrum One professional digital photography design
station; ProductionStation graphics output-device control
system; AZconnect series of software translators; Imagizer
system; SHARP JX Series color scanners

BELL & HOWELL CO./QUINTAR DIVISION 370 Amapola Ave., #106
Torrance, CA 90501-1493
(800)223-5231
(213)320-5700 (in CA)
Color Digital Imager-IV slide maker

BOCA RESEARCH 6413 Congress Ave.
Boca Raton, FL 33487
(407)997-6227
Graphics display adapters: VGA and DGA boards; computer enhancements; memory boards

BRILLIANT IMAGE   7 Penn Plaza, 11th Floor
New York, NY 10001
(800)727-FAST
(212)736-9661
Computer-slide service bureau

BRODERBUND SOFTWARE   17 Paul Dr.
San Rafael, CA 94903-2101
(800)521-6263 (customer service)
(415)492-3500 (in CA)
PrintShop and KidPix graphics software

BROWN-WAGH PUBLISHING, INC.   160 Knowles Dr.
Los Gatos, CA 95030
(408)378-3838
FAX: (408)378-3577
Multimedia software: Curtain Call; Animation software: PC
Animate Plus

BUSINESS AND PROFESSIONAL SOFTWARE   139 Main St.
Cambridge, MA 02142
(800)DIAL-BPS
(617)494-1155 (in MA)
FAX: (617)494-8810
Graphics software packages; Presentation Express II;
GraphWriter II

BUTTONWARE   P.O. Box 96058
Bellevue, WA 98009
(800)J-BUTTON
(206)454-0479 (in WA)
PC-File 5.0 database manager

CALCOMP   2411 W. LaPalma Ave.
Anaheim, CA 92801
(800)CALCOMP
(714)821-2000
Plotters; printer-plotters

CANON U.S.A.   One Canon Plaza
Lake Success, NY 11042
(516)328-6700
Printer systems: inkjet; image scanner; color laser copier

CLARIS CORPORATION   5201 Patrick Henry Dr.
Santa Clara, CA 95054
Drawing software: MacDraw II; Hollywood (Windows)

COMPUADD COMPUTER CORP.   12303 Technology Blvd.
Austin, TX 78727
(800)627-1967; (512)250-1489
Hardware: Multimedia upgrades and systems

COMPUGRAPHIC 200 Ballardvale St.
Wilmington, MA 01887
(508)658-5600
Professional phototypesetting equipment

COMPUTER & CONTROL SOLUTIONS, INC. 1510 Stone Ridge Dr.
Stone Mountain, GA 30083
(404)491-1131
FAX: (404)493-7033
Hardware: Multimedia systems

COMPUTER ASSOCIATES 10505 Sorrento Valley Rd.
San Diego, CA 92121
(800)645-3003
(619)452-0170 (in CA)
Super Image; Superchart; CA-Cricket Graph; CA-Cricket
Presents software packages

COMPUTER PERIPHERALS 667 Rancho Canejo Blvd.
Newbury Park, CA 91320
(800)854-7600
(805)499-5751 (in CA)
Graphics display boards; PC and laser-jet memory boards;
fonts; modems

COMPUTER SUPPORT GROUP 15926 Midway Rd.
Dallas, TX 75244
(214)661-8960
Arts & Letters Graphics Composer and Editor; Arts &
Letters Graphics Editor; Arts & Letters Apprentice; Arts &
Letters Picture Wizard; Arts & Letters Scenario

COREL SYSTEMS CORP. 1600 Carling Ave.
Ottawa, Ontario K1Z8R7
Canada
(613)728-8200
Drawing software: CorelDRAW and Corel Artshow (award-
winning design examples on CD-ROM)

CREATIVE LABS INC. 1901 McCarthy Blvd.
Milpitas, CA 95035
(408)428-6600
FAX: (408)428-6611
Hardware: Multimedia upgrades

DATA TRANSFORMS 616 Washington St.
Denver, CO 80203
Contact: Bob Van Arsdale
FAX: (303)832-1501
Fontrix software and font assortment library

DATAEASE 7 Cambridge Dr.
Trumbull, CT 06611
(800)243-5123
(203)374-8000
Express for Windows Developer Series

DECISION GRAPHICS P.O. Box 2776
Littleton, CO 80161
(303)796-0341
DGI ArtShop plotter support and graphics program and
DGI Text plotter

DELTAPOINT 2 Harris Ct., Ste. B-1
Monterey, CA 93940
(800)367-4334
(408)648-4000
DeltaGraph 2-D and 3-D charting and graphics for Macintosh computers

DISCUS DISTRIBUTION 8020 San Miguel Canyon Rd.
Salinas, CA 93907
GEM-compatible graphics programs: GEM Draw plus,
GEM Paint, GEM Graph, GEM Presentation Team, GEM
WordChart

DIVA CORPORATION 222 Third St., Ste. 3332
Cambridge, MA 02142
(617)491-4147
Video editing software: Video Shop

DOLCH COMPUTER SYSTEMS 372 Turquoise St.
Milpitas, CA 95035
(408)957-6575
FAX: (408)263-6305
Hardware: Multimedia systems

DUKANE 2900 Dukane Dr.
St. Charles, IL 60174
(312)584-2300
LCD projection panel

ECLIPSE TECHNOLOGIES INC. 1221 W. Campbell Rd. #125
Richardson, TX 75080
(800)456-6434; (214)238-9944
Multimedia software: Madison Ave.

ECOLOGICAL LINGUISTICS P.O. Box 15156
Washington, DC 20003
(202)546-5862
Fonts for many alphabets for MAC and Windows

E-MACHINES 9305 S.W. Gemini Dr.
Beaverton, OR 97005
(503)646-6699
Display systems

EMULEX 3545 Harbor Blvd.
Costa Mesa, CA 92626
(800)854-7112
(714)662-5600
Designs and manufactures a full line of hardware and
software servers for Local Area Network (LAN) and Wide
Area Network (WAN) connectivity in the UNIX, Novell,
IBM, Apple and DEC computer environments.

EPSON AMERICA 20770 Madrona Ave.
Torrance, CA 90503
(800)922-8911
(310)782-0770
Printer systems: dot matrix, inkjet, laser, plotter

EXPRESS COMPUTER SUPPLIES 1684 Market St.
San Francisco, CA 94102
(800)422-4949
(415)864-4949
Color ribbons; laser products; peripherals; computer
supplies

FTG DATA SYSTEMS 8381 Katella Ave., Ste. J
Stanton, CA 90680
(800)962-3900
(714)995-3900
Light pens

GENIGRAPHICS 2 Enterprise Dr.
Sheldon, CT 06484
(800)638-7348
Computer-slide service bureau

GOLD DISK INC. 5155 Spectrum Way #5
Mississauga, Ontario
L4W 5A1
Canada
(416)602-4000; (310)320-5080
Animation and multimedia software: Animation Works
Interactive, ShowMaker, Astound

GTCO 7125 Riverwood Dr.
Columbia, MD 21046
(800)344-4723
(301)381-6688
Graphics tablets

HEWLETT-PACKARD	3000 Hanover St. Palo Alto, CA 94304 (415)857-1501 ScanJet image scanner; LaserJet laser printers
HEWLETT-PACKARD	16399 W. Bernardo Dr. San Diego, CA 92127-1899 (619)487-4100 Plotters
HEWLETT-PACKARD	19310 Pruneridge Ave. Cupertino, CA 95014 (800)752-0900 Business graphics software: Graphics Gallery, Charting Gallery and Drawing Gallery
HSC SOFTWARE	1661 Lincoln Blvd. #101 Santa Monica, CA 90404 (310)392-8441 FAX: (310)392-6015 Multimedia software: QuickShow
THE HYPERMEDIA GROUP, INC.	5900 Hollis St., Ste. O Emeryville, CA 94608 (510)601-0900 Animation and audio clips: Hyperclips
IBM	Old Orchard Rd. Armonk, NY 10504 (800)426-2468 (dealer listings) (914)765-1900 Graphics software: PC Graphing Assistant (presentation graphics); PC Drawing Assistant (freehand drawing); Storyboard Live! (an enhanced slide presentation & presentation scripting program); plotters; hardware systems
IBM	Multimedia Information Ctr. 4111 Northside Parkway H1101 Atlanta, GA 30327 (800)426-9402 Multimedia software and hardware tools for the Ultimedia system
IMAGE CLUB GRAPHICS	1902 11 St. S.E., #5 Calgary, Alberta T2G 3G2 Canada (800)661-9410 Clip-art package; PostScript fonts

IMAGE LINE INC. 401 E. Main St., Ste. 100
Richmond, VA 23219
(800)368-3773
(804)644-0766
PC PicturePak image libraries for PC Storyboard & desktop
publishing; Show Partner presentation programs; Custom
logos & presentations

IMSI 1938 Fourth St.
San Rafael, CA 94901
(415)454-7101
Mouse Systems

IN FOCUS SYSTEMS 7770 SW Mohawk St.
Tualatin, OR 97062
(800)327-7231; (503)692-4978
LCD Projection Products

INFORMIX SOFTWARE 16011 College Blvd.
Lenexa, KS 66219
(800)438-7627
(913)599-7100 (in KS)
Wingz graphic spreadsheet

INTEX SOLUTIONS 35 Highland Ave.
Needham, MA 02194
(617)449-6222
2D and 3D graphics enhancers and Graph Array for Lotus
1-2-3

JDR MICRODEVICES 2233 Samaritan Dr.
San Jose, CA 95124
(800)538-5000
Memory chips and computer components

KILLER TRACKS 6534 Sunset Blvd.
Hollywood, CA 90028
(800)877-0078
FAX: (213)957-4470
Audio clips: Killer Tracks MM Library

KINETIC PRESENTATIONS 240 Distillery Commons
Louisville, KY 40206
(502)583-1679
Kinetic Words, Graphs & Art graphics software

LASERGRAPHICS 17671 Cowan Ave.
Irvine, CA 92714
(714)660-9497
Lasergraphics Film Recorder (LFR)series of high-resolution
film recorders of IBM PCs and compatibles, PS/2, Macintosh and mainframes

LINOTYPE-HELL 425 Oser Ave.
Hauppauge, NY 11788
(800)633-1900
(516)434-2000
High-resolution phototypesetting output devices

LOTUS DEVELOPMENT 55 Cambridge Pkwy.
Cambridge, MA 02142
(617)577-8500
Presentation software: Freelance Plus; Business graphics
software: Graphwriter II; Multimedia software: Multimedia
SmartHelp for Lotus 1-2-3 for Windows.

MACROMEDIA 600 Townsend St.
San Francisco, CA 94103
(415)442-0200
Multimedia software: Action, Magic, MacroMind Director,
Videoworks, Videoworks II. Clip-art and multimedia clip
packages. Videoworks II Accelerator, Videoworks II
Hypercard Driver, MacroMind Accelerator, MacroMind
CD-ROM, MacReader Sound System.

MAGICORP 777 Old Saw Mill River Rd.
Tarrytown, NY 10591
Elmsford, NY 10523
(914)592-1244
Computer-slide service bureau

MAINSTAY 5311-B Derry Ave.
Agoura Hills, CA 91301
(818)991-6540
Macflow; Macschedule; Capture; AntiToxin; Click Paste;
Mark-up; MarcoPolo; VIP-C; VIP-BASIC; WINflow;
WINschedule; Phyla (an "object-oriented database")

MANAGEMENT GRAPHICS 1401 E. 79th St., Ste. 6
Bloomington, MN 55425
(612)854-1220
Sapphire Precision Color Slide Recorder; Solitaire Image
Recorders; MGI Colorfit and Q-bit software

MANHATTAN GRAPHICS 250 E. Hartsdale Ave.
Hartsdale NY 10530
(800)572-6533
Standout

MARKETING GRAPHICS 4401 Dominion Blvd., Ste. 210
Glen Allen, VA 23060-3379
(800)368-3773
(804)747-6991
PC PicturePak image libraries for PC Storyboard and Show
Partner presentation programs

MATHEMATICA, INC. 402 S. Kentucky Ave.
Lakeland, FL 33801
(800)852-6284
FAX: (813)686-5969
Multimedia software: Tempra Show

MATROX ELECTRONIC SYSTEMS, LTD. Matrox Video Products Group
1055 St. Regis Blvd.
Dorval, Quebec
H9P 2T4
Canada
(800)361-4903; (514)685-2630
FAX: (514)685-2853
Video and multimedia production software: Matrox Studio

MEDIA CYBERNETICS 8484 Georgia Ave., Ste. 200
Silver Spring, MD 20910
(800)992-4256
(301)495-3305
Dr. HALO freehand painting program; Image-Pro image
processing program

MEDIA VISION, INC. 47221 Fremont Blvd.
Fremont, CA 94538
(800)845-5870; (510)770-8600
Hardware: Multimedia upgrades

MEISEL IMAGE CENTER 9645 Webb Chapel Rd.
Dallas, TX 75220
(800)527-5186 (Meisel Photographics)
(214)350-9442
Computer-slide service bureau

MICROGRAFX 1303 Arapaho Rd.
Richardson, TX 75081
(800)733-3729
(214)234-1769
Windows Graph; Windows Draw; Charisma

MICRORIM 15395 SE 30th Pl.
Bellevue WA 98007
(800)628-6990
(206)649-9500
DB Graphics presentation graphics program, compatible
with Ashton-Tate dBase III and R:base files

MICROSOFT 1 Microsoft Way
Redmond, WA 98052-6399
(800)426-9400
(206)882-8088
PowerPoint 3.0 for MAC and Windows; Presentation software: PowerPoint; Multimedia software: Multimedia Works; Business graphics software: Chart; Video software: Video for Windows

MICROTEK LAB 680 Knox St.
Torrance, CA 90502
(213)321-2121
Color and grayscale image scanners

MITSUBISHI ELECTRONICS 991 Knox St.
Torrance, CA 90502
(213)515-3993
Large-screen color monitors

MOUSE SYSTEMS 47505 Seabridge Dr.
Fremont, CA 94538
(510)656-1117
Mouse systems

MULTI-AD SERVICE 1720 W. Detweiller Dr.
Peoria, IL 61615-1695
(800)447-1950
(309)692-1530 (in IL)
Clip-art software packages

NEC TECHNOLOGIES INC. Personal Computer Division
1414 Massachusetts Ave.
Boxboro, MA 01719
(508)264-8000
Multisync multiple frequency color monitors; laser printers

NEC TECHNOLOGIES, INC. 1255 Michael Dr.
Wood Dale, IL 60191-1094
(800)632-4636; (708)860-9500
Multimedia upgrades

NEW DEST 4180 Business Center Dr.
Fremont CA 94538
(510)249-03305131
Optical scanners

NEW ENGLAND SOFTWARE Greenwich Office Park 3
Greenwich, CT 06831
(203)625-0062
Graph-in-the-Box RAM-resident graphics enhancement software

NUMBER NINE COMPUTER 18 Hartwell Ave.
Lexington, MA 02173
(617)492-0999
Graphics display adapters

NUMONICS 101 Commerce Dr.
Montgomeryville, PA 18936
(215)362-2766
Graphics tablets

NVIEW CORP. 11835 Canon Blvd.
Suite B-107
Newport News, VA 23606
(804)873-1354
LCD projection panel

ODESTA 4084 Commercial Ave.
Northbrook, IL 60062
(800)334-6041
(312)498-5615
Geoquery map and geographic software

OKIDATA 532 Fellowship Rd.
Mt. Laurel, NJ 08054
(609)235-2600
Dot matrix and laser printers

ORCHID TECHNOLOGY 45365 Northport Loop West
Fremont, CA 94538
(415)490-8586
Graphics display boards

PAUL MACE SOFTWARE 400 Williamson Way
Ashland, OR 97520
(800)523-0258
(503)488-2322 (in OR)
GRASP

PANASONIC INDUSTRIAL Computer Products Division
2 Panasonic Way
Secaucus, NJ 07094
(800)233-8182
(201)348-7000
Image scanner

PANSOPHIC SYSTEMS 2400 Cabot Dr.
Lisle, IL 60532
(800)544-8309
(708)505-6000 (in IL)
Studioworks

PC-SIG 1030 D. Duane Ave.
Sunnyvale, CA 94086
(800)245-6717
(408)730-9291 (in CA)
Gantt Pac

PC SOFTWARE 11627 Calamar Ct.
San Diego, CA 92124
(619)571-0981
Executive Picture Show presentation software

PCPI (PERSONAL COMPUTER PRODUCTS) 11590 W. Bernardo Ct., Ste. 100
San Diego, CA 92127
(800)225-4098
(619)485-8411
Laser printers; graphics display adapters

PHILIPS CONSUMER ELECTRONICS CO. P.O. Box 14810
Knoxville, TN 37914-1810
(800)851-8885; (800)722-6224
Hardware: Multimedia systems

PLOTTER SUPPLIES 10475 Irma Dr., #2
Denver, CO 80233
(303)450-2900
Type-Setter

POLAROID Presentation Products Group
549 Technology Sq.
Cambridge, MA 02139
(800)343-5000
(617)577-2000
Film recorder; slide maker; computer slide maker; graphics
accessories kit; Palette, Palette Plus and Turbo Palette
Computer Image Recorder; Bravo Slide Marker

POWER UP SOFTWARE 2929 Campus Dr., Ste. 400
San Mateo, CA 94403
(800)851-2917
(415)345-5900 (in CA)
Express Publisher presentation package

PRESENTATION GRAPHICS GROUP 270 N. Canon Dr. #103
Beverly Hills, CA 90210
(310)277-3050
Audio clips: Digisound Starter Disc

PRESENTATION TECHNOLOGIES 779 Palomar Ave.
Sunnyvale, CA 94086
(800)782-2543
(408)730-3700
Film recorder

PROSOFT 7633 Bellaire Ave.
North Hollywood, CA 91605
(818)765-4444
Fontasy font generation and page makeup programs

PROSONUS 11126 Weddington St.
North Hollywood, CA 91601
(800)999-6191
FAX: (818)766-6098
Audio clips: Musicbytes

PYXEL APPLICATIONS 2917 Mohawk Dr.
Richmond, VA 23235
(804)320-5573
Batchprint; Pyxel Visuals; Formlab

Q/COR One Mecca Way
Norcross, GA 30093
(800)548-3420
CGA-, EGA- and VGA-compatible graphics adapter boards

QMS (QUALITY MICRO SYSTEMS) One Magnum Pass
Mobile, AL 36618
(800)858-1597
(205)633-4300
Laser printer systems (PostScript and non-PostScript)

QUME 1515 Centre Point Dr.
Milpitas, CA 95035
(408)942-4000
Printer systems: dot matrix, laser

RADIUS 1710 Fortune Dr.
San Jose, CA 95131
(408)434-1010
Display systems

RICOH 3001 Orchard Pkwy
San Jose, CA 95134
(408)944-3366
Laser printers

RIX SOFTWORKS 18023 Skye Park Circle, Ste. J
Irvine, CA 92714
(714)476-8266
ColoRIX (VGA paint); PolaRIX; ScanRIX for scanners;
WINRIX (a windows-based 24-bit image-editing package);
Present for Windows (a windows-based presentation
maker)

ROLAND DIGITAL GROUP 1961 McGaw Ave.
Irvine, CA 92714
(714)975-0560
Plotters

SAMSUNG INFORMATION SYSTEMS AMERICA, INC. 301 Mayhill St.
Saddle Brook, NJ 07662
(800)446-0262
FAX: (201)712-4378
Hardware: Multimedia upgrades and systems

SHARP ELECTRONICS CORP. Sharp Plaza
Mahwah, NJ 07430
(210)529-8731
LCD projection panel

SIEMENS NIXDORF 20 Olney Ave.
Cherry Hill, NJ 08034
(609)751-7000
High-resolution inkjet printers

SIGMA DESIGNS 47900 Bayside Pkwy.
Fremont, CA 94538
(510)770-0100
Graphics display adapters; computer monitors

SOFTCRAFT 16 N. Carroll, Ste. 220
Madison, WI 53703
(800)351-0500
FancyFont laser printer fonts (HP LaserJet-compatible)

SOFTWARE PUBLISHING 1901 Landings Dr.
Mountain View, CA 94043-7201
(408)986-8000
Presentation software: Harvard Graphics and Harvard
Graphics for Windows; Harvard Draw for Windows

SPSS 444 N Michigan Ave.
Chicago, IL 60611
(312)329-2400
(800)543-2185
SPSS Base for Windows

STB SYSTEMS 1651 N. Glenville
Richardson, TX 75081
(214)234-8750
Graphics display adapters

SUMMAGRAPHICS 60 Silvermine Rd.
Seymour, CT 06483
(203)384-1344
Graphics tablets; plotters

SUPER MAC TECHNOLOGY 485 Potrero Ave.
Sunnyvale, CA 94086
(408)245-2202
Video Spigot hardware and software

SYMANTEC 10201 Torre Ave.
Cupertino, CA 95014
(800)441-7234
(408)253-9600
Presentation software: More II

SYMSOFT 916 Southwood Blvd.
P.O. Box 10005
Incline Village, NV 89450
(702)832-4300
FAX (702)832-4310
Hotshot Presents

SYSTEM GENERATION ASSOCIATES 60 Woodside
Prescott, AZ 86301
(602)778-4840
Image 1 Plus

TANDY CORP. 700 One Tandy Center
Fort Worth, TX 76102
(817)390-3011
Hardware: Multimedia upgrades and systems

TECH-NIQUE 920 Alvion Ave.
Schaumburg, IL 60193
(800)959-7888
(708)529-7888
Mail-order Canon-cartridge refill

TECMAR 6225 Cochran Rd.
Solon, OH 44139
(216)349-0600
Graphics display boards

TELEX COMMUNICATIONS 9600 Aldrich Ave. S.
Minneapolis, MN 55403
(612)884-4051
LCD projection panel

THREE D GRAPHICS 860 Via de la Paz
Pacific Palisades, CA 90272
(310)459-7949
Perspective 3-D charting program; Perspective Junior;
Junior OS/2 and Junior Option Pak, Perspective for FoxPro

3-D VISIONS 2780 Skypark Dr., Ste. 175
Torrance, CA 90505
(310)325-1339
Graftool

3M Visual Systems Division
6801 Riverplace
Austin, TX 78726
(512)984-1800
Computer-slide service bureau; overhead transparency
supplies

TRUEVISION 7340 Shadeland Station
Indianapolis, IN 46256
(317)841-0332
Video digitizer software

TURTLE BEACH SYSTEMS, INC. P.O. Box 5074
York, PA 17405
(717)843-6916
FAX: (717)854-8319
Hardware: Multimedia upgrades

VECTRIX 204 S. Olive St.
Rolla, MO 65401
(314)364-7500
Computer graphics cards

VENTURA SOFTWARE INC. 15175 Innovation Dr.
San Diego, CA 92128
(800)822-8221
Ventura Publisher desktop publishing program

VIDEOTEX SYSTEMS 8499 Greenville Ave., #205
Dallas, TX 75231
(214)343-4500
(800)888-4336
Chromatools, T-Base, T-Tools, & T-Sep

VISUAL COMMUNICATIONS NETWORK 238 Main St.
Cambridge, MA 02142
(617)497-4000
VCN Concorde

VISUAL INFORMATION DEVELOPMENT 16309 Doublegrove
La Puente, CA 91744
(818)918-8834
Presenter Professional

VOYETRA TECHNOLOGIES 333 Fifth Ave.
Pelham, NY 10803
(914)738-4500
Audio clips: Musiclips, Musiclips Digital Audio

WARP SPEED LIGHT PENS 1086 Mechem Dr.
Ruidoso, NM 88345
(800)874-4315; (505)258-5713
FAX: (505)258-3911
Computer light pens and associated software and hardware

WESTERN GRAPHTEC 11 Vanderbilt
Irvine, CA 92718
(800)854-8385; (714)770-6010 (in CA)
Recorders

WYSE TECHNOLOGY 3471 N. First St.
San Jose, CA 95134
(408)473-1200
High-resolution monochrome and color monitors

XEROX CORPORATION PO Box 24 (125E)
Rochester, NY 14692
(800)TEAM-XRX, ext. 125E
Presentation software: Xerox Presents

YALE GRAPHICS 895 Central Ave.
Cincinnati, OH 45202
(513)579-0455
Graphstation; Imagestation

ZENOGRAPHICS 19752 MacArthur Blvd., #250
Irvine, CA 92715
(714)851-6352
Mirage/Autumn and Pixie freehand and presentation
software

ZENY COMPUTERS 4033 Clipper Court
Fremont, CA 94538
(510)659-0386
Mouse

Z-SOFT (800)227-5609
PC Paintbrush freehand painting program

GLOSSARY

Additive color—Color produced by the combining of beams of light. Red, green and blue (RGB) are the additive primaries; receptors in the human eye are sensitive to red, green and blue.

Alignment—Arrangement or positioning of type elements in a straight line, along the left margin, the right margin, or on center.

Annotation—Titles, labels, etc., added to charts, graphs, diagrams and other illustrations to identify units of measurement, special symbols, etc.

Ascender—The extension or upward stroke of any of the tall lowercase letters, such as b, d and t.

Aspect ratio—The ratio of an image's width to its height. The typical aspect ratio for presentation slides is approximately 3:2; for overhead transparencies, 4:5; for video monitors, 4:3.

Bar graph—A single-scale graph drawn with parallel bars, used to compare quantities at a specific time, or show the activity of one thing through time.

Baseline—The imaginary line on which type rests. Descenders of lowercase letters fall below it, giving variety and establishing character identity. (*See* Descender.)

Bitmapped—Made up of individual dots, as opposed to lines or other discrete shapes, in vector- or object-based graphics.

Blank frame—A frame in a slide presentation used as a place-holder. Useful for a pause while members of the audience ask questions, etc.

Blinds—Transition technique to draw in or erase out an image in horizontal strips, much like venetian blinds opening or closing.

Boldface—A heavier or darker version of a typeface, often used to distinguish headings from text.

Build sequence—A series of frames, in which each new frame adds or emphasizes a new point. Useful technique for pacing information, working from the simple to the more complex in bullet lists, tables, graphs and diagrams.

Bullet list—A list whose items are introduced by small graphic symbols (bullets)—often filled-in circles—that set items apart from each other and from headings and other copy.

CD-ROM—Acronym for <u>c</u>ompact <u>d</u>isc <u>r</u>ead-<u>o</u>nly <u>m</u>emory. A compact disc player can read the information stored on such a compact disc, but can't record new data. These 120mm compact discs can hold files totalling 683mb.

Centering—A type alignment scheme in which lines are centered over one another on a vertical axis, making left and right margins uneven (ragged). This is the most formal, conservative alignment format. (*See* Alignment.)

Class interval—A range of points between observations in a chart or graph, particularly a histogram. (*See* Observation; Histogram.)

Clip art—Previously created illustrations, available commercially. In computer disk form, clip-art graphics can be scanned into your computer or reduced in size by photographic techniques.

Color wheel—A circular chart depicting the colors of the spectrum, showing primary, secondary and complementary relationships. Used as a reference for describing color.

Complements—Colors opposite one another on the color wheel, such as blue and orange, which when added together create a neutral color.

Condensed type—A variation on a given typeface that retains the design of the original, but characters are narrower and taller, permitting more type to fit into a given amount of space.

Critical Path Method (CPM) diagram—A project management diagram, often in the form of a Gantt chart, showing a succession of project activities from beginning to end. (*See* Gantt chart.)

CYM (subtractive) color—A method of mixing pigment based on the subtractive primary colors cyan (greenish blue), yellow and magenta (purplish red). These three colors and black are the process colors used to print full-color graphics. Pigment used to apply color onto a medium is mixed in CYM.

Data symbols—Points, bars, lines and other graphics that represent values in a graph.

Descender—Portion of a lowercase letter, such as g, p and y, that drops below the baseline. (*See* Baseline.)

Deviation bar graph—A graph with bars to the left or right of the reference axis, indicating the area of standard deviation emphasizing differences from the expected value.

Digital audio—Audio tones that are stored as machine-readable binary numbers (as on compact discs) rather than with analog recording methods (as on cassette players).

Display type—A typeface usually selected for style rather than readability, designed to be used in large sizes for titles or other special uses.

Dissolve—A transition effect between two frames, in which the first gradually fades out as the second gradually fades in. The two images share the screen for the duration of the effect.

Dissolve unit—A device used to work two or more slide projectors at once, making slide changes virtually seamless. This device will not permit moving a slide tray backward from a remote control, however.

Divided bar graph—A complex bar graph showing more detail and elaboration. Its concept is similar to that of a pie graph but more precise. (*See* Bar graph.)

Dot map—A map or graph on which colored dots represent data collected at discrete locations, similar to the colored pushpins on a military strategy map.

Double-scale graph—A graph in which two vertical scales present two values or variables; e.g., one scale for product price and one for number of products sold.

Drop (flat) shadow—A shadow placed behind a graphic element to make it appear three-dimensional. Drop shadows are made by copying the element, shading it black, and placing it slightly below and to one side of the original image.

Dry mounting—Method of mounting posters for presentation on rigid board so that they can be displayed on an easel.

E

Em space—A typographic space equal to the space required for an uppercase M in a given type size; e.g., an em space in 12-point type is approximately 12 points wide. A convenient measuring unit for a paragraph indent, dash length or bullet size.

En space—A typographic space half the width of an em space. (*See* Em space.)

Exploded graphic—A three-dimensional representation of an object, created with perspective drawing to detail the object's component parts. The object is drawn as though it were exploding and flying apart.

Extended type—A variation on a given typeface that retains the original design, but characters are wider and therefore fill up more space.

Extent—The ending point of the part of a graph on which you present data (the window), typically the upper right-hand corner.

F

Fade—Transition technique for the gradual closing or opening of a frame, usually to or from black.

Figure/ground—Relationship of type or other graphic element to the design, texture, color and quality of the background on which it's imposed.

Fillet—A decorative curved corner used to join rules together to form a frame or border.

Flip book—A tabletop display, similar to a flip chart but smaller, placed close to the audience.

Flip chart—Unmounted posters of presentation materials; the posters are bound together into a large book whose pages are turned by the presenter.

Flush-left alignment—Type aligned with the left margin, leaving a ragged-right margin.

Flush-left/flush-right alignment—(Same as justified alignment.) Type aligned with both left and right margins.

Flush-right alignment—Type aligned with the right margin, leaving an uneven (ragged) left margin.

Font—The full alphabet, number and symbol set in one weight and style of a typeface. (*See* Typeface.)

Frame—An individual slide or overhead transparency in a presentation; also an individual video or film image.

Frame grabber—Software and hardware working in combination to isolate and store one individual frame from a videotape or live video signal.

Frequency—The number of times an event, value or variable occurs in a given period, as represented in a graph.

Frequency distribution—The size or magnitude of an observation recorded in a graph.

Gantt chart—A process diagram representing activities along a time line. (*See* Process diagram.)

Graduated color—Also called ramped color, a special graphic effect that allows one color to modulate into another with no discernible break. Some computer software lets you specify end colors, number of steps in creating a color blend, and horizontal/ vertical or diagonal/radial direction.

Graph window—The portion of a graph on which you present your data, with a beginning and an ending point. (*See* Origin; Extent.)

Grid—A rectangular pattern of perpendicular intersecting lines on a graph; or simply the intersection of a graph's two axes.

High resolution—See Resolution.

Histogram—A type of graph that shows frequency data in two-dimensional rectangles. The width of each rectangle represents the class interval, while the height represents the number of occurrences. (*See* Frequency; Class interval.)

Horizontal bar graph—A graph with only one scale, used to show relationships between people, products, regions or companies. Observations, represented by horizontal bars, are usually ranked by size with the largest on top.

Hot button—An area of the screen that the designer specifies as the means of accessing further screens of information. The presenter or viewer may click on the button to bring up the detail screen, or simply bypass it and move to the next point.

Hue—A specific color (e.g., red or green).

I

Interactive media—Programs that rely on the viewer to choose the content areas and depth of detail in the presentation, actively participating in the flow and order of the information. These programs are based on providing random access (rather than linear structure) to information screens and sequences, and frequently involve videotape or videodisc players as well as the interactive computer "shell" program.

Intercharacter information—Coding in a computer typeface font file that automatically proportions the space between characters to produce a smooth, readable visual effect.

Italic—A slanted version of a typeface, often used to emphasize words or denote titles of publications.

J-K

Justified alignment (justification)—Type aligned with left and right margins.

Kerning—Automatic adjustment of space between letters to improve the appearance and readability of text.

L

Leading—Space added between lines of type to enhance readability and appearance. (*See* Line spacing.)

Legend—A caption or notation explaining symbols used in an illustration.

Line graph—A graph used to illustrate trends, consisting of plotted observation points joined by curved or straight lines.

Line spacing—Space between lines of type, usually measured in points. (*See* Leading.)

Links—Combined with nodes, the building blocks of many kinds of diagrams. Links show process and flow, such as chains of command or the branches in a decision tree.

Live area—The display area of an overhead transparency or slide; the size of the visual minus a mounting allowance.

Location map—A scaled representation of a three-dimensional surface (such as a building) seen from above.

Logarithmic scale—A scale with a progression based on mathematical logarithms rather than whole numbers, so that values are consistently compressed or expanded as they change.

Loupe—A small magnifying glass set in a stand that is designed to hold it at the correct focal distance from film or paper. Used especially to examine 35mm slides on a light box.

Low resolution—See Resolution.

Mechanical—A page or layout prepared as an original for photomechanical reproduction. It may be a finished page, ready for single-shot photography, or a page with hinged overlays for making successive exposures on the same negative. (*See* Overlay.)

MIDI—Acronym for <u>m</u>usical <u>i</u>nstrument <u>d</u>ata (or digital) interface, a standard interface system for digital audio and electronic music.

Multimedia presentation—An electronic presentation that combines material from a variety of different media sources (audio effects or tracks, video clips or single frames, graphics and illustrations, text, animated sequences, and so forth) into a coherent program operating under the control of a computer software program.

Nodes—Items, representing static entities, linked together in a diagram to show process and flow. (*See* Links.)

NTSC video—A signal provided by many computers that lets you record graphics on videotape or output graphics to video monitors and projectors.

O

Observation—An item of measurement or value represented by a plotted point on a graph.

One-point perspective—A method of drawing three-dimensional objects so that all depth vanishes to a single spot. More difficult to draw than parallel projection, but the results look more realistic. (*See* Parallel projection.)

Organic layout—Positioning type and other graphic elements without a distinct alignment plan. An approach often applied to one or two graphics, but usually not to a whole series of frames.

Organizational diagram—A chart often used by institutions and corporations to show hierarchy, titles and responsibilities of individuals and departments.

Origin—The starting point in a graph window, usually the lower left-hand corner. (*See* Graph window.)

Overhead—A sheet of clear film used as a presentation medium, to project graphic images onto a screen. Less expensive than slides, overheads can be produced in color or black-and-white; computer presentation software can make these easier and quicker to produce.

Overlay—A flap of thin, transparent plastic mounted to a piece of artwork to produce colored or screened graphics via multiple-exposure photography. Also may be manually added to an overhead transparency or poster at the time of presentation.

Palette—A subset of the colors of the spectrum selected from the total possible combinations available.

Parallel projection—A method of drawing three-dimensional objects in axonometric or oblique projection. For example, an isometric cube is drawn with all sides of equal length and all opposite edges parallel. This is the most common and easiest way to draw objects in an exploded view. (*See* Exploded graphic.)

PERT chart—A type of chart used for management planning, showing the correct order of events and activities in a particular project. Nodes represent events, while activities requiring time are shown as lines linking the events. (*See* Links; Scale.)

Pica—A typographic unit of measurement (six picas to an inch, 12 points to a pica).

Pie graph—A single-scale, circular graph that shows proportions in relation to a whole: each pie wedge represents an observation.

Pigment—Coloring matter, derived primarily from metallic and organic compounds, used in inks and paints.

Pixels—Tiny dots of light that form an image of a character or picture on a computer monitor. Resolution quality depends upon the number of pixels that make up the screen display.

Point—A unit for measuring typographic elements (12 points to a pica and 72 points to an inch). (*See* Pica.)

Popping (buzzing or vibrating)—A visual effect that can result when certain fully saturated colors that reside opposite one another on the color wheel are placed next to each other.

PostScript—A page layout language written by Adobe Software, describing images and text; capable of extremely high resolution.

Presentation graphics—High-quality slides, overhead transparencies, posters or computer images used to illustrate information presented to an audience.

Primary colors—Colors that can be combined in various proportions to produce another color. In the light spectrum, primaries are red, green and blue. In inks, paints and other pigments, the primaries are generally blue, yellow and red—or, specifically, cyan, yellow and magenta.

Process diagram—A type of diagram that shows a procedure from beginning to end, resulting in a product or conclusion. It involves nodes, sequences, conditional branches, relationships, functions and changes. When many details must be included, presentation graphics often represent the process over a series of frames. (*See* Nodes.)

Q

Question frame—A frame in a slide show or overhead presentation, often displaying a single question mark or the word "Questions," that gives an audience a chance to ask the presenter to clarify a point.

Quick cut—A transition effect: rapid replacement of one image with another, without an optical transition.

Ragged-right or ragged-left—See Flush-left alignment; Flush-right alignment.

Ramped color—See Graduated color.

Range—The spread between minimum and maximum values of data as shown in a graph. The range determines the graph size and scale necessary to allow room for all values in a data set. (*See* Scale.)

Raster—The pattern of horizontal lines on a computer or video monitor that is described by the electromagnetic beam sweeping across the screen to illuminate the dots that form characters and images. (*See* Pixels.)

Reference values—The terms of progression from the starting point for observation counts or measures in a map or graph (e.g., 100 for indexed data or sea level for mapping elevations).

Regression line—A line drawn in a scattergram whose slope and position on the vertical axis are calculated to represent the trend of the data set and its scatter of points. (*See* Scattergram.)

Resolution—The sharpness and clarity of an image produced on film, transparency, paper, computer screen or other media. Usually expressed in terms of dots or points per inch or points per millimeter. High resolution may contain 1,200 dots or more per inch, while low resolution may have only 300 to 400 dots per inch. (*See* Pixels.)

RGB color—See Additive color.

Roman type—Upright, unslanted type normally used for body copy in magazine and book typography.

Rule—In typography and graphic design, a horizontal, vertical or diagonal line varying in width, texture and color, used to border, accent or define other page elements. Often measured in printers' points.

Sans-serif type—Typeface characters designed without serifs (small strokes on the ends of the main character stems). Usually simply designed, with little contrast in stroke width, sans-serif typefaces are ideal for presentation graphics. (*See* Serif.)

Saturation—The intensity of a given hue or color.

Scale—To reduce or enlarge an image according to a fixed ratio; in an illustration, the proportion the image bears to the thing it represents; the measuring marks along the X or Y axis of a graph.

Scale drawing—A smaller or larger rendition of an image, drawn proportional to the original.

Scattergram—A graph that shows how two data sets correlate. Points are plotted in reference to two scales, but the points representing each observation are not linked. The pattern alone reveals the nature of the relationship.

Scheme—In computer color software, a palette of colors sequenced in the order in which they're to be used. (*See* Palette.)

Screen—An illusion of gray for filling areas in graphic design, created with various densities of black-and-white patterns. Also the process of breaking up a photograph into dots of black and white for easier printing.

Screen grabber—Software and hardware that allows the user to import a "snapshot" of all or part of a particular frame into another program.

Script—A decorative typeface designed with flowing character strokes that resemble handwriting. Usually too ornamental for presentation graphics.

Secondary color—A color derived from mixing two primary colors. In the typical color wheel where the primaries are red, blue and yellow, secondary colors are purple, green and orange.

Serif—Small finishing stroke at the end of a letter's main character stems. Serif type is easy to read, since it combines thick strokes on the vertical and thin strokes on the horizontal.

Single-scale graph—A graph that uses only one unit of measure.

Spectral neighbors—Colors that sit side by side within the spectrum as shown on the color wheel; e.g., blue and green or red and orange.

Statistical map—A graphic representation of activities observed by geographical site, showing the prevalence, intensity or density of target activities. Symbols on these maps represent tangible things.

Storyboard—A visual and textual outline of your presentation, showing its layout in frame sequences. Titles and illustrations are consistently sized and placed and type size and line lengths specified. Some computer systems let you create and also make changes to a storyboard.

Subtractive color—Color formed by the combination of pigments, which absorb various wavelengths of light, reflecting only the colors we see. (*See* CYM color.)

Thematic map—A graphic representation of activities observed by geographical site, showing the prevalence, intensity or density of target activities. Symbols on these maps represent factors and forces that cannot be seen on the ground.

Thumbnail sketch—Rough drawing of a frame, or the layout of a presentation, showing space allocated for headings, copy and artwork. The simplest form of layout used to present or evaluate ideas for a presentation (followed by a storyboard in the design stage). (*See* Storyboard.)

Tick mark—Mark used to call attention to detail, to indicate value, or to serve as a division in a grid.

Tiling—Creating an enlarged graphic by pasting together several 8.5 by 11-inch laser-printed pages.

Time line—A line plotted in a diagram or graph designed to show historical perspective in telling a story. A standard time line is the horizontal axis of a time-series graph, freed from the vertical axis. (*See* Time-series graph.)

Time-related graph—See Time-series graph.

Time-series graph—A graph that uses vertical lines or bars rising from the horizontal axis, with variables counted or measured as time passes.

Title slide—Normally the first slide or overhead transparency in a series; usually shows the presenter's or sponsor's name, or a corporate logo, in addition to the title or subject of the presentation.

Track kerning—A feature of many computer programs that lets you adjust for tighter or looser spacing between letters. Transparencies and slides can often benefit from a slight increase in the normal spacing between characters. (*See* Kerning.)

Transition device—In screen shows and multimedia presentations, the technique used to move from one frame to another; often the controlling software allows the user to specify the duration and direction of the transition. These devices are often used to create motion and the effect of animation. Transition devices include blinds, dissolves, fades, quick cuts and wipes. (*See* specific devices.)

Transparency—See Overhead.

Trend line—A line in a graph that shows a trend based on known values.

Triad—A group of three primary colors, three secondary colors, or any set of three hues spaced equidistant from each other around the color wheel.

Type family—A typeface grouping that includes several variations on one typeface design. A small family might consist of roman, italic, bold and bold italic; using these family members together would let you vary type treatment throughout a presentation without adding a second typeface.

Typeface—A particular design interpretation of the letters of the alphabet, numerals and other character symbols. Hundreds of typefaces are available, some of which work especially well for presentations.

Typography—The selection, arrangement and fitting of type elements on a page, slide, overhead transparency or other medium. Also, the terminology of, and rules for using, different typefaces. (*See* Typeface.)

Two-point perspective—A method of drawing three-dimensional objects so that all depth vanishes to two spots. More difficult to draw than isometric or one-point perspective, but the results look more realistic. (*See* One-point perspective; Parallel projection.)

U-V

Units—In graphing, the terms of measurement (e.g., dollars or percentage points). Units and their scaled values are indicated along the axes of the graph.

Value—Shade or degree to which a color approaches black or white.

Variable—The set of observations for each activity depicted in a graph. (*See* Observation.) A plotted variable is a collection of points on a graph used to shape a bar, trend line or other graphing symbol.

Vertical bar graph—A type of time-series graph in which each observation in a series is marked by a bar, rising or falling from the horizontal axis. Bar heights show differences in the values through time. (*See* Observation.)

Video clip (full motion)—A sequence of video frames transferred from a source tape.

Window—See Graph window.

Wipe—A transition effect that replaces one image with another in a set pattern. The second image seems to be pushing the first off the screen from left to right, for instance, or from top to bottom.

X-height—The height of a lowercase x in any given typeface. The ratio of the x-height to the type's body size determines the visual importance of lowercase letters in a given typeface.

FURTHER READING

BOOKS   Arnheim, Rudolf. *Visual Thinking*. Berkeley, CA: University of California Press, 1980.

Beaumont, Michael. *Type: Design, Color, Character & Use*. Cincinnati, OH: North Light Publishers, 1987.

Boom, Michael. *Music through MIDI*. Redmond, WA: Microsoft Press, 1987.

Bove´, Tony and Rhodes, Cheryl. *Que's Macintosh Multimedia Handbook*. Carmel, IN: Que Corporation, 1990.

Bove´, Tony and Rhodes, Cheryl. *Using Macromind Director*. Carmel, IN: Que Corporation, 1990.

Busch, David D. *The Hand Scanner Handbook: Mac & PC Editions*. Homewood, IL: Business 1 Irwin, 1992.

Carter, Rob, Day, Ben, and Meggs, Phillip. *Typographic Design: Form and Communication*. New York: Van Nostrand Reinhold, 1985.

Cole, Margaret and Odenwald, Sylvia. *Desktop Presentations*. New York: AMACOM Books, 1989.

Corbeil, Jean-Claude. *The Facts on File Visual Dictionary*. New York: Facts on File Publications, 1986.

Fenton, Erfert. *The Macintosh Font Book*. 2d ed. Berkeley, CA: Peachpit Press, 1991.

Fraase, Michael. *Macintosh Hypermedia Volumes I and II*. Glenview, IL: Scott, Foresman and Company, 1990.

Goodman, Danny. *The Complete HyperCard 2.0 Handbook*. New York: Bantam Books, 1990.

Gosney, Michael, Odam, John and Schmal, Jim. *The Gray Book: Designing in Black & White on Your Computer*. Chapel Hill, NC: Ventana Press, Inc., 1990.

Greenberger, Martin, ed. *Electronic Publishing Plus: Media for a Technological Future*. Cherry Hill, NJ: GK Hall, 1985.

Holmes, Nigel. *Designer's Guide to Creating Charts and Diagrams*. New York: Watson-Guptill, 1991.

Jones, Mimi and Myers, Dave. *Hands-On HyperCard: Designing Your Own Applications*. New York: John Wiley & Sons, Inc., 1988.

Kaehler, Carol. *HyperCard Power Techniques & Scripts*. Redding, MA: Addison-Wesley, 1988.

Kemp, Jerold E. *Planning, Producing, and Using Instructional Media*. 6th ed. New York: HarperCollins, 1990.

Lakoff, George and Johnson, Mark. *Metaphors We Live By*. Chicago: University of Chicago Press, 1981.

Lambert, Clark. *The Business Presentations Workbook*. New York: Prentice Hall, 1988.

Laurel, Brenda, ed. *The Art of Human Computer Interface*. Redding, MA: Addison-Wesley, 1990.

Laurel, Brenda. *Computers as Theatre*. Redding, MA: Addison-Wesley, 1991.

LeBoeuf, Michael. *Imagineering: How to Profit From Your Creative Powers*. New York: Berkley Publishers, 1990.

Mambert, W.A. *Presenting Technical Ideas: A Guide to Audience Communication*. Ann Arbor: Books on Demand, 1968.

Mandell, Steve. *Effective Presentation Skills: A Practical Guide for Better Speaking*. Los Altos, CA: Crisp Publications, Inc., 1987.

Meilach, Dona. *Dynamics of Presentation Graphics*. 2d ed. Homewood, IL: Dow Jones-Irwin, 1990.

Morrisey, George L. *Effective Business and Technical Presentations*. Reading, MA: Addison-Wesley, 1975.

Morrissette, Christine, and Fenton, Erfert. *Canned Art: Clip Art for the Macintosh*. 2d ed. Berkeley, CA: Peachpit Press, 1991.

Nemoy, Sheldon, and Aiken, C.J. *Looking Good With CorelDRAW!*. Chapel Hill, NC: Ventana Press, Inc., 1993.

Nemoy, Sheldon, and Levine, Jason. *Looking Good With PageMaker*. Chapel Hill, NC: Ventana Press, Inc., 1993.

Parker, Roger C. *Looking Good in Print*. 3d ed. Chapel Hill, NC: Ventana Press, Inc., 1993.

Parker, Roger C. *The Makeover Book: 101 Design Solutions for Desktop Publishing*. Chapel Hill, NC: Ventana Press, Inc., 1989.

Perfect, Christopher, and Rookledge, Gordon. *Rookledge's International Typefinder*. Mount Kisco, NY: Moyer Bell Limited, 1986.

Pfeiffer, Katherine Shelly. *Word for Windows Design Companion*. Chapel Hill, NC: Ventana Press, Inc., 1992.

Potter, Chris, and Rabb, Margaret. *Harvard Graphics Design Companion*. Chapel Hill, NC: Ventana Press, Inc., 1991.

Potter, Chris, and Rabb, Margaret. *Harvard Graphics Design Companion-Windows Edition*. Chapel Hill, NC: Ventana Press, Inc., 1992.

Robertson, Bruce. *How to Draw Charts and Diagrams*. Cincinnati, OH: North Light Books, 1988.

Smith, Terry C. *Making Successful Presentations: A Self-Teaching Guide*. 2d ed. New York and Toronto: John Wiley & Sons, Inc., 1991.

Stevenson, George A. *Graphic Arts Encyclopedia*, 2d ed. New York: McGraw-Hill, 1979.

Stockton, James. *Designer's Guide to Color: Over One Thousand Color Combination Choices*. San Francisco, CA: Chronicle Books, 1984.

Stockton, James. *Designer's Guide to Color Two: Over One Thousand Additional Color Combination Choices*, vol. 2. San Francisco, CA: Chronicle Books, 1984.

Swann, Alan. *How to Understand and Use Design and Layout.* Cincinnati, OH: North Light Publishers, 1991.

Thorell, Lisa G., and Smith, Wanda J. *Using Computer Color Effectively: An Illustrated Reference to Computer Color Interface.* Englewood Cliffs, NJ: Prentice-Hall, 1989.

Tufte, Edward R. *Envisioning Information.* Cheshire, CT: Graphics Press. 1990.

Tufte, Edward R. *The Visual Display of Quantitative Information.* Cheshire, CT: Graphics Press, 1983.

White, Jan V. *Graphic Idea Notebook.* 2d ed. Rockport, MA: Rockport Publishers, 1990.

Wilson, Stephen. *Multimedia Design with HyperCard.* New York: Prentice Hall, 1991.

Winkler, Dan. *HyperTalk 2.0: The Book.* New York: Bantam Books, 1990.

Zelazny, Gene. *Say It with Charts: The Executive's Guide to Successful Presentations in the 1990's.* Homewood, IL: Business 1 Irwin, 1991.

PERIODICALS

Bove´ & Rhodes Inside Report on Multimedia, Box 1289, Gualala, CA 95445.

Computer-Aided Engineering, Penton Publishing, 1100 Superior Ave., Cleveland, OH 44114. (Monthly)

The Equipment Directory of Audio-Visual, Computer, and Video Products, International Communications Industries Association (ICIA), 3150 Spring St., Fairfax, VA 22031-2399. (Yearly)

Font & Function: The Adobe Type Catalog, Adobe Systems, Inc., Mountain View, CA 94039-7900. (Thrice yearly)

Genigraphics Presents (newsletter), Genigraphics Corporation, Two Corporate Dr., Ste. 340, Shelton, CT 06484. (quarterly)

HOW..., F & W Publications, Inc., 1507 Dana Ave., Cincinnati, OH 45207. (Bimonthly)

Infoworld, 1060 March Rd., Menlo Park, CA 94025. (Weekly)

MacroMind Developer Letter, Bove´ & Rhodes, Box 1289, Gualala, CA 95445.

MacWEEK, 525 Brannan St., San Francisco, CA 94107. (Weekly)

MacWorld, International Data Group, 501 Second St., San Francisco, CA 94107. (Monthly)

MPC World/The Multimedia Magazine, 524 Second St., San Francisco, CA 94107. (Bimonthly)

New Media Magazine. 901 Mariner's Island Blvd., Ste. 365, San Mateo, CA 94404. (Monthly)

PC Publishing and Presentations, PO Box 941909, Atlanta, GA 30341. (bimonthly)

PC World, International Data Group, 501 Second St., San Francisco, CA 94107. (Monthly)

Practical Presentations (newsletter), C&M Communications, PO Box 3235, Mammoth Lakes, CA 93546. (Monthly)

Presentation Development & Delivery, PTN Publishing Company, 445 Broad Hollow Road, Melville, NY 11747. (monthly)

Presentation Products Magazine, 23410 Civic Center Way, Ste. E-10, Malibu, CA 90265 (monthly)

Print, RC Publications, Inc., 3200 Tower Oaks Blvd., Rockville, MD, 20852. (Bimonthly)

Publish!, Integrated Media Inc., 501 Second St., San Francisco, CA 94107. (Monthly)

U&LC, International Typeface Corporation, 866 Second Ave., New York, NY 10017. (Quarterly)

Verbum: The Journal of Computer Aesthetics, 2187-C San Elijo, Cardiff, CA 92007. (Quarterly)

COMPACT DISCS

MultiMedia HANDisc: Introduction to Multimedia. CD Technology. 1991.

SEMINARS AND TRADE SHOWS

Powerful Presentation Skills That Work, CareerTrack Seminars, 3085 Center Green Dr., Boulder, CO 80301-5408. (Available on audio and videotape)

GRAPH EXPO, Graphic Arts Show Company, 1899 Preston White Dr., Reston, VA 22091-9958.

Seybold Seminars, 29160 Heathercliff Rd., Ste. 200, Malibu, CA 90265. (April and October)

INDEX

A

Abbreviations & acronyms   24–25
Acronyms
    See Abbreviations & acronyms
Adobe Type Manager   88
Alignment   63–65
    centered   64, 238
    flush-left   63–64
    flush-right   64
    justified   65, 239
    mistakes   237–239
Animation
    See Motion effects
Art   16–17
Ascender   104
Aspect ratios
    electronic presentations   44
    overhead transparencies   38
    slides   30, 32
Audience
    color geared to   113–115
    defining   5–6
    distance from screen   28
Audio elements   220–221
    editing   227
Avant Garde typeface   86, 97
Axonometric projection   287

B

Background
    clutter   235
    graduated color   132–134
    multiple colors   126–127
Baseline   103, 105
    distorted   233–234

Bitmapped images   88
Black & white
    See Monochrome
Blank frames   159
Blinds   224–225
Board meetings   258–260
    content & design   259
    media choice   259
Bodoni typeface   85
Bookman typeface   107
Borders   71–72
    mistakes using   234–235
Boredom
    avoiding   263–265
Boxes   72
    mistakes using   234–235
Build sequences   151–153
    diagrams   197
Bullet lists   146–153
    build sequences   151–153
    defined   146
    entries   147–149
        maximum per frame   149
    headings   147
    subentries   150–151
    summaries   151
    symbols   149–150

C

Capital letters   241
Centered alignment   64, 238
Century typeface   94, 98
Charts
    See Gantt charts; Organization charts;
    Posters & flip charts

D

Explore the Internet

The Macintosh Internet Tour Guide, Second Edition 🌐
The Windows Internet Tour Guide, Second Edition 🌐

$29.95, 424 pages, illustrated
Windows part #: 174-0, Macintosh part #: 173-2

This runaway bestseller has been updated to include
Ventana Mosaic™, the hot Web reader, along with
graphical software for e-mail, file downloading, newsreading
and more. Noted for its down-to-earth documentation, the
new edition features expanded listings and a look at Net
developments.

Walking the World Wide Web, Second Edition 🌐

$39.95, 800 pages, illustrated, part #: 298-4

A listing that never goes out of date! This groundbreaking
bestseller includes a CD-ROM enhanced with Ventana's
WebWalker™ technology, and updated online components
that make it the richest resource available for Web travelers.
More than 30% new, the book now features 500 listings
and an extensive index of servers, expanded and arranged
by subject.

Internet Business 500 🌐

$29.95, 488 pages, illustrated, part #: 287-9

This authoritative list of the most useful, most valuable
online resources for business is also the most current list,
linked to a regularly updated *Online Companion* on the
Internet. The companion CD-ROM features the latest
version of *Netscape Navigator*, plus a hyperlinked version
of the entire text of the book.

HTML Publishing on the Internet for Macintosh
HTML Publishing on the Internet for Windows

$49.95, 512 pages, illustrated
Windows part #: 229-1, Macintosh part #: 228-3

Successful publishing for the Internet requires an understanding of "nonlinear" presentation as well as specialized software. Both are here. Learn how HTML builds the hot links that let readers choose their own paths—and how to use effective design to drive your message for them. The enclosed CD-ROM includes Netscape Navigator, HoTMetaL LITE, graphic viewer, templates conversion software and more!

Netscape Navigator Quick Tour, Second Edition

$16.95, 250 pages, illustrated
Windows part #: 371-9, Macintosh part #: 372-7

This national bestseller, updated for Netscape Navigator 2.0, highlights the latest enhance-ments to the hottest browser on the Internet. Includes step-by-step instructions and expanded Web listings. *Online Companion*: links to top listings plus the latest versions of featured utilities and other Web resources.

SGML Publishing on the Internet

$24.95, 500 pages, illustrated, part #: 366-2

This new-generation publishing tool is actually an old standard for creating complex electronic documents. Learn the code, along with the keys to effective planning and execution. Covers SoftQuad Author/Editor, the acclaimed SGML authoring software.

 Books marked with this logo include a free Internet *Online Companion*™, featuring archives of free utilities plus a software archive and links to other Internet resources.

Publish in Style

The Makeover Book, Second Edition

$29.95, 208 pages, illustrated, part #: 132-5

Design fundamentals and solutions highlight this project-oriented handbook for beginning-to-intermediate users. Includes a gallery of makeovers and 24 pages of full-color professional examples. *Online Companion*: Ventana Online's desktop publishing archive of utilities and resources, plus links to other online resources.

Looking Good in Color

$29.95, 272 pages, illustrated, part #: 219-4

This cross-platform guide addresses basic theories of color, design and production. Features four-color illustrations throughout. Includes advice on choosing and using scanners, digital cameras, digitizing tablets to import color and much more. *Online Companion*: Ventana Online's desktop publishing archive of utilities and resources, plus links to other online resources.

Looking Good in Print, Third Edition

$24.95, 464 pages, illustrated, part #: 047-7

More than 300,000 copies in print! The recognized standard throughout the industry—covers design fundamentals and professional techniques. For use with any software or hardware, this desktop design bible has become the standard among novice and veteran desktop publishers alike. Includes new sections on photography and scanning.

Photoshop f/x, Mac Edition

$39.95, 360 pages, illustrated, part #: 179-1

With full-color examples throughout, this step-by-step guide walks users through an impressive gallery of professional projects. The CD-ROM includes free Paint Alchemy 1.0, sample filters, photos, textures and demos. Ventana's *Online Companion* includes Photoshop shareware plus links to continually updated online references and resources.

Advertising From the Desktop

$24.95, 464 pages, illustrated, part #: 064-7

With only seconds to make an impression, advertisers need this book to ensure success. Includes tips on fonts, illustrations and special effects to win the battle for readers' attention. *Advertising From the Desktop* is an idea-packed resource for improving the looks and effects of your ads.

Newsletters From the Desktop, Second Edition

$24.95, 392 pages, illustrated, part #. 133-3

Design basics spiced with hands-on tips for building great-looking publications. Includes color gallery of professionally designed newsletters. Features advice on applying color; using clip art and other graphic details for the greatest effect; placing pictures, sidebars and pull quotes.

SPAN THE GLOBE IN SECONDS!

The Easiest Way to Explore the Internet's Web

World Wide Web Kit

MACINTOSH VERSION

BONUS! NETSCAPE NAVIGATOR INCLUDED

The World Wide Web makes it possible. The World Wide Web makes it easy. The *World Wide Web Kit* has everything you need—access, tools and instructions— to make the Web your own territory.

🌐 **Connect to the Web through the IBM Internet Connection** service—provided by the IBM Global Network: reliable Internet access at affordable prices.

🌐 **Explore the Web using Netscape Navigator™** —with a convenient new toolbar, turbocharged text flow, tough security modules, built-in sound system and much more. Fully supported!

🌐 **Learn more about Netscape Navigator—** with *Netscape Quick Tour, Special Edition*, the bestselling guide to accessing and navigating the World Wide Web.

🌐 **Find your way**—with *Walking the World Wide Web*, the richly illustrated tour of the Web that includes an interactive CD-ROM with live links to top Web sites once you log on!

🌐 **Plus!** *FREE ACCESS* to the *Walking the World Wide Web Online Companion*™, a regularly updated online version of the book.

All that for only $49.95. Well worth the trip!

Available in Windows or Macintosh versions.

VENTANA

FROM THE PUBLISHER OF THE BESTSELLING *INTERNET MEMBERSHIP KIT*™.

To order any Ventana title, complete this order form and mail or fax it to us, with payment, for quick shipment.

TITLE	PART #	QTY	PRICE	TOTAL

SHIPPING

For all standard orders, please ADD $4.50/first book, $1.35/each additional.
For software kit orders, ADD $6.50/first kit, $2.00/each additional.
For "two-day air," ADD $8.25/first book, $2.25/each additional.
For "two-day air" on the kits, ADD $10.50/first kit, $4.00/each additional.
For orders to Canada, ADD $6.50/book.
For orders sent C.O.D., ADD $4.50 to your shipping rate.
North Carolina residents must ADD 6% sales tax.
International orders require additional shipping charges.

SUBTOTAL = $ _____
SHIPPING = $ _____
TOTAL = $ _____

Name _____ Daytime telephone _____
Company _____
Address (No PO Box) _____
City _____ State _____ Zip _____
Payment enclosed ___ VISA ___ MC ___ Acc't # _____ Exp. date _____
Signature _____ Exact name on card _____

Mail to: Ventana • PO Box 13964 • Research Triangle Park, NC 27709-3964 ☎ 800/743-5369 • Fax 919/544-9472

Check your local bookstore or software retailer for these and other bestselling titles, or call toll free:

800/743-5369